# A War Like No Other

## The Truth about China's Challenge to America

Richard C. Bush
and
Michael E. O'Hanlon

John Wiley & Sons, Inc.

Published by John Wiley & Sons, Inc., Hoboken, New Jersey
Published simultaneously in Canada

Wiley Bicentennial Logo: Richard J. Pacifico

For general information about our other products and services, please contact our
Customer Care Department within the United States at (800) 762-2974, outside the
United States at (317) 572-3993 or fax (317) 572-4002.

Wiley also publishes its books in a variety of electronic formats. Some content that
appears in print may not be available in electronic books. For more information about
Wiley products, visit our web site at www.wiley.com.

*Library of Congress Cataloging-in-Publication Data*:

Bush, Richard C., date.
    A war like no other : the truth about China's challenge to America /
Richard C. Bush and Michael E. O'Hanlon.
        p. cm.
    Includes bibliographical references and index.
    ISBN 978-0-471-98677-5 (cloth)
    1. China—Military policy. 2. United States—Military policy. 3. China—
Relations—Taiwan. 4. Taiwan—Relations—China. I. O'Hanlon, Michael E.
II. Title.
    UA835.B88 2007
    355'.033551—dc22

                                                        2006020554

Printed in the United States of America
10 9 8 7 6 5 4 3 2 1

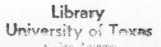

*To Cathy, Grace, and Lily*
—MOH

*To Richard C. Bush Jr.*
*and Mary Ball Bush*
—RCB

# Contents

Acknowledgments                                              vii

1   Thinking the Unthinkable                                   1

2   An Emerging Rival?                                         17

3   Competition versus Opposition                              35

4   The Lost Island                                            57

5   The Taiwan Tinderbox                                       77

6   Adding Fuel to the Fire                                    99

7   China Might Think It Would Win                            125

8   Spiraling Out of Control                                  143

9   From Standoff to Stand-down                               161

Appendix: Why China Could Not Seize Taiwan                   187

Notes                                                        197

Index                                                        223

# Acknowledgments

With gratitude to Dennis Blair, Bernard Cole, Bates Gill, Nina Kamp, Carlos Pascual, Kevin Scott, Hong-jun Park, and Grace Chung, and for the generous support from the TSMC Education and Culture Foundation.

# 1

# Thinking the Unthinkable

I n October 1995, U.S. relations with China had become tense, over the issue of Taiwan. A group of senior Chinese officers were debating with an American named Charles "Chas" Freeman about whether the United States would respond to aggressive exercises that China was planning. The exercises carried a clear signal of China's displeasure toward Taiwan's leaders.

Freeman, a retired foreign service officer, and an interpreter during Richard Nixon's 1972 trip to China, had become a favored unofficial interlocutor for senior Chinese officials thereafter. Freeman said there would be an American response.

Citing America's casualty-averse posture in Somalia, Bosnia, and Haiti, the Chinese were dismissive. One senior Chinese general escalated the rhetoric: "You do not have the strategic leverage that you had in the 1950s, when you threatened nuclear strikes on us. You were able to do that because we could not hit back. But if you hit us now, we can hit back. So you will not make those threats.

"In the end," he said, "you care more about Los Angeles than you do about Taipei."[1]

The remark created a firestorm as China watchers parsed his statement. The only way China can truly harm Los Angeles is with intercontinental ballistic missiles tipped with nuclear weapons.

Freeman insisted later that the Chinese statement was made "in a deterrent context"—that is, it was about whether Washington could make nuclear threats of its own with impunity anymore—and so really did not constitute a warning to the City of Angels.[2] One may also interpret the sentence as saying that China's interest in Taiwan was fundamental, whereas America's was peripheral (what might be called an "imbalance of fervor"[3]). One may further surmise that the Chinese invective was fueled by a bit too much *maotai*.[4] And on its own, neither the "no longer threaten with impunity" thought nor the "imbalance of fervor" thought was remarkable or necessarily false. But if words have meaning, linking the two ideas together could represent a threat to carry out a nuclear strike on California if America were to defend Taiwan.

Although the statement was uttered in the heat of the moment and probably did not reflect Chinese policy at the time, it does reveal something important about how Chinese generals thought about Taiwan, about the United States, and about the use of Chinese military power.

Rather astounding, moreover, was how little time it had taken for the United States and China to begin to think the unthinkable. A few months before, Beijing and Washington had been caught up in diplomatic disputes over human rights, intellectual property, and nonproliferation. Now, at best, they were discussing whether the United States could still engage in nuclear blackmail against China. When in January 1996 American officials learned of the Chinese general's remarks to Chas Freeman, they interpreted them as either bluster or a calculated bluff that should not go unchallenged.

Then, in March 1996, there occurred the most significant military standoff between the United States and China in almost forty years.[5]

The root cause of this standoff, strangely, was a simple visit to Ithaca, New York. The person making the visit to Ithaca and to Cornell University there was Lee Teng-hui, the president of Taiwan, which, to the confusion of most Americans, is officially known as the Republic of China. (What we typically refer to as China is the People's Republic of China, or PRC.) The leaders of the People's

Republic of China took that visit as a serious challenge to their definition of what Taiwan was and its place in the world (or lack of one). Specifically, they regard Taiwan as legally part of the People's Republic. Only through accidents of history has it not come under their sovereign control. They expect that someday it will be reunified as a subordinate unit, as Hong Kong was in 1997.

Until that day arrives, they think it perfectly logical that Taiwan leaders limit their international activities. So, in 1995, they had expected the administration of President Bill Clinton to follow their wishes and block Lee's trip. When it did not, China initiated a sharp deterioration of relations with both Taiwan and the United States and engaged in aggressive military exercises involving the firing of ballistic missiles that landed near Taiwan's coasts. While China never had any intention of going to war, American officials understood then that accidents could happen. They also knew that they could no longer take peace in the Taiwan Strait for granted. The combination of Taiwan's democratic politics, the vision of its president, China's orthodox policy toward the island, and Washington's complex stance toward the two sides of the Taiwan Strait had triggered an emotional reaction. The region would never be the same.

Taking office in 1988, Lee had completed the hard work of transforming the Taiwanese political system into a democracy, and the culmination of that effort would be a direct presidential election in 1996. Lee was proud of those achievements, and he believed they gave him a moral authority that his authoritarian counterparts in the Chinese capital of Beijing lacked. Armed with that legitimacy, he wanted to break the diplomatic quarantine to which China had long subjected Taiwan because it believed the island was a wayward province of China that had yet to "return to the embrace of the motherland." Lee had started his campaign to break the blockade by making trips to neighboring Asian countries. But the big prize was the United States. He had other reasons as well. Political dialogue with Beijing was at a stalemate, and Lee needed to make a point to gain negotiating leverage. An American trip would help him do that, he thought (incorrectly, as it turned out). It also would help him boost his electoral chances at home (on this point, Lee was proven right).

Lee had another, final reason to go to Ithaca: he was angry at the Clinton administration. In April 1994, he had planned to go through Hawaii on the way to South America. The United States had allowed other senior Taiwan leaders to make similar transit stops as long as they kept a low profile. But Lee wanted to raise the profile and stay long enough to indulge his passion for golf. The Clinton administration refused and allowed only a brief refueling stop. Some of Taiwan's friends in Congress heard about Lee's treatment and began working on legislation to restrict the executive branch's flexibility concerning his travel. Lee went further. Through a private organization he controlled, he hired an American lobbying firm, which soon mounted a highly sophisticated effort to pressure the administration to permit him to visit Cornell, contrary to past policy. If persuasion worked, fine. If not, Congress would pass binding legislation. What harm would it do for the leader of a friendly democracy to visit his alma mater and give a speech?

China was taken aback by this turn of events. Under the rules of the game adopted after Washington established diplomatic relations with Beijing in 1979 (and simultaneously ended them with Taipei), senior Taiwan leaders could only transit through an American city on the way to visit one of the island's diplomatic partners. And they could do so only stealthily. There could be no public events. This system provided convenience to Taiwan but preserved the Chinese claim that Taiwan was not its own country.

Lee Teng-hui's proposal would destroy that previous facade, but the Clinton administration never gave Congress and the media a persuasive answer to the question of what harm it would do. China's diplomats démarched the State Department to convey China's strong opposition. Secretary of State Warren Christopher assured China's foreign minister, Qian Qichen, that such a visit was inconsistent with U.S. policy, but he also sought to warn Beijing that Congress was about to take away the president's flexibility. China heard the assurance but ignored the warning.

In the end, Clinton bowed to Capitol Hill and permitted Lee to come. The administration then sought to place limits on the political character of the visit, with little success. In response, and under pressure from some generals and civilian politicians, the Chinese

leadership decided that a stiff response was required to demonstrate the seriousness with which it viewed this action and to deter
future transgressions. It branded the visit evidence of a secessionist
plot by Lee. It suspended cross-strait dialogue between the organizations designated to forge cooperative arrangements between the
two sides, on the grounds that Lee had poisoned the political atmosphere. It canceled normal exchanges of officials between the
United States and China, recalled the Chinese ambassador to
Washington, and delayed its concurrence with Clinton's selection of
the new American ambassador to Beijing.

And the Chinese leadership engaged in military intimidation.
Routine exercises were given publicity. Of even greater concern,
ballistic missiles were fired into the sea in an area eighty-five miles
north of Taiwan in mid-July. That had an immediate psychological
effect on the island, where the stock market fell. Air and naval
maneuvers by China, complete with the firing of antiship missiles,
followed in August.

Amid this and a host of other problems, there were efforts to get
the U.S.-China relationship back on track. Chinese president Jiang
Zemin met with Clinton in New York in late October. But Beijing's
campaign of intimidation was resuming as well. It was at this time
that the senior Chinese general made his "you care more about Los
Angeles" remark to Chas Freeman. In late November, a week
before legislative elections on Taiwan, China's People's Liberation
Army (PLA) conducted a relatively large-scale amphibious exercise
on a coastal island to simulate an invasion of Taiwan. Lee's Kuomintang Party did badly in the elections. Thus perhaps encouraged,
the PLA prepared for the presidential election in March 1996. This
time it chose to compress in time the various exercises that it had
conducted over several months in 1995 (missile firings, air and
naval maneuvers, amphibious landings) and move the missile firings
closer to the island.

It happened that a senior Chinese foreign policy official, Liu
Huaqiu, arrived in Washington the very day the first missiles were
fired outside Taiwan's two major ports, March 7, 1996. When Liu
dined with senior administration officials that evening, Secretary of
Defense William J. Perry was particularly harsh in his criticism of

the exercises. He called them "dangerous, coercive, absolutely unnecessary, and risky." He compared the two closure zones to the brackets that artillerymen use to range a target (Perry had been in the artillery corps himself in the U.S. military).

Perry and his colleagues understood that China was not about to attack Taiwan, but he in particular felt strongly that the United States had to demonstrate that it could not be ignored or intimidated. So they quickly decided that action was needed to deter China from doing "something stupid" (and to impress Congress and other domestic audiences that the administration was not weak). On their recommendation, Clinton sent two aircraft carrier battle groups toward the waters east of Taiwan, much to China's surprise and Taiwan's gratitude.

Tensions persisted and the rhetoric flew for a couple more weeks, and then gradually tensions declined and strategists in all three capitals assessed what they had learned.[6]


If the goal of China's leaders was to convince all concerned that China was dead serious about Taiwan, they succeeded with the missile tests and other exercises in the second half of 1995 and early 1996. They also had demonstrated the vulnerability of Taiwan's economy to coercion. But they paid a high price, as well. They caused great doubt in Asia about their commitment to peace and gave Americans one more reason to wonder whether China was a friendly country. By triggering the deployment of American carrier battle groups, they sharply reduced past ambiguity about whether Washington would defend Taiwan against Chinese attack. On Taiwan in particular, there was a growing feeling that the United States would defend the island under any circumstances. And for anyone who noticed, the 1995–1996 episode revealed that while the PLA could undertake displays of force, its ability to wreak significant damage on Taiwan was quite limited. It began a program to close that gap.

For the United States, the episode also had exposed a not-so-latent tension between Taiwan's democratic politics and China's desire to complete its mission of national unification. Leaders in

Taipei and Beijing had previously shared a general belief that Taiwan was part of China and that unification should occur. They just disagreed on which government should rule the reunified state. Now a democratic Taiwan was asserting a right to participate in the international system, and China did not like what it was seeing. Worse, China would respond aggressively—even forcefully—to challenges to its unification goal. Washington, which had assumed before that this dispute would solve itself, now concluded that Beijing and Taipei might not act as rationally as it had expected and that the only way to protect the American interest in peace and security was to become more deeply involved.

Though it hasn't always been at the top of the American public's mind, this dangerous dynamic of Taiwan action, Chinese reaction, and American intervention, often accelerated by politics in each capital, would recur with alarming regularity over the next few years.

- In 1999, Lee Teng-hui made a statement about Taiwan's political status—declaring that Taiwan and the PRC should interact on the basis of "state-to-state relations"—that China regarded as akin to a declaration of independence. The PLA's air force jets patrolled aggressively in the strait. The United States sought to dampen the dispute diplomatically.
- In early 2000, in the run-up to the next Taiwan presidential election, China announced that "Taiwan independence means war." Beijing also believed that the goal of the opposition Democratic Progressive Party (DPP) was in fact Taiwan independence. So did a victory by the DPP candidate, Chen Shui-bian, mean war? The Clinton administration worried that it could and worked with both sides to calm the situation.
- In the 2003–2004 Taiwan presidential campaign, Chen sought reelection by playing to his political base and stoking China's fears. Washington worried that Chen was taking its support for granted and that Beijing might overreact. It worked to restrain Taiwan and calm China.

Managing these minicrises—and preventing them in the first place—are difficult because the two sides really do now disagree on the core issue: the fundamental desirability of unification. A large part of Taiwan's reluctance is that China's model for unification—the one used for Hong Kong and referred to as "one country, two systems"—would put Taiwan in a subordinate position. Taiwan's leaders believe strongly that they are a sovereign entity, equal to the mainland government, and that if unification is going to take place, it has to occur on that basis, and it could theoretically. (There are people on Taiwan who want to have nothing to do with China and who want a totally separate country, but that is another story, and those people are in the clear minority.)

That disagreement is bad enough. On top of it, however, leaders also misperceive each others' motives, have to worry about political rivals and public opinion, and lack adequate communications channels to keep molehills from becoming mountains. So when Taipei leaders assert the island's sovereignty, Beijing leaders tend to see a separatist plot. China has refused to have an authoritative channel with Taiwan's president since 1999 unless the latter provides a major political reassurance—in effect, that he guarantee that he will not pursue independence. Taipei worries about the negotiating purposes to which such a concession will be put and so refuses to give it. Unlike buildings in an earthquake zone that are built flexibly to withstand most tremors, there is a rigidity in the China-Taiwan relationship that makes it vulnerable to even minor incidents.

This rigidity is not just a problem between China and Taiwan. Recall two cases between the United States and China. In May 1999, during the Kosovo War, NATO planes accidentally bombed the Chinese embassy in Belgrade. The episode created a firestorm of protest in China, with demonstrators attacking the American embassy. It is clear from official Chinese media sources, however, that within twelve hours of the attack the leadership had decided on the key factual issue: determining incorrectly that the bombing was intentional—that is, that the Chinese embassy was bombed because it was the Chinese embassy. This was after the U.S. government had declared that a mistake had been made, just as President Clinton was issuing an apology, and long before it was possible to determine what had really happened. (That investigation would reveal that inexperienced U.S. government analysts gave the physical coordinates of the embassy to NATO targeters, mistakenly thinking it was the location of a Serbian government building.) China, based on its initial and wrong assessment of American intentions concerning the attack, then made a series of demands on the U.S. government, including punishment of those responsible for the attack.

The other episode was the clash in April 2001 over international waters between a U.S. EP-3 naval reconnaissance plane and a Chinese naval air force fighter. The Chinese pilot flew so close to the American plane that he caused a collision and crashed into the sea. Miraculously, the American EP-3 landed at a Chinese military base without being shot down, despite not being able to raise the tower. The information reaching Beijing was that the slow-moving American plane somehow turned and rammed the higher-speed Chinese jet, and the Foreign Ministry too quickly and on faith made that the basis of its demands on the United States.

Compounding these rushes to judgment—drawing invalid conclusions from available data or failing to question subordinates' information—was an absence of communication. In both cases, American leaders and diplomats sought to use available channels to contact their Chinese counterparts and got little or no response. If the key to effective crisis management is communication, then managing crises with China can be surprisingly difficult.

To be sure, there is much that brings China and Taiwan and China and the United States together. Mutual economic advantage binds all three, as a Dell laptop computer so vividly demonstrates. The microprocessor is made in the United States; advanced components are made in Taiwan's Hsinchu Science Park; Taiwan's Quanta Company does the production management on behalf of Dell; and the assembly is done in China. Washington and Beijing cooperate to at least some extent on a number of foreign policy issues, the most prominent being the nuclear programs in North Korea and Iran. All three countries have much to lose from any conflict and powerful objective reasons to avoid one.

But these crisis episodes show that standing between the objective reasons to avoid war and its outbreak through some stupid accident or miscalculation are precious few fail-safes and institutional buffers.

Among all the complicated issues that China and the United States must balance in their relationship—economic, geographic, ideological, ecological—the fulcrum has become Taiwan. If we go to war against the world's number-one rising power in the twenty-first century, the main cause and spark will most likely result from a dispute over that small island of about twenty-three million people, or one-sixtieth of the PRC's population. And as counterintuitive as it may seem, the risks of such a war are real.

Just because there are good reasons why war *should not* break out does not mean that it won't (just as the fact that there are reasons why war *could* occur does not mean that it will).

Here's how war could happen. A crisis similar to the 1995–1996 problem, sparked by Taiwan's growing sense of separate identity and China's continued unwillingness to tolerate any such thing, recurs. Taiwan could take a major political step toward strengthening its sovereignty that its leaders might believe is reasonable and moderate but that China views as a separatist declaration of independence. Alternatively, even if Taiwan remains comfortable with the status quo, China could grow impatient about Taiwan's refusal to agree to prompt unification on its terms. In a fog of miscommunication and politics, an enraged China prepares to attack the island while Taiwan's leaders assume American support. The United States, bound by decades of promises and a strong sense of moral obligation to Taiwan, warns that China should not use military force and strongly suggests that the United States will defend the island. No one backs down—each has too much at stake.

Thus the first direct major military clash between two nuclear powers begins. Perhaps Chinese submarines sink a couple of ships headed toward Taiwan, leading the United States and Taiwan to undertake antisubmarine warfare operations, or perhaps Chinese missile strikes lead to reprisal attacks by the United States and Taiwan against the missile launchers on PRC soil. Resisting escalation in such a conflict will be very difficult. So it's war, with the prospect that atomic weapons will be used and that the judgment/threat with which we began—"you care more about Los Angeles than you do about Taipei"—might actually be tested. Even if we're lucky and the nuclear threshold is not crossed, tens of thousands of people could die from the direct effects of conventional war in the waters and airways near Taiwan.

There would also be further, earth-shattering repercussions. American-Chinese relations would change radically, probably plunging the region, if not the world, into another cold war that could last for decades. The U.S. economy would sink—not irreparably, but in a way that could take a decade or more to recover from. The Asia-Pacific region would begin to split into two opposing and even hostile camps, with the possibility of more wars—say, between China and Japan over oil buried in the seabeds between them— much greater than it is today.

A terrifying scenario, to say the least. Can it happen? Yes. Is there anything we can do to stop it? Absolutely. In fact, some of the right measures have been adopted, and as a result the chances of war may have been at least temporarily lowered. Ambassador Freeman estimated that the odds might have been as high as 25 percent in the 1990s; right now, the figure is substantially lower. But given the stakes, it is still way too high for comfort, and it could increase if the wrong steps are taken by one or more parties. Also, with China growing into its role as the dominant regional power, even if tensions don't get higher, the stakes will.

More needs to be done, and the sooner the better.

First, the public needs to understand the possible dangers of conflict over Taiwan so that we have a strong base of support for the only policy that makes sense—a clear commitment to ensuring Taiwan's security, combined with a strong resolve to dissuade Taiwan leaders from actions that would upset the status quo and undermine peace and stability. Policy elites in the United States understand the need for this balancing act, but their thinking may not always carry the day without understanding and support from the American people.

Second, our friends in China need to understand how strongly Americans feel about Taiwan, and not underestimate this country's commitment to its well-being. Third, our friends on Taiwan need to be responsible. They already have *de facto* independence, replete with economic prosperity, a vibrant democracy, and a reasonably secure territory. While we understand the desire of some for outright independence, totally separate from China, that would risk war, even nuclear war, involving more than 1.5 billion people and a fundamental change in the international order. It is a luxury that cannot be afforded, not now or in the foreseeable future.

Finally, military planners in both China and the United States must avoid the temptation to develop war plans that would lead to rapid escalation in any future crisis pitting their two countries against each other. There are natural military pressures and desires for such escalation, but strategically it would be hugely counterproductive. We must, of course, do everything possible to prevent conflict. But if, heaven forbid, it occurs, we must do everything possible to minimize the risks of all-out war.

If we fail to take these steps out of complacency or mistaken views about the nature of the Taiwan Strait challenge, our country may be faced with a crisis more critical than terrorism. Indeed, it could result in our greatest military threat since the Cuban missile crisis, and perhaps not one resolved peacefully this time around. It also will present us with our gravest economic challenge at least since the oil shocks and stagflation of the 1970s.

Let us be clear: we do not worry that the United States may fight China over Taiwan because we have an ideologically negative view of China. Far from it. That country has made incredible, and positive, strides over the past thirty years. China is not an evil empire, as Ronald Reagan termed the Soviet Union, nor is it ruled by menacing tyrants. The men and women who run China (mostly men) have been more successful than the leaders of any other Communist system in reforming an inefficient and outmoded Stalinist system. They still have many challenges and have not yet addressed the issue of political reform, but they have engineered sustained economic growth, have reduced poverty significantly, and are beginning to create a middle class. They have done so by relying, among other things, on American markets, investment, and technology, and a benign U.S. foreign policy. (America has become dependent on China as well, for low-priced consumer goods and its purchase of our debt.) Moreover, there is some hope that perhaps Washington and Beijing might work together diplomatically, along with other great powers, to manage the international system for the good of all.

Yet there are reasons to think the dynamic will worsen for reasons beyond what reasonable politicians can accomplish. A special interaction occurs in the international system when a formerly weak country quickly accumulates money and military muscle and thereby reorders the previous power hierarchy. And it is usually the strongest and most established state, the one that has the greatest stake in the existing order, that watches the upstart most carefully.

Some scholars claim that world politics are actually the most unstable when a rising power confronts the leading status quo power. Whether it was Britain challenging France in the eighteenth century, or Germany testing Britain in the late nineteenth and first half of the twentieth, or the Soviet Union probing American positions in the mid-twentieth, there is a "not enough room in this town for the both of us" dynamic that makes rivalry difficult to manage. Much of the dynamic is psychological, born of the uncertainty that each party feels about the intentions of the other. Each hopes for the best but prepares for the worst, and in doing so confirms the other's worst fears. Finally, this rivalry, fueled by uncertainty, is often accelerated by specific issues that neither can completely control. Thus World War I was triggered, literally, by an assassination in Sarajevo.

Still, skeptics might wonder why the world's two most important states of the twenty-first century would really fight each other over a small island, however impressive as small islands go. But there are major reasons why China and the United States care so much about Taiwan.

For the Chinese leadership, Taiwan is a touchstone of the Communist Party's legitimacy. It represents the last vestige of the imperialist division of China during the "century of humiliation" (from the mid-nineteenth through the mid-twentieth century). Even if that did not happen, there is the anxiety that China's long-delayed quest to reenter the ranks of the world's great powers, something denied them for the past half century, would be incomplete until the Chinese flag flies over Taiwan. In this mind-set, a divided nation is still a weak nation. Then there is the anxiety that if Taiwan were allowed to secede, Tibet in the southwest and Xinjiang Autonomous Region in the northwest could be next—with a potential domino effect that could splinter the middle kingdom. So handling the Taiwan issue well is a key test of any Chinese leader's ability.

For leaders in Washington, America's ties to Taiwan have been strong for more than half a century, and the United States has threatened force against China before (in the 1950s) over the issue. In the past decade or so, as Taiwan has become both democratic and rich, America's moral and political commitments to Taiwan have only strengthened. In the 1995–1996 crisis, as we described above, the Clinton administration sent aircraft carriers near China as a show of force. In 2001, George W. Bush promised that the United States would do "whatever it takes" to help Taiwan defend itself. So American values, history, and concerns about credibility are all at issue over Taiwan.

Abandoning Taiwan in its moment of acute need would surely make many around the world question the continued trustworthiness of the United States. Traditional allies such as South Korea and Japan would likely reassess the security calculus. Would they accommodate fully to China as the new hegemon in East Asia? Would they develop nuclear weapons to ensure their own security as a result? It's hard to predict what they would do, but it is certain that there would be a fundamental tilt *away from* the United States. Countries such as Saudi Arabia might do the same, or feel the need to curry favor with powerful but aggressive neighbors such as Iran to ensure that they would not wind up at war with them.

None of these reasons is powerful enough to justify war. But all are convincing enough to many leaders in Beijing and Washington to justify taking some *risk* of war to protect their key interests. That means a process can begin that, if mismanaged, can escalate out of control. It should not. But it could.

China, we believe, will be the world's next great power—most likely all alone in the number-two spot within a few decades and perhaps even laying claim to the title of the world's other super-power sometime in this century. This poses a fundamental challenge to the United States and to the leaders of both countries.

There is no guarantee that a rising China will challenge the United States for dominance in East Asia, much less in the world. China's leaders have not, as far as anyone knows, decided what kind of great power they want their country to be. A relationship of cooperation and coexistence is certainly conceivable. Yet it is not assured, and as a result, both Beijing and Washington have begun to hedge in case things do not turn out for the best. Far and away the most likely trigger of a U.S.-China war and of long-term enmity, in spite of our shared interests, is Taiwan. Get that issue right and the U.S.-China relationship—as well as the overall power structure of the international system—are likely to prosper. Mismanage it and the result could be catastrophic.

# 2

# An Emerging Rival?

During 2005, the world took notice of China like never before. Each major newsweekly had its provocative China cover story. *Newsweek* forecast "China's Century" and pictured the very chic actress Zhang Ziyi in jeans and a Chinese-style blouse. *Time* had a retro look, with a picture of the late chairman Mao Zedong and a proclamation of "China's New Revolution." But then the title had a twist: "Remaking our world, one deal at a time." The *Economist* had a street sign that punned, "Great Wall St." and a caption that promised an exposé of "how China runs the world economy." The more highbrow *Atlantic Monthly* thought it had discovered a far more ominous trend. On a cover that portrayed a scowling, heavy-browed Chinese sailor on the deck of a warship was the title "How We Would Fight China."[1] In 2005, the number of Lexis/Nexis hits to Napoleon Bonaparte's early 1800s statement about China ("Let China sleep. For when China wakes, it will shake the world.") was more than double the number in 2004, which in turn was triple in any previous year.[2] Obviously, something was going on.

Actually, China had not been totally ignored before 2005. You cannot simply dismiss the world's most populous country. A full decade before, the guardians of American power had already realized that China was a force to be reckoned with. The executives of major U.S. corporations had concluded that China had become a key to their very survival. If they did not include the country in their business plans, either as a production platform or as a future market or both, they risked the very extinction of their companies. And these corporate executives have already been proven largely correct in their bets.

China has become a global economic powerhouse, with ramifications for all other economies and in some surprising ways.

China was noticed in another way. The People's Liberation Army's military exercises near Taiwan in the second half of 1995 and early 1996 after Lee Teng-hui's Cornell visit caught the attention of Americans who were trying to divine the new organizing principles of the international system that would replace the strategic muddle that followed the bipolar simplicity of the cold war. Did the Taiwan minicrisis, they asked, foreshadow the world to come? In May 2000, Kurt Campbell, an American defense expert who had advised Secretary William J. Perry in the Clinton Pentagon, wrote a seminal essay in the *New York Times* on how strategic thinkers who knew little about China welcomed its growing military power like the answer to a maiden's prayer. Those on the lookout for new threats to American interests, Campbell wrote, "now have a sense of renewed purpose after a prolonged period of melancholy and nostalgia."[3]

Ever since World War II, the premise of U.S. security strategy in the Pacific has been to deny hegemony to any rival naval and air power by preserving hegemony itself. Never again would a country be allowed to gain a relative advantage so that, like Japan in December 1941, it could attack U.S. interests with impunity. This was a concept that found new resonance in the Bush administration's strategy documents. A September 2002 National Security Strategy document stated: "Our forces will be strong enough to dissuade potential adversaries from pursuing a military buildup in hopes of surpassing, or equaling, the power of the United States." In a passage in the February 2006 *Quadrennial Defense Review* that appeared right after a discussion of China's military buildup, the report said that the United States "will also seek to ensure that no foreign power can dictate the terms of regional or global security. It will attempt to dissuade any military competitor from developing disruptive or other capabilities that could enable regional hegemony or hostile action against the United States or other friendly countries, and it will seek to deter aggression or coercion."[4] Throughout the post–World War II period, American military dominance was reinforced through alliances, bases, and political relationships. America's role at the center of the global economy was assured by creating a trading system based on free trade and supported by a network of multilateral institutions: the International Monetary Fund, the World Bank, and the General Administration of Trade and Tariffs (later the World Trade Organization).

It is only common sense that a stronger China will inevitably affect the interests of the United States and the postwar Pacific order it created. The only question is the degree of that impact. The growth of Chinese economic, military, and political power will certainly create friction, and we would not want to minimize the challenge China poses for the United States. In facing that challenge it will be easy to get it wrong, in part because subjective factors are as powerful as objective ones. As a very wise man, former Pentagon official and Harvard dean Joseph Nye, is fond of saying, if Washington treats China as its enemy, it will become its enemy, because of the way it perceives U.S. intentions and readjusts its behavior. But we believe that Washington is capable of managing most of the ways in which China's challenge will manifest itself. Indeed, in most respects, America's future is in its own hands, and the question is whether we possess the national will to seize that future.


In the early 1990s, ironically, the Chinese economic trajectory was uncertain. The brutal suppression of the Tiananmen demonstration had put on hold the gradual 1980s movement toward a market economy. Conservative forces who emphasized planning and ideology had made something of a comeback. But in the wake of the collapse of the Soviet Union in 1991, Deng Xiaoping revived the idea that the best way to keep the Communist Party in power was to promote prosperity. To that end, he advocated doing whatever was necessary to enhance economic growth, except, of course, turn over power. This was, after all, the same Deng Xiaoping who had led the

Tiananmen crackdown. Under the slogan of "reform and opening up," his policies facilitated external investment, permitted private and foreign ownership, enhanced the role of markets, and permitted partnerships (i.e., collusion) between local officials and businessmen.

All of these things had occurred before. Deng had declared the end of Maoist ideology and first offered the prosperity-for-legitimacy bargain in 1979. What changed in the early 1990s was the scale of the internal and external liberalization, breaking through even more taboos and fueling a new explosion of growth. Even more important was the timing. It came just as a wave of globalization swept the world during the 1990s and allowed China to become a key link in the international global supply chain. As tariff walls and transportation costs fell, multinational companies looked for the cheapest platforms to produce and assemble goods. China, with its low wages, low land prices, permissive environmental policies, and political stability, became their default option for manufacturing, processing, and assembly. This was true not only for the labor-intensive goods that sell in Wal-Mart but also for more high-end products such as notebook computers that are purchased on the Internet.

The best measure of this new role is a measure called "manufacturing value added" (MVA), which is more or less the value of finished Chinese products minus the value of the imported raw materials and components they were manufactured from. From 1990 to 2001, the last year for which data are available, China's MVA grew by 3 1/2 times, from $116.6 billion to $407.5 billion. It contributed almost 30 percent of the global growth in MVA and was responsible for most of the MVA growth in East Asia.[5] Since 2001 and the global recession, China's share of manufacturing has only accelerated, as Japanese, South Korean, Taiwanese, American, and other companies move more and more operations to China to remain competitive.

Buoyed by exports, China's economic achievements have been impressive. Its gross domestic product has been growing at about 9.5 percent per year over the past twenty-five years. Based on new data released at the end of 2005, China now has the fourth-largest economy in the world, trailing only the United States, Japan, and Germany.[6]

That it continues to grow at a 9.5 percent rate on a base that continues to expand is a remarkable feat itself. (Even if we were to adopt the more conservative figure of 8 percent, output is still doubling every nine years.) Although more than one hundred million Chinese are still very poor, many times that many have been lifted out of poverty over the past quarter century. In the coastal areas, a middle class is emerging, and economists estimate that China will become the world's second-largest consumer market by 2014.[7]

One reason for China's performance has been the growing quality of the Communist Party leadership and the skill with which it has addressed an array of challenges. Each cohort is better than the last. They are committed Marxists in terms of their long-term goals, but they are not ideologues. They are technocrats, seeking the best solutions to the daunting problems they face, within the circumstances of one-party rule and China's current position in the international economy and global balance of power. They are quite conscious of the problems they must address even though they do not always have answers. They are also nationalists. They aim to make their country a world-class power in this century and will not be content with the subordination and sometime humiliation that China suffered for the past two centuries. They are not resigned to their country forever, for example, assembling notebook computers, with the advanced components produced someplace else. Rather, they look to the day when those components will be designed, developed, and produced in China. To this end, China is producing a growing number of engineers, graduating six hundred thousand people with some level of engineering skills in 2004.[8] China's leaders understand that it will take a long time to fulfill that ambition and to ensure a comfortable standard of living for most of their country's population. But they are serious about their goal.


China's economic growth has created mutual dependency with the United States. America is the market of choice for its manufactured exports. Fully one-third of China's exports go to the United States, and as the following table shows, U.S. imports from China increased more than tenfold from 1991 to 2004. American exports to China increased significantly over the same period, by almost six times. American producers shipped over $28 billion more in goods in 2004 than they did in 1991. The U.S. trade deficit vis-à-vis China has mushroomed: $12.69 billion in 1991, it was $161.98 billion in 2004 and $201.63 billion in 2005. Millions of Chinese depended on the American market for their jobs, just as millions of Americans depended on China for consumer goods at reasonable prices. According to Morgan Stanley, low-cost manufacturing in China has saved American consumers $600 billion over the past decade.[9] (It should be noted that the U.S. trade deficit with East Asia as a whole has remained fairly constant over time; the countries with which it runs bilateral deficits are changing as manufacturing moves.)

### Total Exports vs. Imports to China 1991–2004[*]

|      | U.S. Exports to China | U.S. Imports from China | Balance, U.S. perspective |
|------|-----------------------|-------------------------|---------------------------|
| 1991 | 6,286,833             | 18,975,798              | −12,688,965               |
| 1992 | 7,469,573             | 25,675,509              | −18,205,936               |
| 1993 | 8,767,104             | 31,534,834              | −22,767,730               |
| 1994 | 9,286,759             | 38,781,143              | −29,494,383               |
| 1995 | 11,748,447            | 45,555,432              | −33,806,985               |
| 1996 | 11,977,921            | 51,495,276              | −39,517,356               |
| 1997 | 12,805,416            | 62,551,934              | −49,746,518               |
| 1998 | 14,257,953            | 71,155,860              | −56,897,908               |
| 1999 | 13,117,677            | 81,785,930              | −68,668,252               |
| 2000 | 16,253,029            | 100,062,958             | −83,809,929               |
| 2001 | 19,234,827            | 102,280,484             | −83,045,656               |
| 2002 | 22,052,679            | 125,167,886             | −103,115,207              |
| 2003 | 28,418,493            | 152,379,236             | −123,960,742              |
| 2004 | 34,721,008            | 196,698,977             | −161,977,969              |
| 2005 | 41,836,534            | 243,462,327             | −201,625,969              |

[*] TradeStats Express TM–National Trade Data 2005 ($USD in thousands), www.tse._export.gov (various pages).

There is mutual dependence of another sort. China earns dollars from its American trade surplus. One of the ways it recycles those dollars is to purchase U.S. Treasury securities. According to the Department of the Treasury, China held $60.3 billion in these securities at the end of 2000, $78.6 billion in 2001, $118.4 billion in 2002, $157.7 in 2003, and $193.8 in 2004. China's participation in Treasury auctions has helped keep interest rates low, in spite of fiscal deficits.

Within this relationship is a shift in the balance of power. The CIA estimates that China's gross domestic product (GDP) in 2005 was $8.883 trillion and that of the United States $12.18 trillion, using the purchasing power parity method of calculation.[10] Because China's economy is growing faster than America's, at some time in the not too distant future China's GDP will surpass that of the United States. Granted, GDP is not the only or the best measure of economic power. America's GDP per capita will probably exceed China's for centuries. The United States still has significant resources in science, technology, and finance if it chooses to husband and exploit them. If, however, China emerges as a true economic rival to the United States, might China challenge the terms of the bilateral economic relationship or even the postwar global economic system itself?

There is another point that needs to be made about China's economic miracle: it has, without overstatement, conducted the most successful antipoverty program in the history of the world, based on the sheer size of the country and the enormous progress it has made in the past quarter century. One can debate the exact measurements, but by a rough accounting, some 300 million to 500 million people have been lifted out of a previously destitute existence. Many now have Western-style middle-class living standards within their likely reach in the next few decades. A country once known for some of the worst mass starvations of modern times has become, despite its human rights problems and the continued poverty of much of the country's interior and other challenges, a reasonably good place to live for a large fraction of its citizens—certainly by developing country standards. With their long-standing interest in the well-being of their fellow human beings, Americans can feel gratified by this development. Of course, natural disasters or other tragedies still could strike China, but overall, a country that was once one of the world's main objects of charity and worry has now learned to stand on its own two feet. In this sense, given its values and ideals, America has really had little choice other than to root for and do its part to promote China's growth.

It was also in the early 1990s that China's military, the People's Liberation Army, had a rude awakening. During the previous decade, it had embarked on a leisurely modernization of its military capabilities, lulled into a complacency that its previous rivals—the United States and the Soviet Union—were becoming less threatening. Civilian leaders told the generals in this more peaceful environment that military power would have to grow only as fast as broader economic growth. There was no need for a more rapid buildup. It didn't matter that China's own defense industries were woefully backward or that China performed badly in a brief conflict with Vietnam in early 1979. Military modernization would be gradual.

Then three things happened. First, China shifted its threat perception of the United States in the wake of the Tiananmen incident. Previously Beijing believed that America's aid to China's economic development far outweighed any danger it might pose to the regime. After the 1989 crisis, however, Washington's intentions were seen through a paranoid lens. Any negative policy—economic, security, human rights—was interpreted as somehow targeting the Communist regime. This was not in fact American policy, but many Chinese believed that the United States had again become a threat to the country's national security. At best, it had resumed a policy of containment.

The second development was the U.S. military's stunning victory over Iraq in the first Persian Gulf War. This was significant in two ways. First, China's own military was very much like Iraq's: heavy on Soviet-style ground forces and prepared for a low-tech war of attrition. Second, the Chinese military saw for the first time how a high-tech, highly mobile military with substantial air and naval assets like the United States could perform in combat.

So China's leaders faced the shocking realization that their own military was weaker than they thought and that the U.S. armed forces were more capable than they assumed at the very time when anxieties about U.S. intentions were growing. To make matters worse, China's more robust defenses were against the former land enemy, the Soviet Union, not against the potential Pacific adversary, the United States.

Then there was a third trend: Taiwan. As we will elaborate in chapter four, China's hopes for a peaceful reconciliation with the island waned in the mid-1990s. Instead, fears festered that Taiwan's leaders had begun a campaign of irreversible separation with Washington's witting or unwitting support. We believe that China's assessment of Taiwan's intentions was incorrect, but its sense of threat to its national security was no less real. All three drivers—U.S. policy, U.S. military strength, and Taiwan—led Beijing in one direction: a buildup of military power. The pace began slowly in the mid-1990s and accelerated at the end of the decade.

There is no debate in the United States that the People's Liberation Army is stronger today than it was in the early 1990s. Nor is there any question that the PLA is accumulating the ability to project power beyond the Chinese mainland in ways that were never before possible and that may eventually come in contact with the projected power of the United States. But there is a debate on precisely how strong China is at any given time, on how soon the friction with U.S. armed forces may come, and on what China's strategic intentions are. It would be surprising if there were no argument, for the simple reason that the Chinese government is not transparent about most details of its military modernization. It is likely that the leadership itself has not defined its long-term strategic objectives beyond the general goal of restoring China to the position of regional and global preeminence it occupied centuries ago. How it would do so and how it would manage the implications for other powers have not been spelled out.

As a result of that lack of transparency, there has been, for example, a long-running discussion among outside experts about the size of the Chinese defense budget as one measure of the scale and pace of the modernization effort. All agree that the government's publicly stated budget figure is understated. Different views have been offered as to what fraction of the total the public figure represents: a quarter? a third? a half? There is a growing consensus outside of China that the stated figure is now roughly comparable to half of what makes up a Western defense budget. And that metric may not be the most revealing for American security interests. It may, for example, be more useful to focus on what capabilities China is acquiring that will be projected against the United States, or those that are relevant for a conflict over Taiwan. Here, a rough but interesting measure is China's spending on foreign military equipment. The Stockholm International Peace Research Institute estimates that foreign deliveries to China of major conventional weapons totaled $2.58 billion from 1992 to 1995, $3.59 billion from 1995 to 1999, and $10.26 billion from 2000 to 2003.[11]

Every year, the Department of Defense provides a lengthy report on Chinese military power in response to a congressional mandate. These reports include a wealth of information on the PLA's acquisition of capabilities, both equipment and institutional structures. They also seek to interpret what those capabilities might mean for China's future intentions, even as they emphasize the difficulties of doing so. "Secrecy envelops most aspects of Chinese security affairs. The outside world has little knowledge of Chinese motivations and decision-making and of key capabilities supporting PLA modernizations."[12] Thus the 2005 report, released in July, was cautious in predicting China's future direction, but one scenario it did identify was that Beijing might use its economic clout, reinforced with military power, "to attempt to dictate the terms of foreign security and economic interactions with its trading partners and neighbors." Moreover, the Pentagon noted that Chinese military acquisitions could not be explained simply as preparations for a possible war against Taiwan, as many of them can. Missiles have a range that extends beyond Taiwan. Current and likely air and naval systems, such as aerial refueling, advanced destroyers, submarines, and sophisticated command and control, all suggest missions that reach well beyond an island only a hundred miles from China's coast. The DOD report warns: "China does not now face a direct threat from another nation. Yet, it continues to invest heavily in its military, particularly in programs designed to improve power projection. The pace and scope of China's military build-up are, already, such as to put regional military balances at risk."[13]

That is, the Pentagon was, in effect, inferring that China was doing the very thing President Bush's 2002 National Security Strategy warned potential adversaries not to do: "pursuing a military build-up in hopes of surpassing, or equaling, the power of the United States." The unstated implication: China's power projection would someday bump up against U.S. power projection in the western Pacific.

There was another American perspective made public in the summer of 2005 on the Chinese military buildup. This was the *Atlantic Monthly* cover story, "How We Would Fight China," by Robert Kaplan, the acclaimed author of *Balkan Ghosts*. It was quickly dismissed by specialists for being overly alarmist, but there was one reason why it should have been taken seriously. The article was worth dismissing because it was a combination of false advertising and misplaced analogies. The title was a misnomer, for the article forecast more a cold war than a hot war between America and China. And Kaplan saw China as the new Soviet Union, the Pacific Ocean as the new North German Plain, and the savvy sailors and airmen of the U.S. Pacific Command as the latter-day analogue of NATO.[14] Yet Kaplan's article should have been taken seriously given the principal sources of his information: the officers in the Pacific Command, an arm of the Department of Defense. It should be very significant that the individuals in command of America's front lines in the Pacific apparently believe there is a cold war in our future. For like their bosses in the Pentagon, they have some power to act on their perceptions of the trajectory of Chinese military power.

Economically and militarily, China's rise may be a gradual thing. In its regional political influence, China has already made tremendous strides. At just about every point of the compass, Beijing has had improved relations with its neighbors during the past decade or more.

Simultaneously, and usually by neglect, the United States has lost influence.[15]

In 1992, China established diplomatic relations with South Korea. There were compelling economic interests to do so, given South Korean strengths in technology, management, and finance. And Beijing pulled off this coup without offending its longtime ally North Korea too much. The South Korean public saw China in an increasingly attractive light as they grew to resent the U.S. military presence in their country and Washington's policy toward North Korea. As time went on, moreover, China emerged as the pivotal player in peninsular diplomacy, sponsoring multilateral talks and mediating between North Korea and the United States, gaining leverage over both in the process. On balance, China had emerged a clear winner.

Regarding post-Communist Russia, China developed a very friendly relationship after decades of hostility with the Communist Soviet Union. Russian presidents Boris Yeltsin and Vladimir Putin have held frequent summits with Chinese leaders Jiang Zemin and Hu Jintao. Russia is China's main source for advanced weapons systems and an outside source of energy. The two often line up against the United States on key foreign policy issues—Iran's nuclear program, for example.

To its west, China took the lead in forming the Shanghai Cooperation Organization (SCO), a multilateral organization that tied Beijing to Russia and the countries of central Asia that emerged from the fall of the Soviet Union. It began with a focus on nontraditional security threats such as terrorism, an emphasis that only became more important after September 11. It has since expanded both in membership and in functional scope to include confidence-building measures and economic issues. In 2005 the SCO supported Uzbekistan's demand that "foreign forces" depart from the region. The appeal was an obvious reference to the military bases the United States had employed after 9/11.

On the Indian subcontinent, China for decades was allied with Pakistan against India, which was aligned with the Soviet Union. After the latter's collapse, Beijing began a slow process of repairing its hostile relations with New Delhi. Most progress has occurred in the economic arena, and suspicion remains strong on the security side. But the level of tension has declined significantly. The United

States has not been absent here. Indeed, the Bush administration has worked hard to improve relations, even resolving disagreements over India's nuclear program. But China probably has come further with India in a shorter period of time.

Another zone of significant Chinese progress has been Southeast Asia. The region has many of the raw materials that China's manufacturing base requires (but its own manufacturing industries worry about the competition). China's leaders have accommodated themselves to the norms of the Association of Southeast Asian Nations (ASEAN) and proposed to make it the foundation of a free-trade area and a regional community organization. Since 9/11, meanwhile, U.S. policy toward Southeast Asia has focused single-mindedly on counterterrorism and offended Islamic sensibilities in the process. Most governments in the region know it is in their interest for the United States to remain in the region to balance China, but they are perplexed that Washington has allowed Beijing to gain an advantage so easily.

The only exceptions to this string of diplomatic successes have been Japan and Taiwan, where that lack of progress is remarkably telling. Both are cases of "warm economics, cold politics." That is, their companies depend on manufacturing platforms in China to ensure economic growth at home, but Tokyo and Taipei each faces a unique set of obstacles to harmonious political relations. We will explore Taipei's in the next chapter. Between China and Japan there is a complex set of issues that subvert any objective potential for cooperation. These include:

- Rivalry over which country will be number one in East Asia.
- The history issue: memories in China about Japan's aggression in China in the 1930s and 1940s; the Chinese Communist Party's exploitation of those memories to bolster its legitimacy; the whitewashing of the past in Japanese historiography, including some school textbooks (though many fewer than in the past); and mutual resentment over how each side handles the history issue.

- Military buildups on each side, plus Japan's closer security alignment with the United States and Chinese fears that Japan may assist "Taiwan separatists."
- Competition for energy resources, particularly in the East China Sea.
- The tendency of political leaders on each side to be swept along by nationalist sentiment rather than to contain it.

In one sense, China's regional gains should not be surprising. Many have been a natural result of its geographic position, human resources, and economic strategy of reform and opening up. It was only when the three melded in the late 1980s and 1990s that China took full advantage of the opportunities that had existed for some time. On balance, economic ties have been mutually beneficial. And China is served by a cadre of highly skilled diplomats who, while not flawless, generally do an outstanding job in reassuring the neighborhood that their country's intentions are benign.

Yet what China has achieved politically on its periphery seems to be more than catchup. It is asserting leadership of a kind that was once reserved for the United States. As early as 1997, as the Asian financial crisis spread through much of Asia, China earned high marks by keeping its currency steady and providing assistance. In the fall of 2002, when George W. Bush and Hu Jintao made back-to-back visits to Australia, it was Hu who made the better impression by far. His visit to Latin America in the fall of 2004 made an even starker contrast. The United States is losing its soft-power appeal, often for reasons that have nothing to do with East Asia. In a variety of ways, deepening security ties with Japan may not be sufficient to counter the proliferation of Chinese political influence.

We therefore have the makings of a danger that historians and strategists instruct leaders to ignore at their peril. The Greek historian Thucydides wrote almost twenty-five hundred years ago that the root cause of the Peloponnesian War was the growth of Athens' power and the sense of insecurity that caused in Sparta, the dominant power of the day.[16] To state the proposition generally, international conflict is most likely when global and regional balances of power shift. China is gaining economic power and translating that into military power and political influence. All of these gains are occurring to some degree at the expense of the United States, whose presence as East Asia's "external balancer" has kept the peace and whose global economic centrality has fueled the region's prosperity. In short, will the challenge that a rising China ineluctably poses to the United States result in a conflict that damages both them and the East Asian region? To be blunt, is it inevitable that war—or at least an unpleasant, competitive, and potentially dangerous rivalry—will occur between a rapidly ascendant China and a still-strong United States? According to a traditional saying in Southeast Asia, "When two elephants fight, the grass gets trampled." (Southeast Asians have a sense of humor; and the saying goes on, "When two elephants make love, the grass also gets trampled.")

It is worth noting that with China's rise, something more is going on than simply a previously poor, weak country flexing its new muscles. A unique historical consciousness is energizing China's contemporary ambition. It is the only world civilization or great power to have fallen on hard times and then had a realistic hope of revival and return to glory. Two millennia ago, China's Han Dynasty was more or less the equal of the Roman Empire. Both collapsed, but while Europe was mired in weakness and division for another thousand years, traditional Chinese civilization remade itself twice, in the Tang Dynasty and the Song Dynasty. These dynasties were wonders of the world at those times and, relatively speaking, combined economic vitality, social coherence, political effectiveness, military power, and cultural brilliance. At their height, these dynasties ruled over a territory more or less equal to that of China today and one hundred million people; the United States did not reach a population that large until the 1910s. Historians of science tell us that a thousand years ago, during the Song Dynasty, and some eight centuries before the West, China possessed the ingredients for an industrial revolution but somehow failed to put those ingredients together.

Most educated Chinese, if not most Chinese, are deeply proud of this cultural heritage and past greatness. They feel a sense of shame that their civilization was unable to meet the challenge of the West (and still resent the West for having posed the challenge over the past two centuries). China's economic growth over the past twenty-five years and spreading international clout provide Chinese today with some optimism that their country and civilization can return to greatness, as well as with a strong sense of historic responsibility to bring that about.

Is there any way that a rising China and a globally dominant United States can avoid a negative relationship, with a growing chance of war, in the twenty-first century? For some theorists of international relations, any time a great rising power encounters an established one, war is likely as they sort out their relative places in a new international order. China's willingness to play by the rules of today's international system, in their eyes, is just a means of playing for time. For other observers, it is obvious that the Middle Kingdom, after being humiliated by the Western powers and Japan in the nineteenth and twentieth centuries, will resurge with a vengeance as it establishes itself, and even throw its weight around as it rights old wrongs that are seared on the national memory. These are deterministic predictions based on broad power trends and historical realities. Still other specialists focus on the specifics of today's world. They argue that war could occur as the two countries compete for diminishing Persian Gulf oil supplies. Or they think China may attack Japan (or even Russia) over disputed resources and disputed views of their respective histories, possibly dragging the United States into war indirectly through alliance relations.

We disagree. We think that all of the above issues are well within the capacities of the Chinese and American peoples and governments to handle peacefully, and even in most cases cooperatively. There will be untold numbers of challenges, to be sure, requiring the diligent efforts of thousands of business leaders, government officials, and private citizens on both sides of the Pacific. But for reasons we explain below, we think it highly likely—if admittedly not inevitable—that war can be avoided, and in fact generally friendly relations maintained, between the world's two twenty-first-century behemoths.

That is, we feel confident about this conclusion for every issue but Taiwan. Taiwan is the one big issue dividing the two sides that China views as a matter of sovereign pride and territorial integrity, and that the United States views as a matter of maintaining its commitment to fellow democracies as well as a stable and dependable global alliance system. It is the one big subject where the use of force has been explicitly viewed by both sides as a possible tool in resolving the issue. And it is the one fundamental problem involving the two big countries where the actions of a third party beyond either of their control can have an unpredictable and incendiary effect on their interactions with each other.

For these reasons, much of this book is about Taiwan—why it is a big problem, how it became one, what we can do about it, and most of all how to avoid an escalating war should a crisis erupt despite our best efforts to prevent one. The next chapter, by contrast, is more optimistic in its findings. We attempt to explain why several hypothetical causes of U.S.-China war are in fact either implausible or highly unlikely to cause direct military conflict, debunking them one by one.

# 3

# Competition versus Opposition

I n the past ten years—if not the past fifty, for that matter—American perceptions of China have oscillated dramatically. Candidate Bill Clinton talked of the "butchers of Beijing," but as president, in 1997, he declared the goal of "moving toward a constructive strategic partnership" with the PRC. Candidate George W. Bush termed China a strategic competitor and seemed braced for an adversarial relationship until September 11 changed American security priorities dramatically. With his penchant for alliteration, President Bush soon talked of ties that were candid, cooperative, and constructive. In fact, as former secretary of state Colin Powell was fond of noting, the American relationship with China cannot be reduced to a slogan on a bumper sticker. The interactions between the two huge countries, the world's only established superpower and its main rising power, are far more complex than that and will remain so. There will be many issues on which the two sides cooperate because they benefit enormously from doing so (as with economics), or because for the sake of their own nations and the world they must (as on human health matters). There will be others on which they keep a wary eye on each other as they cooperate and compete.

Some students of history and theorists of international relations argue that much more often than not, great powers wind up in adversarial relationships with a high likelihood of going to war. Great writers of the past, from Thucydides to Hobbes, have explained the tendency of strong states to assert themselves. This could be described as the international relations equivalent of Darwin's theory about the survival of the fittest. In particular, rising powers tend to want more say in how the international system is run than established powers tend to peacefully grant them, often leading to war. This is in large part the story of what happened with Germany and Japan in the early twentieth century.[1] And China is headed in a very impressive direction. Even if its annual economic growth rate slows from the meteoric average of about 9 percent of the past quarter century to about 5 percent, by 2025 it will probably begin to approach the U.S. GDP (as measured in purchasing power parity at least), and its defense budget could easily approach $200 billion a year.[2] Moreover, China has used the tools of coercion and military force in its past, suggesting that its national character is not inherently different from those of other great powers in history—and that it could again become assertive as its strength grows.[3] Whereas there is a conventional wisdom that Chinese statesmen have a cultural proclivity to rely more on diplomacy than on coercion and military force, careful scholarship has proven that this is not the case.[4]

But "power-transition theory" is not an iron law of history, and many things are different today. One is the example of what happened when Germany and Japan behaved the way they did. Few if any believed world wars killing tens of millions to be possible when the guns of August sounded in 1914. Almost a century later, the world is probably wiser, at least about the risks of all-out war.[5] Second, nuclear weapons reinforce the painful historical lesson about the risks of large-scale conventional war, making the thought of great-power conflict over a general competition for influence seem absurd to all but the most irresponsible of leaders. As none other than Henry Kissinger recently put it, "The European system of the nineteenth century assumed that its major powers would, in the end, vindicate their interests by force. Each nation thought that a war would be short and that, at its end, its strategic position would have improved. . . . Only the reckless could make such calculations in a globalized world of nuclear weapons."[6]

In addition, wealth and power no longer depend nearly as much on the direct physical control of large landmasses as they once did. Indeed, what works for China in particular is integration into the global economy, even though the rules of that economy were largely established by the United States and its allies. China's own scholars and leaders say as much; its actions speak even louder than these words; its decision to join the World Trade Organization in 2001, and its continuing to open its economy to outsiders, reaffirm its beliefs and its resolve. Integration with the international economy makes good political sense as well, for it employs tens of millions of people and ensures domestic stability. While a rising power in one sense, China is also a status quo power, in that its rise—and the Communist Party's rule—are facilitated by the current international economic and political system, making it highly doubtful that China would seek to challenge it once strong enough to do so. The character of the modern global economy makes colonialism much less appealing; it also reduces the attraction of invading other countries. None of this suggests that people have become fundamentally nicer, only that the rules of the road and lessons of history have been clarified sufficiently to radically shift the tables against imperialistic war. [7]

Clearly this argument is somewhat theoretical and conjectural, especially as it pertains to China. But we do have a certain amount of real evidence from the past sixty years. Since World War II ended, very few wars have been fought among countries. The frequency is even less since the Cold War ended. Civil conflicts have been as prevalent as ever, reinforcing the point that the human race may not have collectively progressed very much. And new kinds of dangers, arising from terrorists and other small, irregular actors using modern technology in extremely destructive ways, underscore the severe dangers of the modern world.[8] But the nation-state system appears to have gained enough stability that countries rarely take up arms against each other.[9]

❀          ❀          ❀

Look at it in another way. One hundred or two hundred years ago, if one great power could gain primary access to a resource like oil, it would likely try to control the land under which the oil lay, if necessary invading the territory and establishing a friendly government or colonial administration there. It would then enjoy preferential access to that oil at the expense of not only the local inhabitants, but also other major powers in the international system. And that oil (or other resource) would also allow it to further build up its economic power, thereby furthering its military potential as well. This type of competitive world put everyone on edge, watching each other's every move and worrying about the consequences while also trying to beat other countries to the punch when key resources were up for grabs. In other words, both fear and greed were abundant.

Today, what happens is essentially this. The United States uses far more oil than any other country, so the international system clearly serves its interests. But it does not control Saudi Arabia or Iran or, for that matter, even Iraq in the process. It pays the same price every other country does for oil from those regions. In effect, it pays a net cost for the privilege of being the superpower, because its military takes primary responsibility for defending the global oil system that other major industrial states depend on. This American approach is not so much selfless as enlightened; it creates broad support for an international system that serves U.S. interests in expanding global trade and investment. But it also greatly reduces the odds that a rising power would see the status quo as unfavorable—as, for example, Germany did a century ago when it was essentially shut out of the competition for African and Mideast territories by the more established European colonial powers.[10] As Richard Haass writes, "Countries tend to challenge the status quo when they see it as being inconsistent with their national aspirations and vulnerable to challenge."[11]

On the specific matter of energy, there are further reasons not to worry too greatly about the potential for clashes. The U.S. and Chinese economies are so intertwined and interdependent that either would suffer greatly if the other were deprived of energy. As scholars such as

Amy Jaffe, David Zweig, and Bi Jianhai have argued, the fact that both China and the United States are both major energy importers should bind them together. They might, for example, agree to counter the strength of suppliers, and the uncertainties of the global oil economy, by agreeing to create much larger joint reserves.[12] They also might embark on joint projects to develop alternative energy supplies.

In broader terms, China's rise is, we believe, much less destabilizing than Germany's or Japan's in the first half of the twentieth century. First, it is rising fast, but still gradually—the world is adjusting to its importance over decades (for all the hoopla about the PRC's meteoric growth, Japan's economy is still more than twice as large as China's by standard measures even if not by purchasing power parity measures). Second, it is rising at a time in which the international system is still economically and strategically dominated by the United States-led alliance system, which comprises roughly 75 percent of global GDP and military strength.[13]

China's emergence as a center for global manufacturing has suddenly made it a key buyer of commodities of all kinds, particularly oil, and created a seller's market in the process. Chinese companies roam the world in search of providers of those commodities and, where possible, try to lock up exclusive supply relationships to ensure that the raw materials for Chinese factories will be available when they are needed. Beijing's diplomats have followed quickly behind its traders and investors, causing comment about China's growing influence. In some cases the influence is not all positive, for the commodity deals and infrastructure projects have provided protection to some bad actors (e.g., Hugo Chavez in Venezuela) and undermined environmental protection and good governance.[14] But in today's world, China must negotiate, not intimidate.

There is another difference from the classic rising-power–established-power dynamic: the established powers, particularly the United States, have regarded the gradual integration of China into the international political system as a force for stability, not instability.

Great-power cooperation, not competition, is the current vision. The seed of this idea was sown during World War II by Franklin Roosevelt, and was why China became a permanent member of the United Nations Security Council. It sank real roots in the 1970s, when Nixon and Kissinger opened up relations with Mao's China, and grew once Mao was replaced by more pragmatic and less ideological leaders. China was seen as a potential partner to be engaged, in the hope that it someday would work with Washington in running the international system. And in recent years at least, Chinese leaders appear to have understood that this is the American strategy.

There is another way some arrive at the broad conclusion that a rising China and the United States will likely clash, less by reference to China's GDP or defense budget or population than to its system of government. In short, it is not a democracy; it is an autocracy. Its leaders are not accountable to the public and, as smart as they may be, make decisions on external policy in general and on war and peace in particular with less reference to public opinion than democratic systems do. Indeed, the fact that democratic leaders must be responsive to their publics and accountable for their actions is the basis for the "democratic peace theory," the idea that established democracies do not tend to fight each other. Clearly, that idea does not apply to China, because it is not a democracy, much less an established one. Some would state the basic hypothesis differently and emphasize that this dictatorship is animated by Communist ideology, and note that this ideology was historically associated with expansionist foreign policy ("exporting revolution").

Let us be clear: China's government is authoritarian; it is not the best one for its people or its neighbors; and it can be brutal and ruthless toward its political opponents. Chinese leaders need to understand that as long as they suppress their own citizens' political activities, imprison their dissidents, mandate abortions as a population control mechanism, curtail religious rights, force North Korean political refugees back to their country of origin (to be tortured or killed) when they reach Chinese soil, and turn a blind eye on Sudan's and Iran's human rights abuses to cultivate oil deals, United States-China relations will not elevate to the level of true friendship or alliance. Partnership, yes; true and trusted friend, no.

But today's China is not an old-fashioned Communist state. Chinese leaders have done three enormous things right in the past thirty years.

First, at home they have adopted pragmatic (and often capitalistic) economic policies that have resulted in the most massively successful antipoverty campaign in the history of the world. Rapid growth has fostered economic inequality between those who have done very well and those who have been left behind. But the leadership understands the need to reduce this gap. Second, even if China remains a far more oppressive state than it should be, the scope of oppression has shrunk. By and large, those who feel the harsh hand of the state are those who challenge its authority. Those who simply wish to be left alone are now, unlike the situation during the Mao period, left alone. (Yet for all the accomplishments, Chinese know how far they still have to go in addressing huge problems of poverty, corruption, societal and political unrest, reform of a still-bloated and inefficient state economic sector, and other problems. If China's power and wealth and growth rates dwarf those of most other countries, so does the scale of its remaining challenges in a country of 1.3 billion people.[15])

Third, in their dealings with other countries they have put aside the more aggressive posture of the Mao period and taken a much more pragmatic and cooperative approach.

They have stopped trying to subvert the governments of neighbors in an effort to foment Communist takeovers. Over the past almost three decades, they have instead built effective business and political relationships with solid capitalist countries such as South Korea and Australia. Whereas Beijing supported Communist parties in Southeast Asia before 1979, it distanced itself from them (or even shut them down) thereafter because they became obstacles to good-neighborly relations as well as trade and investment. With Taiwan itself, the economic interaction is stunning in scope. From next to nothing as recently as 1990, Taiwan's cumulative investment in China probably exceeds $100 billion, and cross-strait trade is now approaching $70 billion a year.[16] In some ways, China has gotten better at regional diplomacy than the United States itself, especially in recent years, while Washington has been focused primarily on the war on terror.[17] Perhaps this latter approach, often described as China's policy of "peaceful rise," is a disguise, intended to lull neighbors into a false sense of complacency while China is still building up its strength. If so, China has done a magnificent job of masking its true intentions—one far more sophisticated than any old-school Stalinist thug ever managed. And should it become more hegemonic in the future, after its strength has increased, many of the countries now hedging their geostrategic bets and alignments—South Korea, Australia, Vietnam, Indonesia, Russia—will likely become more inclined to strengthen their ties with the United States.[18]

China's leaders have given up the export of revolution. They export goods, and lots of them. The Communist Party has not necessarily given up its ideals, even as it has used capitalistic methods to restore its legitimacy and improve the livelihood of the Chinese people. What is driving Chinese foreign policy today, however, is national interest, as is the case with most other countries in the world. China wants to expand its influence, particularly vis-à-vis the United States. It envisions and even desires a reduction in American power. Recent polls among its elites show that about two-thirds of all respondents admire America's wealth and domestic policies but resent its purported hegemonism.[19] And its more perceptive and open analysts, such as Wang Jisi, dean of the School of International Studies at Peking University, see China's relationship with the United States as inherently complex and difficult. But these same observers seem to be aiming for a multilateral world, with China perhaps "first among equals" in Asia and one of the world's key powers, rather than anything akin to global hegemony or a systematic displacement of America's current role in the international system.[20]

China's ambition is colored by history and specific issues such as Taiwan. In former American government official Robert Suettinger's apt words, it is a "moderately discontented regional power, angry about American support for Taiwan . . . and resentful of American leadership pretensions and of what it perceives as overbearing American behavior."[21] Or to paraphrase Richard Solomon, former U.S. assistant secretary of state for East Asian and Pacific affairs, China is hypersensitive about being treated equally and as a great power, and self-righteous in believing it has been wronged in the past and thus is deserving of special treatment in the future.[22]

These mind-sets do not always make dealing with China easy. But an ideological crusader intent on overthrowing the international system China is not. It has demonstrated a continually improving maturity and reasonableness in most of its judgments in recent years. This is not to say that China has stopped watching out for number one—only that it now sees its own interests increasingly harmonious with those of the broader international economy and global order. It is Communist, it is true, but it is also capitalistic, and increasingly interconnected with the rest of the world— and it is even becoming increasingly open, step by step, with its own people. It is also increasingly run by competent, serious people who have jettisoned ideology for professionalism. As a Singaporean scholar, Kishore Mahbubani, put it admiringly, "to watch the world's most populous society experience the world's most rapid growth is like watching the fattest kid in school win the 100-meter hurdles."[23]

Ironically, even if ideology has not been driving Chinese foreign policy, many Chinese believe that it has driven American foreign policy toward their country. After the Tiananmen tragedy of 1989, they interpreted various elements of American policy as designed to undermine the Chinese Communist Party. Trade disputes (e.g., on intellectual property rights) were designed to retard China's growth. Support of Taiwan and the Dalai Lama were part of a separatist plot. And the purpose of the American human rights agenda was to weaken the Leninist system. None of this paranoia had a basis in fact. But these American "policies" seemed more dangerous precisely because China was now more open. This sense of anxiety has waned as China has become more confident and as American leaders have assured their Chinese counterparts that they have no intention of carrying out "regime change." The focus on democracy as a goal of George W. Bush's foreign policy has caused cobwebs of doubt to linger in Chinese minds, but on the whole their anxieties have diminished.

If ideology itself is not a source of worry, what about the authoritarian nature of the political system and the fact that leaders are not accountable to the public? In theory that could make them more extreme and thus more dangerous. What we do know, however, suggests that the regime is actually more moderate than the most outspoken sector of the Chinese public when it comes to the United States. When tensions increase on Taiwan, when American jets bombed the Chinese embassy in Belgrade, and when a Chinese fighter crashed after ramming an American surveillance plane, Chinese citizens offered their opinions on the United States and what their government should do. (They are allowed to broach such topics in newspapers and blogs and magazines, even though internal political matters remain taboo.)

In most such cases, the public believes the government is too weak in responding to America. The Foreign Ministry is known as the "sell-the-country ministry," which almost rhymes with the Chinese for foreign ministry. Public opinion has gotten too large to suppress when these episodes occur. Rather, the government allows people to vent and propose standing up to the United States. It cannot allow this to go on too far because at some point criticism of America may turn into criticism of the regime. So at an appropriate point, the leadership lays out in some fashion the reasons why a hard-line response is not in China's interests (including economic dependence), and the crisis subsides.

Would China's leaders go to war to rally public support at a time of domestic difficulty? The Communist Party does manipulate nationalism, but it does so within limits. Even nationalist demonstrations against Japan or the United States quickly become a two-edged sword for the regime because they can always be turned inward.

There may be circumstances under which China's leaders might decide to go to war with outside powers. But they will have much to lose in any such war, notably China's role in the international economy. They would need to convince themselves that there was very good reason to fight. Ideology disappeared long ago as a reason, if it ever was one.

Even if a rising, Communist China shows no interest in picking a fight with the distant United States, might it wind up causing a war by attacking a key ally, such as longtime regional rival Japan? It is this very mechanism that we worry about in regard to Taiwan. But as for America's major regional allies—notably Japan and South Korea—as well as Thailand and the Philippines, together with distant allies such as Australia and close partners such as Singapore, there is less reason to think war truly plausible.

In theory one could tell several types of stories about how war could break out. Perhaps with the Philippines as a target, China might enforce its claims to seabed resources in the South China Sea, where various countries argue that they own disputed islands—and thus the resources surrounding them. Or China could pick a fight with its neighbor Japan—a historical nemesis, even if economic interests have often coincided in modern times. Disputed islands and seabed resources could provide the spark, but the real motivation in fighting Japan would perhaps be nationalism.

Such conflicts are remotely possible but seem extremely unlikely. For example, while the South China Sea does hold some valuable resources, it is no Persian Gulf or even North Sea. China would be making enemies with half a dozen countries at once (and risking access to their markets) if it pursued its aims in this way. In addition, all of China's moves in the past decade have been away from aggressively pursuing access to these seabed areas. As scholar Sheldon Simon put it, "China accepted the UN Law of the Sea as a basis for negotiations, achieved bilateral understandings with Malaysia and the Philippines, raised the prospect of joint development, and agreed to discuss the Spratly [Island]s with ASEAN multilaterally."[24] Moreover, the sea lanes are already entirely available to China; it does not need to fight a war to control them. In addition, the United States has made it clear that it does not interpret its alliance commitment to the Philippines to include fighting on Manila's behalf for disputed islands in the South China Sea (though this position can admittedly work both ways, weakening deterrence by making the chance of some kind of conflict greater than it might otherwise be, since China might not fear American reprisal).[25]

The bigger question is probably Japan. Here there really is a certain amount of genuine bad blood, largely the legacy of Japanese imperialist aggression in the 1930s and 1940s. Both sides are capable of being riled up against the other; both are too proud to see disputed territories, even if uninhabited islands, seized by the other by force. But both are also highly codependent countries, and leaving aside the direct military risks of war, the economic fallout of conflict would be staggering in its likely effects on both (since it is very hard to imagine normal trade and investment patterns resuming after a violent conflict). For all the ongoing worries stoked by disputes over competing claims to seabed resources, differences of opinion about history, and raw nationalism, the two countries are quite pragmatic.[26] For Japan in particular, even as it has increased its security role in recent years, the limits on that role are still stark.[27] One can begin with the fact that even as it deployed forces to Iraq, it placed them under such restrictive rules of engagement that other foreign troops were needed to protect the Japanese self-defense forces there. Japan's recent moves toward a more normal and unencumbered security posture are better interpreted as a form of what former Bush administration official Michael Green calls its "reluctant realism" than any latent militarism.[28] And as Japan expert Mike Mochizuki notes, whatever Japan's enduring problems with "the history question," allegations about its willingness to whitewash history are often exaggerated. For example, an overwhelmingly high percentage of its textbooks accurately describe the atrocities that Japanese forces committed in China in the 1930s and 1940s.[29]

On top of all of the above is an additional stabilizing factor: the role of the United States in the region. The bottom line is that as long as America remains firmly committed to its Asian allies, it is far more likely to deter China from attacking them than to be dragged into conflict. China could not seize any substantial amount of territory, or cause any notable amount of damage, to these countries without making a war against the United States nearly inevitable. And half a century of American presence in the region has largely conveyed this message.

By contrast, China may doubt America's commitment to Taiwan, where China has the strong sovereign claim to control (at least in its own eyes), and where the United States has no formal security treaty or even diplomatic relations. But leaders in Beijing could hardly doubt the U.S. resolve to stand by its major state partners in the region. So stability seems overdetermined. The stakes are too low to justify even a successful war—the economic fallout would be disproportionately great; and any war would in fact probably not be successful due to intervention by the United States.

But are there newer dynamics in the U.S.-China relationship that could lead to war—or at least a fundamental deterioration short of war? Is it possible, for example, that economic ties, which are principally what bind the two countries together, could sunder? After all, severe economic problems led to real wars in the past. To take the most recent major example, in the 1930s worldwide economic depression and the devastating economic legacy of World War I helped produce the political brew that allowed for Hitler's rise (although they were not the drivers of his aggression). Does China's more aggressive economic diplomacy, which includes investment in companies in Asia, Africa, and indeed Latin America as well as the United States itself, also raise questions about whether it has the intent of gaining geostrategic influence in the Western Hemisphere—with possible security implications?

Just because U.S.-China economic relations have been significantly positive over the past three decades does not, in and of itself, mean that they will continue to be positive. There are a couple of areas that, if not adequately addressed, could weaken the belief in the United States that trade with China is a mutually beneficial proposition. That belief is particularly important in the American business community because it is the source of political support in Congress and elsewhere for the relationship.

The first area of concern is macroeconomic asymmetry between China and the United States. Americans spend too much and Chinese save too much. That is the fundamental reason for the huge American trade deficit with China (just over $200 billion in 2005), which China helps finance with its purchase of U.S. Treasury securities (keeping U.S. interest rates low in the process).

Other problems emerge as symptoms of this basic asymmetry, one of which is the undervalued Chinese currency. Ultimately there must be an adjustment to reduce this asymmetry. The question is whether it will be gradual or sudden. Far preferable is a gradual, mutual adjustment to increase saving on the American side and increase domestic demand on the Chinese side. In China, that in turn requires creation of a social safety net and funding of health, unemployment, and pension systems, particularly as the population ages and as more old people are dependent on fewer young people. In the absence of that social safety net, meanwhile, Chinese families are driven to save at very high levels and do not spend. Chinese companies export to survive.

The second area of concern is China's failure to protect foreigners' intellectual property rights. Too much of China's economic growth is being powered by the theft of knowledge created by American and other foreign companies. This is not the first time that piracy of intellectual property has occurred, to be sure, but it is occurring on a much larger scale than before. Unchecked, it can negate the fair-trade premise on which the free-trade system is built.

China's leaders understand the need to create a social safety net to stimulate domestic demand and the need to protect intellectual property rights. The question is whether they can do so. Until now, they have lacked robust institutional capacity to carry out these goals and, in the case of the safety net, they also have lacked the financial recourses. The corruption that the Communist Party has condoned to stay in power is another serious obstacle. One can speculate, in a worst-case scenario, that macroeconomic imbalances and intellectual property piracy abuses become so entrenched that for the U.S. and Chinese governments, like America and Japan in the 1980s, trade and investment become daily headaches—or worse—and not sources of opportunity.

There are other economic issues that create foreign policy problems. One is China's investment in companies around the world, particularly those that produce oil and other natural resources. President Hu Jintao used his November 2004 visit to South America at the time of the the Asia-Pacific Economic Cooperation (APEC) summit in Chile to sign a whopping $100 billion in investment commitments to Latin America. China or Chinese firms with ties to the PRC government also have shown an interest in potentially strategic assets—such as the UNOCAL energy bid in the United States in 2005 (later withdrawn).[30]

Another very sensitive issue is China's effort to obtain foreign technology illicitly (both for economic purposes and for more immediate military purposes). As an assistant director of the FBI's counterintelligence division put it, "China is the biggest [espionage] threat to the U.S. today." The FBI believes that China may have set up more than three thousand front companies in the United States to acquire military or industrial technology illegally.[31] Nor are the Chinese beyond trying to steal classified information or materials, as several investigative panels have documented.[32] For example, Congress's so-called Cox Commission in the late 1990s explained how China stole design information for U.S. nuclear warheads and obtained classified information on rocket technologies as well.[33]

So there is the nontrivial potential that an accumulation of economic issues between the United States and China could "tilt" the relationship into a conflicted mode. Unlike the difficulties between Washington and Tokyo in the 1980s, there would be no alliance to compensate. Indeed, security concerns about China's direction— plus continuing human rights problems—would only aggravate the economic problems. As Ted Fishman writes in his best-selling book *China, Inc.*, "As China's new economic might helps it acquire geopolitical clout, its growing political power and strategic presence also hinder the rest of the world's ability to force China to compete on a level playing field."[34]

Again, however, while a war over currency or illegally burned DVDs alone is theoretically possible, it seems practically implausible. The more likely scenario is for the two sides to muddle through and find ways to manage the economic tensions rather than be trapped by them. Their codependence is just too strong. As noted above, China's leaders understand what they must do. Their challenge is to create the capacity to do it. They also understand that the United States, with its vast market, is the destination point for much of China's manufacturing, and sustaining that manufacturing at a high level is key to solving three major domestic problems. First, job creation remains a constant challenge. The number of job entrants is more than twenty million a year, about the population of the state of Texas. Second, the reform of the inefficient state sector, with hundreds of millions of employees, is not yet anywhere near complete. Third, creation of an efficient mechanism for the allocation of capital is in its early stages. In the meantime, state banks weighed down with nonperforming loans keep inefficient state-owned enterprises afloat. Just as Chinese leaders know that they need economic growth and the American market to grow out of the old system of state planning, so American companies know that the China market remains a good bet for a profitable future. Both sides are prepared to muddle through.

Moreover, China's trade practices are hardly predatory. It has chosen to base its economic growth on the strategy of opening up to the global economic system and to foreign direct investment—a very different strategy than Japan pursued. Indeed, according to one of the world's top experts on China's economy, Nicholas Lardy, it is "perhaps the most open of all emerging market economies." It has become the location where many manufactured goods are assembled because of its efficiencies, economies of scale, and low-cost workforce—as well as its openness to imports of foreign manufacturing capacity, raw materials, and constituent parts for finished goods. While its trade surplus is large with the United States, it is not so large with the world as a whole. Although China is a substantial threat to those who are losing their jobs due to the migration of manufacturing to the PRC, most of those jobs have moved from other places in East Asia, not from the United States. As a measure of that, the aggregate U.S. deficit with East Asia as a whole has actually fallen in recent years. Moreover, the China trade has been a great boon to many consumers in the form of less expensive goods.[35]


Even in the event of trade tensions, and whatever the degree of conflict they might cause, the proper approach is to draw on the repertoire of available policy instruments rather than force a deterioration in the bilateral relationship into a cold-war state. Economic complementarity and codependency are facts of life and are liable to remain so. The countries are likely to still need each other's markets and to value their economic relationship, even as one of them seeks to curtail it somewhat. And they are likely to avoid economic collapse even as their relationship potentially sours. Among the remedies available to the United States are the dispute-settlement mechanism of the World Trade Organization, which was one of the important reasons to bring China into the WTO in the first place. In addition, several authorities are available under U.S. trade law that could be used as necessary.

As for China's acquisitions of foreign companies, they need to be watched, but they also need to be placed in perspective. China's investments in overseas national resources reflect as much its dependence on external suppliers as they do global ambitions. It is more plausible to interpret them as efforts to spread Chinese "soft power" and to expand China's economic interests, in a way similar to how the United States itself acts around the world, than as a cunning creation of Trojan horses all over the planet. And they may not always work out to China's advantage. There is some question, for example, as to whether all of President Hu's November 2004 investment commitments in South America will be honored, and whether some acquisitions in Africa will be profitable.

That a Chinese-run firm proposed for a time to acquire UNO-CAL, an American energy company, was not the danger to the national security that some portrayed it. UNOCAL accounts for much less than 1 percent of global oil production. Most of its assets are in Asia, where China understandably has substantial interests, and even with this acquisition, China would have controlled less of global oil production than the nearly 10 percent it consumes. It also would have continued to have far less investment in the United States than Americans have in China. Most likely, the proposed acquisition reflected a desire to assure future energy supplies in light of China's growing dependence on external sources.[36]

The U.S. government does have a mechanism for assessing foreign purchases of American companies. It is the Department of the Treasury's Committee on Foreign Investments in the United States (CFIUS), and in the aftermath of the Dubai Ports World brouhaha in early 2006, CFIUS is scrubbing its procedures to make them more effective for today's world. Ultimately, however, a balance must be struck. The United States must remain open to foreign

capital if only because we support the policy of American investment in other countries, including China.


Another place where a balance must be struck is in the field of dual
use technologies—that is, know-how that has a legitimate civilian
use but military applications as well. One example would be a
super-computer that might be used for both weather forecasting
and tracking missiles. Since the American military advantage over
China lies in its technological advantage, the United States has considerable interest in slowing the flow of know-how where there is
reason to believe that the end user will be the Chinese military, not
a civilian entity. Key areas of relevance concern high-energy lasers;
advanced optics; submarine quieting equipment; stealth technologies; and perhaps of greatest concern in the PRC case, high-
performance computers. Yet controlling dual-use exports has
become very complicated. The fast pace of technological change
means that factories in China are now assembling desktop computers that are more sophisticated in terms of their processing speeds
than units the U.S. government prohibited on security grounds fifteen or twenty years ago. Furthermore, the United States is not the
only provider of these technologies. Unless export controls are multilateral, China will get what it wants from other countries. For the
most sophisticated items, however, the ones for which the United
States is the only source, there are established procedures for
reviewing which ones should receive a license for China and which
should not. When transfers occur without a license, stiff penalties
should be imposed.[37]

On the espionage front, we should assume that China will continue to try to steal technology it cannot purchase legitimately.
While such espionage is hardly unique to China, it is nonetheless
unfriendly in character and potentially dangerous to American
interests, and it is one factor that will continue to preclude a close
U.S.-PRC friendship. The United States should maintain a powerful counterintelligence tool kit for opposing that theft, including
criminal sanctions. That will both help deter the activity and defend
our "crown jewels."

Economics is about competition, so a certain amount of friction in our relationship is inevitable. We can manage that friction with strong and sound trade policy, export controls, and counterintelligence tools. What will prevent trade competition from becoming the source of deep-seated foreign policy conflict is mutual benefit that outweighs the competition. In that regard we should recall that for all the talk of its great economic strength, China's problems and challenges are staggering—and virtually all will require engagement with the international community to mitigate for decades to come. They begin with the simple fact that China remains a relatively poor country, with a per capita income only one twenty-fifth that of the United States.[38] The need to address that poverty plus the high U.S. standard of living and size of the American market create a complementarity that works in favor of mutual benefit. And we have economic tools to retaliate against China proportionately if and when it cheats.

None of these major structural realities about the rise of China or the nature of U.S.-China relations should spell war or conflict short of war. Still, there is obviously real tension in their relationship for some of the above reasons. This tension, combined with the specific spark of a Taiwan problem, could contribute to a real crisis even if it is highly unlikely to produce confrontation on its own. For all the mutual dependency and cooperation, Washington and Beijing remain uncertain about each other's intentions.

The best way to characterize what is happening is that each country is hedging against the other. Because neither can take the positive declarations of the other at face value and must take seriously evidence to the contrary, each takes steps to ensure that it is prepared in case things turn out for the worst. In each capital's policy, cooperative approaches coexist with competitive or defensive ones.

Each country's military treats the other as a potential foe, and shapes acquisition, budgets, and planning accordingly. Beijing's and Washington's diplomats each seek to expand their nation's influence in Asia and beyond. Each seeks to strengthen regional institutions that serve its respective interests. The United States is quite explicit

that it is pursuing a two-handed approach. The Pentagon's Quadrennial Defense Review, released in February 2006, stated: "Shaping the choices of major and emerging powers requires a balanced
approach, one that seeks cooperation but also creates prudent
hedges against the possibility that cooperative approaches by themselves may fail to preclude future conflict."

Neither can be completely confident that the other's declarations of benign motives are believable. Take China, for example.
Beijing was pleased in the latter part of 2005 when Deputy Secretary of State Robert Zoellick proposed that the United States and
China work together as "stakeholders" to take special responsibility
for the peace and stability of the international system.[39] That
appeal, an elaboration of the FDR vision of sixty years before, constituted an American acknowledgment of China's great-power status and essential equality with the United States. On the other
hand, Beijing watched as the Pentagon was transforming the global
posture of the U.S. military. Most relevant to China was the buildup
of Guam as a major deployment point and the strengthening of
security relations with Japan, Australia, and India (the Guam
buildup had global purposes, too, but China would naturally look at
the regional impact). China also has not liked the annual Pentagon
reports about China's purportedly troublesome and threatening
military buildup.[40] Simultaneously, economic frictions were rising
and with them the possibility of anti-China legislation or action in
the World Trade Organization, or both. So which would be more
telling for China: American words or deeds?

The United States is in the same ambivalent position. The
premise of China policy for more than three decades has been that
we can shape the PRC's interests and values by integrating China
into the institutions of the existing system while simultaneously
benefiting from access to the Chinese economy. At the same time,
we watch China's military buildup, its past history of proliferation,
and its repressive policies at home.

In this context, neither Washington nor Beijing is prepared to
jump to the conclusion that the other is a permanent adversary, for
that would create an insidious dynamic: if strategists and military
planners on both sides were to assume that a cold war is the best

that China and United States can expect, they will prepare accordingly and create a self-fulfilling prophecy. Some version of containment would be the result. Joseph Nye's advice remains sound: if Washington treats China as its enemy, it will become its enemy. The same goes for how Beijing treats Washington. Leaders on each side understand this danger and the need to reassure the other that its intentions are in fact benign.[41]

There are some problems with a hedging strategy. The first is that there needs to be coordination between the cooperative and defensive elements. Leaders in Beijing and Washington need to ensure that the relevant bureaucracies do not in their mindless pursuit of their mission end up working at cross-purposes. Specifically, if defense establishments run amok, it will destroy the delicate balance that comes with hedging. Second is the issue of domestic support. Public opinion in each country tends to be wary about the intentions of the other and supports the negative side of the hedging policy. It is up to leaders to remind publics of the broader, positive vision for U.S.-China relations. And third, in an environment of strategic uncertainty and reciprocal hedging, issues arise that can exacerbate mutual suspicions and trigger the crisis that neither side wants. Between the United States and China, we believe that Taiwan is easily the most likely trigger.

Generally, when it comes to future relations between the United States and China, there is good reason for cautious optimism.[42] To be sure, inherent difficulties occur when a new power seeks to insert itself into an international system that it did not create and when the established power that created that system faces such a challenge. And given the demands of managing a U.S.-China relationship in which future intentions are unclear, the temptation to hedge is strong. But the odds are good that with strong leadership on both sides, a mutual accommodation between China and America is possible, one that can gain public support in both countries. More broadly, in the messy, globalized world of the twenty-first century, the United States, China, Japan, Europe, Russia, and perhaps India and

Brazil probably have sufficient interests in the survival of the international system as a whole that they may see the value of subordinating their narrow national interests to work cooperatively to preserve that system and promote peace, stability, and prosperity. That China is a permanent member of the UN Security Council gives it reasons to do so. In the process, there will be absolutely no need for China and the United States to fight for relative supremacy—over ideology, over economics, or because of the actions of a U.S. treaty ally such as Japan.

There is one precondition to this assessment, however: the resolve of the United States to continue to play the kind of leadership role it has played since World War II. On a variety of dimensions, America is losing the lead and the edge that have allowed it to set the agenda for the international system and to set the terms of mutual accommodation for newly rising powers such as China. Because the United States has global responsibilities, it must maintain a lead in each major region, including East Asia. And because America has always led as much by example as by effort, with both soft power and hard power, it must devote equal attention to both. Regaining America's lead will require returning to what made the United States strong in the first place: a sound fiscal policy; ample resources for building science and technology; a high-quality education system that is accessible to all; the institutional infrastructure for a knowledge-based economy; and a strong defense. These in turn will require political leadership and a broad-based public consensus. But they are achievable, and we expect that they can and will continue to be achieved in the future.

We are much more troubled over the matter of the Taiwan Strait. This is not because the two sides of the strait want war; far from it.

But war could happen.[43] Unlike the hypothetical danger of war from great-power competition or economic clashes or ideological disagreement, a Taiwan crisis is more plausible because it would involve a concrete matter of intense interest to both large powers, and a matter over which a third party has the ability to shape many events.[44]

# 4

# The Lost Island

A true war between Taiwan and China might seem implausible, since the people have a lot in common and too much to lose. Signs of friendship abound. In early 2005 and 2006, for example, Chinese airliners transported Taiwan businessmen home for the lunar New Year holiday. In the spring of 2005, Taiwan's political opposition leaders traveled to China to be received warmly by the country's president, Hu Jintao.

There are a number of reasons why conflicts often occur that are simply not the case here. War will not happen, for example, because the people on the two sides of the strait are like Israelis and Palestinians or Bosnians and Serbs, riven by a deep, tribal animosity. It will not occur because of ideological differences between communism and its opposite. We will explain these reasons by telling the story of Taiwan and its complex history with China. We will then turn to why war could *very well* happen.

Look below the surface and you will see seeds of a conflict rooted in the soil of history. While there may not be sharp ethnic differences between mainland Chinese and island Taiwanese, powerful and contending national identities are at play. For people in the PRC, returning Taiwan "to the embrace of the motherland" after five decades of Japanese colonialism and five more of Kuomintang rule is part of what it means to be Chinese. For many Taiwanese, however, the key to their identity was that outsiders denied them the right to shape their destiny during most of the twentieth century. For them, China is not a mother figure, and its embrace would constrain rather than comfort.

Taiwan is a leaf-shaped island about a hundred miles off the coast of southeastern China. Taiwan is about equal in size to Connecticut and New Hampshire combined. Until the sixteenth century, it was sparsely inhabited by aboriginal peoples. Then Taiwan became attractive to residents of southeastern China. These Chinese came to trade but especially to farm, since land was becoming scarce on the mainland. They planted their settlements on the broad coastal plain on the western side of the island. Farming was easy, and through intermarriage the settlers soon assimilated the indigenous peoples who were their neighbors on the western plain. These "cooked" aborigines quickly disappeared from history. Chinese who ventured into the central mountainous chain and down the narrow eastern coast usually met with danger from the "raw" aborigines who lived there and who remained, making trouble.[1]

This Taiwan migration is interesting in three ways. First, these were Chinese people. They saw themselves as Chinese and transplanted the Chinese folkways of their native places to their new homes. True, these were the folkways of southeastern China, but it was part of Chinese culture all the same: the Chinese family system, Chinese gods, Chinese language, and so on. Just as the English people who settled the eastern coast of North America and planted English folkways at about the same time continued to see themselves as English men and women, it did not occur to the new residents of Taiwan that they were not Chinese.

Second, this migration was part of the centuries-long spread of Chinese people from the China heartland outward in all directions—to coastal areas in the southeast and south, to Sichuan, central Asia, and Manchuria, to Taiwan, Tibet, Southeast Asia, and ultimately to America. Sometimes the spread was only in the form of people. In other cases, areas of new settlement were incorporated into the Chinese state. In others, the situation was ambiguous.

In the case of early Taiwan, the Manchu imperial government established the island as a prefecture of the southeastern province of Fujian in the late seventeenth century, but that was only form. The stark reality was that the island was still very much a frontier area. Even the Fujian governor had only loose responsibility. For two centuries, conflict was endemic among immigrants from three distinct places on the mainland, unassimilated mountainous aborigines, and weak government forces. Each group was like an armed camp, and the fights were pitched battles.

By the late nineteenth century, Taiwan's society and polity resembled that of mainland China. Farmers grew crops to feed their families, pay the rent to landlords, and sell on the market, just as their cousins did across the strait. Smart young men took exams to enter the imperial civil service. Those who were literate read Chinese texts. Those who were not listened to stories in the dialects of southeastern China. Old and young prayed to images that had been blessed in temples in China and that were returned to those "mother temples" to have their spiritual power revived. In short, Taiwan became a Chinese society, warts and all.[2]

The third point is that growing Sinification of the Taiwan frontier paralleled the European powers' penetration of East Asia. Dutch and Spanish colonialists had outposts on the island for a while in the seventeenth century but soon departed.

By the nineteenth century France and Japan saw a strategic value in Taiwan's position amid regional sea lanes, and it was Japan that took Taiwan as a prize for defeating China in a war in 1895.

Japanese rule was a mixed blessing for Taiwan's people. The army and the police were strict, but officials in charge of agriculture, education, and health fostered economic and social development. On balance, Japanese colonialism probably strengthened the Taiwanese sense of their Chinese identity.

When Chinese forces took over Taiwan from the Japanese at the end of World War II, the Taiwanese were genuinely pleased to see an end to foreign colonial rule. Their experience at the hands of their new rulers was another story, one to which we will return.

But what is relevant for us in this history is the simple conclusion that no deep-rooted tribal animus exists between the people of Taiwan and the people of the Chinese mainland. Ethnically, at least, with the exception of several hundred thousand aborigines (about 2 percent of a total population of some twenty-three million), they are all Chinese. Generally, they have the same physical features. Their spoken dialects stem from the same root language, and the language of instruction in schools tends to be standard—or Mandarin—Chinese. The written languages are somewhat different for reasons that have to do with political history, but they are both based on pictographs rather than Western phonetic script. After taking account of regional cuisines, the food in restaurants in the mainland cities of Beijing and Shanghai and Guangzhou is more or less the same as you would find in the Taiwan cities of Taipei, Taichung, and Kaohsiung. Taiwan children hear the same legends and historical tales as children on the mainland. And when people on each side of the Taiwan Strait pray to Chinese gods, they all pray to Buddha, or the Goddess of Mercy, or Mazu.[3] This is not the hardwired hostility of Israelis and Palestinians or English and Irish or Serbs and Bosnians. If we are looking for kindling with which to start the fires of war, we will not find it in ethnic and cultural differences between the two sides of the Taiwan Strait.

For the four decades after the end of World War II,[4] the Taiwanese suffered under an authoritarian regime in Taipei caught up in a tense struggle with Beijing during the most frigid part of the Cold War. On the mainland were the Communists of Mao Zedong, who vowed to liberate Taiwan. On the island was the exiled Nationalist Party of Chiang Kai-shek, which had lost the mainland in 1949 to Mao and fled to Taiwan. Its priority was a counterattack against the "Communist bandits." Although neither side could seriously threaten the other (particularly since the U.S. Seventh Fleet stood between them), each maintained something of a war footing for political purposes. A state of civil war was a convenient excuse for political repression.

Both claimed to be the true government of China. Internationally, Mao's People's Republic of China and Chiang's Republic of

China competed to represent "China" in international organizations such as the United Nations. The United States regarded Taiwan as a useful ally in the containment of communism, pledged to defend it against Chinese attack, and deployed significant American troops on the island. Taiwan for many years was a leading U.S. aid recipient and a poster child for conservative capitalist economic development, while Mao's China was a major example of radicalism gone inhumanely wrong.

There were a couple of occasions when war, even nuclear war, seemed possible. In 1954, Communist artillery batteries began shelling the Nationalist-held coastal island of Jinmen (then known as Quemoy). Mao's units were able to take some smaller islands and force the evacuation of others. Then in 1958, Beijing again shelled Jinmen and threatened to cut it off from resupply. Although the island had no military value, the United States feared the shock of its loss on Nationalist morale and, at some risk to its own ships, protected a Nationalist resupply effort. The crisis soon abated, but both episodes left Washington worried about being dragged into a war over Taiwan that was really not in U.S. interests. And in both cases, historians learned later, Mao Zedong probably overestimated the political gains he could secure through limited application of military force (coercive diplomacy).[5]

At this point we must shift our focus from what took place *between* China and Taiwan to what occurred *on* Taiwan itself. Here the storyline is how Chiang Kai-shek's Nationalist Party and army ruled the people of Taiwan after they took over the island in 1945 and how the people's response reshaped cross-strait relations once Taiwan became a democratic place. For many Taiwanese, democracy finally gave them—not outsiders—the power to determine their destiny.[6]

The Nationalist regime (known as the KMT, from one English spelling of its Chinese name) ruled Taiwan with an iron hand. Soon after its arrival, its troops, ill-disciplined and fearing a Communist plot, engaged in an islandwide massacre after a minor street incident spiraled out of control in February 1947, searing memories to this day. After Chiang Kai-shek's defeat on the mainland and retreat to Taiwan in 1949, he created a garrison state atmosphere. Political freedoms were restricted on the grounds that a civil war was still under way. Secret police penetrated every corner of the island's life and campuses overseas. Although the Taiwanese were 85 percent of the population, they were given only minimal representation in the token legislature because, the regime said, it was the government of all of China.

KMT repression went further, however. Thinking that Taiwanese had lost their national soul after decades of Japanese colonial rule, the regime embarked on a program to remold them into "good Chinese." Mandarin Chinese became the official language of instruction, even though it is nearly unintelligible to speakers of the local dialect and even though most local teachers did not know it. Soon Taiwanese children who were caught speaking their native tongue at school were punished. The curriculum was Sinified. Students learned about the history, geography, and literature of the Chinese mainland that most of them had never seen, and little of the island where their families had been for generations. In the military, mainlander officers treated Taiwanese conscripts harshly. Mainlanders displaced some Taiwanese civil servants. Taiwan cities were informally segregated socially.

These policies affected Taiwanese at various levels. The violence and arrests of the early years probably affected every family on the island. If a victim (either killed or jailed) was not a relative, it was a teacher in the village school or the local doctor or someone in the landlord's family.

Later, as it became clear that the Nationalists were there to stay and a kind of tense stability emerged, Taiwanese had to choose how to survive in the new order. Most channeled their energies and their frustrations into economic pursuits: first farming, then business, and then industry. Many did very well, and the island prospered. Some sought a haven in scholarship or the professions. For example, a bright young man named Lee Teng-hui pursued agricultural economics, and a poor farmer's son named Chen Shui-bian excelled as a maritime lawyer. They became the two most recent presidents of Taiwan. But there were hundreds of thousands of other examples.

Then there was the option of working for the Nationalist government. In the early years, it approached native Taiwanese to work for it because it needed the locals for their skills, as teachers, policemen, tax collectors, and so on. Later, it was to create the image of a more indigenous regime. For the Taiwanese so approached, this created a dilemma. Most of those who joined the regime simply needed a job, but they also knew that other Taiwanese might blame them for "selling out." Those with superior educational credentials were willing to be co-opted because they thought they might change the system from within in spite of their bitterness at how their people had been treated. Again, Lee Teng-hui is an archetype.

There were yet other strategies of adaptation. Many intelligent individuals continued their education overseas and then stayed because life was comfortable there and political life at home was not. Some of them began to engage in exile opposition politics. Back on Taiwan, some could not control their righteous indignation at KMT repression and became political dissidents early on. They were constantly in trouble. Others engaged in politics more carefully but still took great risks. And still others did not like the KMT regime but made an early decision to avoid politics because it would hurt their careers, only to be drawn in anyway. Chen Shui-bian is a model here.

However various Taiwanese adjusted, the KMT's policies had a perverse and counterproductive effect. This was to alter their consciousness about themselves. We noted earlier that Taiwanese saw themselves as Chinese when Chiang's forces arrived in 1945. But because the KMT sought to force them into a rigid Chinese mold thereafter—through the education system, through military service, and so on—they began more and more to regard themselves as something different. Their logic was, "If the harsh treatment that we are receiving is what it means to be Chinese, then we cannot be Chinese." Thus was born a Taiwanese identity.[7]

Some Taiwanese who came to this conclusion took a further logical step: that Taiwan should be an independent country. They have argued that there is no legal basis for the claim of either the Communist or the Nationalist regime that Taiwan was returned from

Japan to China. Although they will acknowledge that they have an ethnic Chinese heritage, they point to the English background of people in the United States, Canada, Australia, and New Zealand, all of whom have their own country. Some advocates of Taiwan independence fled overseas, first to Japan and later to the United States. (Only native Taiwanese seek Taiwan independence.)

Others on Taiwan have not been so categorical. There are many whose families have been on the island for many generations but who are prepared to admit that they are also Chinese. Then there are the children and grandchildren of the people who came from China as adults in the late 1940s and for whom Taiwan is all they have known. These two groups, with their very different histories, have mixed identities and together constitute about half the population. Then, of course, there are those who see themselves as Chinese only.[8]

What is important about the configuration of identities on Taiwan is that it is shaped by circumstance. Harsh KMT rule created a sense of Taiwaneseness where it did not exist before. Today, polls tell us, when China behaves badly toward the island, it tends to increase the sense of Taiwan consciousness. By inference, when China behaves well, those people with mixed identities will feel more Chinese and less Taiwanese.

There is one more notable dynamic to the notion of Taiwan identity. When it was dangerous to claim to be Taiwanese, few did it. Once it became safe, Taiwan suddenly became cool. (Indeed, at different times on the island, there has been Taiwan fever as well as China fever.)

Then, in the mid-1970s, a change occurred. On Taiwan, Chiang Kai-shek died in 1975, and his son Chiang Ching-kuo (CCK) assumed formal power. CCK had long been groomed to succeed his father. He had started out as head of the security services and enforced the repressive rule of the so-called mainlanders over the "native Taiwanese," those whose ancestors had migrated from China during the seventeenth to nineteenth centuries. He had long had a reputation as a thug. But he subsequently developed a reformist streak and started bringing loyal Taiwanese into the Nationalist Party and expanding the scope of elections.

In 1976, in China, Mao Zedong died. His rule had been such a disaster for the Chinese people and for the legitimacy of the Chinese Communist Party that other Communist leaders, led by Deng Xiaoping, concluded that they had no choice but to pursue anti-Maoist reform. Incrementally, Deng dismantled the worst of the Communist system and began a program of economic liberalization that resulted in the manufacturing powerhouse we see today.

More than fifty years before, in the 1920s, when the Nationalist Party and the Communist Party temporarily were allies on the mainland, CCK and Deng had been classmates. Now, in the 1970s, each finally had the opportunity to carry out reformist agendas. With the nearly simultaneous deaths of Chiang the father and Mao Zedong, the ideological obstacles that their elders had erected to cross-strait pragmatism were crumbling. There were those on each side who sought unrealistic maximal solutions and resisted compromise. Yet in a subtle Chinese way, CCK and Deng chipped away at those obstacles. In 1979 China ended the symbolic, every-other-day shelling of the offshore islands of Quemoy (Jinmen) and Matsu (Mazu) as a gesture of peace. Taiwan traders tested the business waters, seeking to create facts on the ground. For a while, Taiwan tourists slipped quietly across the strait. Then the Taiwan government legalized tourism by saying that elderly mainlanders who had come over with Chiang Kai-shek in 1949 could "search for their relatives." Thus the ideological hostility of the Chinese cold war did not vanish overnight. But as it waned, its power to produce a hot war quickly diminished.[9]

Business was a powerful driver in this slow-motion reconciliation. On the mainland, the economy was in a shambles after the Mao years. There were no indigenous sources of technology or capital, and the populace was in a sour frame of mind. If the Communist Party was going to regain its legitimacy, promoting prosperity was the surest way to do it. Taiwan had a different problem. It had been very successful, marrying American and Japanese technology and capital to relatively cheap yet talented Taiwan labor. But by the 1980s, labor was becoming more expensive, and the Reagan administration was exerting strong pressure to appreciate the Taiwan currency. Taiwan companies had two ways to maintain their competitiveness. One was to move up the technology ladder, into information technology products (which they did). The other was to move labor-intensive production in sectors such as shoes to China, where the wages were low, land costs were cheap, and officials were eager. The China Migration had begun.[10]

Economic interdependence has grown enormously over the past two decades. The recession that began in 2000 propelled much of Taiwan's information technology industry to China. The only way that the companies that assemble Dell computers could remain competitive was to move more operations across the strait. Accurate figures are hard to come by, but direct Taiwan investment on the mainland probably exceeds U.S.$100 billion. Annual two-way trade exceeded $70 billion in 2005. Approximately a hundred thousand Taiwan companies have operations on the mainland and employ about 10 million Chinese. As many as 1 million Taiwan residents spend a good bit of their time in China for business or other reasons.[11]

Business integration should have profound security consequences, in the direction of peace. Both China and Taiwan have a stake in this mutually beneficial arrangement continuing. Taiwan companies profit. People are employed, and in China in particular, employment means political stability. Neither side, therefore, has an interest in a war that would kill the goose that lays these golden eggs.

Nor does the international economy want this arrangement disturbed. In September 1999, Taiwan suffered a serious earthquake that interrupted production in the island's semiconductor factories. Prices of dynamic random access memory chips immediately surged 16 percent.[12] A significant conflict between the two sides of the Taiwan Strait would damage a critical link in the information-technology-sensitive international economy. There is not nearly enough spare capacity globally to replace the network of design shops on the island and factories on the mainland that Taiwan companies have built. Experts estimate that it would take at least a year and a half to replace that production infrastructure.[13]

Economic benefits affect security calculations in another way. China's leaders are still Marxists in at least one sense: they believe that economic interests shape political interests. Applied to Taiwan, this principle dictates that over time, whatever ideological hostility may have existed before between Chiang and Mao, the mainland's economic attraction and the fact that, as Beijing saw it, people on Taiwan were Chinese would sooner or later bring about political reconciliation.

For a while, Beijing's Marxist assumption seemed to be borne out. In the early 1990s, the Chinese and Taiwan governments set up organizations to conduct cross-strait relations. A number of practical problems that stemmed from the growing economic interaction were addressed. Senior statesmen from the two sides got together in a well-publicized meeting in Singapore in April 1993. Secretly, we now know, representatives of the two leaders had a number of productive conversations. Within the Taiwan public there was a China fever, and cross-strait links were forged in religion, sports, education, philanthropy, and museums. It seemed like progress would occur incrementally, in fits and starts, but progress all the same. Perhaps Marx was right.[14]

Then it all came apart. In July 1995 and March 1996, the Chinese missiles landed first north of Taiwan and then close to its two major ports. True, the missiles had dummy warheads and there was never any intention to go to war. But the stock market and the new Taiwan dollar were certainly affected. A shared Chinese ethnicity, the waning of ideology, and mutual business benefit didn't seem to matter.[15] What had gone wrong?

In the past two decades, nothing has reshaped America's interests and views about the cross-strait issue as much as the fact that Taiwan has become a thriving democracy. And nothing has done more to change the way leaders in Taipei deal with the mainland issue. The significance of this change cannot be overstated.

Taiwan became a democracy for several reasons. First of all, a Taiwanese opposition movement arose to challenge Nationalist repression. Some of its members wished ultimately to pursue an independent Taiwan. Others simply wanted to ensure that the mainlander-dominated KMT would not make a deal behind the backs of the Taiwanese majority. The opposition used every opportunity to pressure the regime to allow more freedom. Second, Chiang Ching-kuo had reasons of his own to liberalize. He wanted to appear more reformist than his former classmate Deng Xiaoping. He believed that having fostered economic prosperity, the KMT could stay in office more easily by running in truly competitive elections than by preserving a political monopoly at some cost. Finally, the United States had broken diplomatic relations in 1979 to open ties with China. Chiang needed a new basis for ensuring Washington's support, and values, in the form of a democratic system, seemed to be that basis. That related to another reason: pressure from American liberals in Congress. Their exposure of human rights abuses was causing the KMT bad publicity. Turning Taiwan into a democracy would turn these congressmen into allies.

China viewed these developments with some trepidation. That another Chinese society, Taiwan, should enjoy political freedom was something of an embarrassment, of course, especially after Beijing carried out the harsh crackdown on the Tiananmen demonstrations in 1989. More important than this ideological challenge, however, was democratization's impact on Beijing's principal goal: the unification of China. The Chinese Communist Party had always viewed Taiwan as a matter left over from the unfinished Chinese civil war. For U.S. audiences, they compared it to the American Civil War, to make two points: first, that they were as serious about national unity as Abraham Lincoln had been; and second, that this was a civil conflict, from which all foreigners should butt out.

Beijing could bide its time as long as there was some hope for unification. Actually, it *had* to bide its time because it did not have sufficient military power to bring Taiwan under its military control, particularly if the United States helped defend Taiwan. China had taken some small comfort in the fact that the KMT regime shared its view on the desirability of unifying China; it just disagreed on who should be in charge. And now, in the 1990s, there was the hope that the seductive power of China's economic attraction would weaken ideological barriers. What worried Beijing, however, was that competitive politics on Taiwan would bring to power forces whose goal was antithetical to its own: the permanent separation of Taiwan from China. And if unification became impossible, they believed, war would become necessary. Keeping alive the hope of national unification was at the heart of the Communist Party's legitimacy and the position of its top leaders. Should that hope end, the logic went, the party's legitimacy and the leaders' position would be in dire straits.

And this was not an abstract anxiety for China. The Taiwanese opposition, composed almost completely of native Taiwanese, had formed itself into the Democratic Progressive Party (DPP) in 1986 and incorporated the independence goal into its party charter in 1991. Should *de jure* independence someday become Taiwan government policy, the Chinese leadership would be inclined to act.

At first, however, China focused less on the DPP, which remained a minority, and more on President Lee Teng-hui. Lee was a Taiwanese scholar who had been brought into the KMT as part of Chiang Ching-kuo's effort to broaden the base of the party, and who had acquitted himself well in a variety of posts. In 1984 Chiang, in poor health, had named Lee his vice-presidential running mate, thus signaling that it was time to pass power to the Taiwanese majority.


Chiang died in January 1988, and Lee slowly consolidated his power. At first Beijing had little problem with him, even though he was a Taiwanese president. He proclaimed the goal of unification and stuck to KMT orthodoxy on the issue. Under his leadership, the first signs of reconciliation began in the early 1990s. Lee, for example, proclaimed that as far as Taiwan was concerned, the civil war was over. Then the two sides began to diverge. There were several problems.[16]

The main one was a fundamental difference over the approach to Taiwan's place in a unified China. China's approach was what it called "one country, two systems," which was formulated for territories that did not come under Communist control back in 1949 and that has since been used for Hong Kong and Macau. The one country is China, and the two systems are socialism and capitalism. The term "two systems" is something of a misnomer because China is becoming less socialist and, really, what is important is politics, not economics. The arrangement does permit the territories to preserve a great deal of autonomy in their affairs and for life to go on much as it did before. Hong Kong today operates much as it did under the British before the handover on July 1, 1997.

Yet even under this system of autonomy or home rule, China retains an effective veto over outcomes it fears. It has crafted the political system so that political forces unfriendly to China cannot come to power. Moreover, it dictates how Hong Kong participates in the international system. To put it another way, the PRC government remains the exclusive sovereign over Hong Kong, Hong Kong is subordinate to that central government, and Beijing has intended a similar unification arrangement for Taiwan.

Lee Teng-hui begged to differ on one country, two systems. Although he was not opposed to unification, he asserted that his government, the Republic of China (ROC), was a sovereign state, just like the PRC. Unification would have to take place on the basis of equality. Moreover, he asserted, as a sovereign state Taiwan had a right to participate in the international system.

This was a rather fundamental difference. Either Taiwan (or the ROC) was sovereign or it was not. But Lee was not defining the problem in a way that denied China its basic objective of unification. There are political unions made up of sovereign entities, such as the European Union. He was most assuredly rejecting China's formula for unification.

In addition to this conceptual impasse, other things happened to make matters worse. First, Lee Teng-hui got frustrated. He tried at the beginning of this negotiating process to make it easy for his Chinese counterparts by talking ambiguously. He referred to "equal political entities" instead of "equal states," but China did not reciprocate. It just stuck to the core of one country, two systems and gave him no incentive for restraint.

Second, the dynamics of the democratic process on Taiwan were proving combustible. Public opinion was growing increasingly frustrated at the quarantine Beijing had erected to prevent Taiwan from participating in the international community. When Taiwan people traveled abroad and presented their passports with "Republic of China" on the front, they would become irritated when immigration officers thought they were from the People's Republic of China. The opposition DPP saw an issue and mounted a public campaign for Taiwan to join the United Nations (the ROC had left in 1971 when the PRC entered). Lee's ruling KMT naturally saw the political need to co-opt the issue and so made it a government effort. As we described at the outset, when Lee Teng-hui began preparing for the first direct presidential elections, to be held in March 1996, he decided to boost his popularity by using Taiwan's influence in the U.S. Congress to secure a visit to the United States. The tactic worked and was immensely popular with the island's voters. In Beijing's eyes it was seriously provocative.

Third was the question of arms. The fall of the Soviet Union had created a global buyer's market in advanced weapons that China began to benefit from. Partly in response, Washington and Taipei argued, Taiwan had secured large numbers of F-16s from the United States and Mirage fighters and Lafayette frigates from France. But China then worried that so strengthened, Taipei would be less in a mood to negotiate.

Finally, Beijing looked at all these trends and drew the wrong conclusion. It could have given Lee Teng-hui the benefit of the doubt and viewed his actions as results of substantive differences, negotiating dynamics, and domestic politics—not an ironclad desire to create a new country. Instead, Chinese leaders decided that his actions were part of a plot to separate Taiwan from China. What Lee would call an effort to assert and strengthen Taiwan's sovereignty (but not negate the possibility of unification), Beijing regarded as secession. His goals, they judged, were in fundamental conflict with China's and had to be opposed, by force if necessary.

At the beginning of this book, we described China's response to the Lee visit to Cornell, on both the political and the economic fronts, and Washington's reaction to ensure that Beijing did not do "something stupid." War wasn't that likely because China did not have the resources to prosecute one, and stability soon returned. But look at the missteps on all sides. Did China misunderstand Lee Teng-hui's intentions and then overreact? Almost certainly, but given the complexity of the issues, and the limited amount of high-level interaction between Beijing and Taipei, that is understandable. China's use of coercive diplomacy certainly backfired, by harming its image in East Asia, in the United States, and, most importantly, on Taiwan. Did Lee Teng-hui overestimate Chinese tolerance? Probably. He later suggested he found it significant that a high-level mainland visitor had been in Taipei just at the time that Washington announced his American visit, and China had not reacted harshly. That for Lee suggested that Beijing was relaxed about his visit. But he really did not know. There was simply too little communication between the leaders of China and Taiwan.

Did Lee overestimate the leverage of Congress in the American system? Probably. He got his visit but damaged U.S.-Taiwan relations for a few years to come. Was the United States asleep at the switch? The Clinton administration was at a real disadvantage here. It was still adjusting to a Taiwan where democratic impulses were affecting foreign policy. Moreover, it was still reeling from the Republican takeover of Congress. Lee's lobbying campaign to get permission to make a visit was one of the most sophisticated in congressional history. His agents exploited every point of leverage and played up Taiwan's status as a fellow democracy to put Clinton in a lose-lose situation.

The 1995–1996 crisis had something of a sobering effect. But that effect wore off as new issues surfaced and little happened to clarify misunderstandings about motives.

Fast forward three years to the summer of 1999. Cross-strait relations had warmed somewhat, and the two sides were preparing for their first political negotiations. Lee Teng-hui commissioned a team of experts to work in secret to tighten the definition of Taiwan's legal identity—its sovereignty. The core idea was an explicit statement that there was a state on each side of the Taiwan Strait. The original plan for the special state-to-state formulation was that it would be deployed in private in the negotiations with China, but Lee jumped the gun. Before having a chance to share this concept with all of his advisers, and before he could discuss it with American officials, he made it public. He claimed later that he knew China was going to make its own preemptive statement. China immediately interpreted Lee's statement as an effort to wreck the talks and create the intellectual basis for independence. For several weeks it sent jet fighters into the Taiwan Strait to patrol more aggressively; Taiwan scrambled its jets in response. The United States was miffed because Lee had not bothered to inform it about this significant overture. It was also very concerned about the danger of an incident between a PRC pilot and a Taiwan pilot, with no telling what consequences. Washington rushed its diplomats (including one of the authors) to try to calm the situation. But note that the United States was unhappy with the tensions that Lee's statement created (and the fact that he had not consulted prior to making it), yet it did not criticize the content of what he said. That is, Washington never believed he was staking out an independence position. And some Chinese scholars have in recent years admitted that Lee's formulation is not as bad as it seemed at the time, and they wish they could have it back.[17]

Fast forward only a few months, to March 2000. Taiwan had another presidential election, and suddenly Beijing became extremely nervous. It looked like Chen Shui-bian, the candidate of the Democratic Progressive Party, might win. That was not due to a massive swing in Taiwan opinion in the direction of the DPP and independence. In fact, Chen took a moderate line on China to prove that his party could be trusted in power. The main reason why Beijing was anxious is that the KMT, the party that Lee Teng-hui led for twelve years, had split. China had expected a more acceptable candidate to win, but when it realized that might not happen, it began to threaten that a Chen victory might mean war. Chen then won by a narrow margin, and the United States again worked to moderate tensions. China soon realized that Chen would stick to a cautious course and so backed away from its threats. Still, a line had been crossed. The DPP, a party whose charter included the ultimate goal of independence in spite of its leader's stated moderation, had taken control of the presidency.

Fast forward again, to late 2003. Chen Shui-bian ran for reelection with little to show for his presidency because the conservative opposition was still in charge of the legislature. Gridlock had resulted. But Chen's own base supporters were unhappy since he had not promoted the DPP's more ideological objectives. To energize his supporters, Chen proposed a new Taiwan constitution to be enacted through a referendum. Chen's proposal had the desired effect within the DPP but it alarmed China, which saw it as a thinly disguised declaration of independence. The Bush administration, which had not been consulted, was first surprised and then annoyed. Was Chen taking the American defense umbrella for granted? What if an alarmed China (and China was alarmed) had chosen to increase military tensions while U.S. forces were occupied in Iraq? As it was, Beijing complained to Washington, and a frustrated President Bush was quick to criticize Chen Shui-bian in public. In the end, by dint of superior campaign skill, Chen gained reelection. He backed away from his campaign agenda, and both Beijing and Washington relaxed their guard (but China did so very slowly).

In summary, why do the leaders and the people of China care so much about Taiwan? By now, it is an issue wrapped up in the very ethos of Communist rule.

From the beginning of the Communist period in 1949, the goal of "returning Taiwan to the embrace of the motherland" was not subject to question.

It also was a staple of regime propaganda.

Taiwan had been a Chinese territory lost to foreign countries in the nineteenth century and so was symbolic of the humiliation that China suffered at the hands of the "imperialists." The Japan that annexed the island pursuant to an "unequal treaty" and allegedly "brainwashed" its people was the same Japan the Chinese Communist Party fought from the 1930s until the end of World War II and has been the object of chauvinistic appeals ever since. To make matters worse, Taiwan was the civil war refuge of Mao's nemesis Chiang Kai-shek, and it was from there that Chiang engaged in harassment against the PRC. To make matters even worse, Chiang's ROC regime was the government of China in the eyes of much of the world until the early 1970s. That the United States—Taiwan's protector and Communist China's principal enemy—was in Beijing's eyes the principal obstacle to fulfilling the goal of unification was yet another source of grievance.

For more than five decades, the only message the Chinese public heard on the issue was that Taiwan is an issue of national destiny. Party leaders believed it was a test of regime credibility. No conflicting point of view has been allowed. What has been allowed is a limited public discourse in Internet chat rooms, the blogosphere, and some journals. In those arenas, it never goes out of fashion to take a firm stand in favor of unification and against those who would block it (in Chinese eyes, Lee Teng-hui, Chen Shui-bian, and the United States).

By virtue of history, nationalism, and foreign policy, therefore, a leader who is perceived to have mismanaged the matter and to have been duped by the United States is a leader who is vulnerable to criticism from his colleagues, from foreign policy experts, and even from the public. The danger for the Communist Party is that its already weak legitimacy might be further undermined.

Regaining the island is the brass ring of Chinese politics; to somehow "lose" Taiwan can be the kiss of death.

# 5

# The Taiwan Tinderbox

Looking back over the sequence of cases between 1995 and 2004, the most obvious piece of good news is that there has been no war. In each crisis or minicrisis, China's leaders weighed what its military forces could—and could not—achieve, what the United States might do against it militarily, what it could do to pressure Taiwan diplomatically, and what impact military forces would have on the island's public over the long term. In each case, they concluded that Taiwan's leaders had not posed a challenge that was so great that it was necessary to go to war to protect the sacred political principle that Taiwan was part of China. They were always able to convince themselves that time was on their side in the long term and that when necessary in the short term, the right combination of threats, bluffs, and pressure on the United States would get Taiwan to back down and spare them the need to use force. Over time, they may even have begun to accept, at least subconsciously, that they are unlikely to get Taiwan back during their own lifetimes.

Another piece of good news has been the role of the United States. Successive administrations have understood that they need to help prevent war between China and Taiwan.

The Eisenhower, Kennedy, and Johnson administrations were committed by treaty to the defense of Taiwan but simultaneously worked to ensure that Chiang Kai-shek would take no action against China that would provoke a conflict and draw in the United States.

Washington terminated the treaty when it established diplomatic relations with China in 1979, but retained a vague commitment to defend Taiwan. Known as "strategic ambiguity," its very vagueness was thought to promote stability. According to this logic, China would not run the risk of attacking the island because it could not be sure that Washington would fail to come to Taiwan's defense; Taiwan would not risk something reckless (such as a declaration of independence) because it could not assume that the United States would intervene. Yet strategic ambiguity was more a journalistic bumper sticker than a full description of U.S. policy. And there was always the danger that too much ambiguity might lead China to underestimate and Taiwan to overestimate American resolve.[1]

In any event, since 1995, the approach evolved to take account of the changes in cross-strait relations. "Dual deterrence" is now a better description of U.S. policy.

Deterrence has two elements—warning and reassurance—and Washington usually deploys it toward both China and Taiwan. The United States warns China not to use force against Taiwan; on the other hand, it reassures Beijing that we do not support the permanent separation of the island from China. To Taiwan, Washington warns against political initiatives that would provoke a Chinese attack; it reassures Taipei that we will not sell out its security and democracy for the sake of good relations with China. Since each side knows the message the United States conveys to the other, it amounts to a conditional commitment to the defense of Taiwan—as before—but with a somewhat clearer and more activist American role.

Indeed, Washington does not simply express this approach as a matter of rhetoric. It supplements it with active diplomacy, translating these general principles into specific démarches. The balance of warning and reassurance toward each party depends on circumstances and whether it is disturbing or preserving the status quo. In late 2003 and early 2004, the Bush administration warned Taipei about Chen Shui-bian's campaign rhetoric and reassured Beijing. In early 2005, it warned Beijing about its plans to pass an "antisecession law" and reassured Taipei. The United States has also sought to strengthen Taiwan militarily, to further deter China by raising the costs of war.

Another piece of good news is that there has been some learning. China has become somewhat modulated in its reactions to the challenges it perceives from Taiwan. It used displays of force in 1996, general threats of force in 2000, and pressures on Washington in 2003–2004. The American foreign policy establishment also has learned. Democrats working in the Clinton administration were caught short when Lee Teng-hui initiated his effort to visit the United States to bolster his campaign for election in 1996. Thereafter they tried to keep him and Chen Shui-bian on a short leash. Republican foreign policy gurus thought that treatment was unseemly, and they provided a number of favors to Chen once George W. Bush entered office in 2001. Taipei may have gotten the impression that it had received a "blank check" and bore no responsibility for the conduct of the relationship (hence the failure to consult on matters of importance to the United States). Annoyed by subsequent actions by Taiwan, Republicans became as tough on Taiwan as their Democratic counterparts. Over time, all sides and actors were learning.

Another piece of relative good news is that the ever-deepening economic convergence that began in the mid-1980s is growing deeper every day. That benefits Taiwan companies and the publics on both sides of the strait. The desire to continue that prosperity is a good reason to avoid conflict.

Yet shared economic interests are not a guarantee of peace. Our first piece of bad news is that the migration of manufacturing from Taiwan to China creates economic losers on the island and some political anxiety. Whether it is true or not, some Taiwanese fear that China is gaining economic leverage over their destiny. Moreover, we should recall that there was a fairly high degree of interdependence in Europe early in the twentieth century. There were even pundits who predicted that the sharing of prosperity had made war a thing of the past. Obviously, World War I belied those predictions.

Another piece of bad news is the role of domestic politics in Taiwan, China, and the United States. Politics operates differently in each country, particularly authoritarian China. But it still has an impact, often unpredictable or uncontrollable—and quite often an escalatory effect.

We have already seen some of the ways in which a strong Taiwan identity has stimulated actions by the island's leaders that have provoked their counterparts in China. Lee Teng-hui's 1995 visit to Cornell and Chen Shui-bian's 2003 constitution proposal are cases in point. These leaders also are tempted to exploit popular fears of China for political gain.

In China, mass nationalism is a growing force that affects the leaders' conduct of Taiwan policy. Leaders have helped foster that mentality by permitting only a politically correct discussion of the Taiwan issue and by using their propaganda agencies to stigmatize individuals on Taiwan they do not like. But nationalistic fervor has taken on a life of its own. Taiwan, or Taiwan's resistance to unification, constitutes a thorn in the side of China's return to national greatness. China's Internet chat rooms flood with criticisms when an incident occurs on Taiwan that suggests the Beijing government does not have the situation under control. Ironically, China's Communist government is less able to handle this populist nationalism than Taiwan's democratic system is. To make matters worse, nationalism is the ethos of China's military, as it is of any country's armed forces. The People's Liberation Army exists to defend the nation's unity, sovereignty, and territorial integrity. In most Chinese eyes, Taiwan's leaders represent the most serious threat to those values.

So there exists in China at least a latent coalition between a nationalistic military and a chauvinistic public, arrayed against a relatively moderate civilian leadership trying, in its own mind, to manage a volatile issue.

Politics, broadly defined, also is a factor in U.S. policy. First, the Taiwan government has cultivated members of Congress for decades as an insurance policy against unfavorable executive branch policies. It also has relied on the Republican Party for protection. This influence has not always worked. Witness Richard Nixon's secret opening to China and George W. Bush's criticism of Taiwan after treating it so well at the beginning of his first term, particularly in the promise that the United States would "do whatever it takes" to help the island defend itself. But it does introduce a bias in the conduct of American policy. (The influence of the PRC is not trivial, either, but is less likely to lead to a crisis.) Second, the electoral calendar can have a distorting effect. Presidential candidates stake out positions on China and Taiwan that are outside the mainstream of past policy because they think they are useful for gaining the nomination or winning the election, only to find that the national interest requires them, sooner or later, to return to mainstream policy. In the interim, confusion is sown and damage is done—and the risk of war may, at least temporarily, sometimes increase. Third, the rapid turnover in the American system in both the executive and legislative branches means that the subtleties of China and Taiwan policy get lost as time goes on and as new policymakers come to the fore. Who remembers what is in the three communiqués, the Taiwan Relations Act, the Six Assurances, and so on?[2]

Another piece of bad news is that China has been building up its military power from the beginning of the 1990s and particularly since 1999. It has done so systematically and steadily. As China's economy has grown at about 9 percent per year, the real military budget has grown at a double-digit rate for a decade and a half, including acquisition of advanced systems from Russia, Israel, and other suppliers. Moreover, its program of modernization tends to have a specific target: Taiwan.

Acquisition of equipment, war planning, improvements in command and control, movement toward joint war fighting, and reforms in training and logistics are generally focused on a specific mission and in preparation for a specific conflict.

There is another element to these preparations. Although there may be some lingering ambiguity or conditionality about whether the United States will defend Taiwan in the event of a cross-strait war, Chinese war planners are remarkably conservative, like war planners in most countries. They assume the worst about the wars for which they prepare. And when it comes to a possible Taiwan war, they assume that in some way, the People's Liberation Army will be fighting the United States. This assumption has already been reflected in acquisitions of equipment: Russian destroyers with sea-skimming cruise missiles that could put U.S. aircraft carriers at risk;

Russian submarines that could do the same thing; medium-range ballistic missiles that could target American bases in East Asia.

This raises a very basic question. What strategy guides this military buildup? China's leaders see warfare as a *means* to achieve political objectives, not as an *end* in itself. They would agree with the German military theorist Karl von Clausewitz that war is "nothing but the continuation of state policy by other means." In the Taiwan case, the political goal of China's leaders is unification. But they can use the growing military assets at their disposal in one of two ways. The first is deterrence, to threaten Taiwan with war, but only to dissuade it from taking the step that China cannot abide: the island's permanent, legal independence from China. The second is coercion, to force Taiwan acceptance of political unification on Beijing's terms and preferred time schedule. Each strategy has a different assumption. The assumption of deterrence is that as long as Taiwan can be blocked from independence by threats of war, ever deeper economic integration will ultimately have its desired political impact. The assumption of coercion is that Taiwan is drifting apart politically, in spite of economic convergence. Most American China specialists would probably ascribe a deterrence motivation to China. The U.S. Department of Defense concluded in 2004 that China's strategy was "fundamentally coercive." It stated that the most likely goal of Chinese force development is "to compel Taipei's acquiescence to a negotiated solution by promising swift and effective retaliation if it does not."[3]

When it comes to deterrence, if all Beijing had to worry about were a 1776-style declaration of independence by Taiwan, then its job would be easy. Either there is a declaration or there isn't. But a long time ago Taiwan leaders announced that it would not declare independence because it already was independent! It was already a sovereign state. Understandably, Beijing was not reassured and concluded that it would not have the luxury of an either-or situation. It would have to remain vigilant for actions by Taiwan that were functional equivalents of independence. It would have to watch for accumulations of small actions that taken together constituted a qualitative change in the situation.

The problem, of course, is that it then becomes impossible to draw a clear line, and the evaluation of whether the line has been crossed becomes very subjective. On setting limits, it is necessary to avoid either too much specificity or generality. If China's conditions for force are too specific, then Taiwan might grab for everything except what is clearly specified. If they are too general, then Taiwan does not know what actions to avoid. The result is fuzziness, which only exacerbates subjectivity and instability. If Beijing and Taipei each have their own understanding of what the lines mean according to their respective logics, instability will result.

As an example of the ambiguity under which Chinese decision-makers operate, consider the "antisecession" law that the National People's Congress passed in March 2005. This was an effort to codify deterrence and state the circumstances under which force ("nonpeaceful means") would be used to counter intolerable Taiwan actions. Between the lines, we can detect an effort to strike a balance between specificity and generality. But if the final text reflects how the Chinese leadership will evaluate Taiwan's actions—and how it seeks to shape Taiwan's choices—then it is disturbing:

> In the event that the "Taiwan independence" secessionist forces should act under any name or by any means to cause the fact of Taiwan's secession from China, or that major incidents entailing Taiwan's secession from China should occur, or that possibilities for a peaceful reunification should be completely exhausted, the state shall employ nonpeaceful means and other necessary measures to protect China's sovereignty and territorial integrity.

Clearly, this set of warnings errs on the side of generality and ambiguity. If "the fact of Taiwan's secession" can occur "under any name or by any means," Beijing will be on guard against functional equivalents of a declaration of independence. The phrase "major incidents entailing Taiwan's secession" is vague in and of itself, but it probably represents a warning against actions that might not be problematic in and of themselves but could be part of a separatist plot or trend. Finally, the possibility of unification might disappear (whatever the reason).

Not only are these Chinese criteria for the use of force general and ambiguous, they also are highly subjective. Instead of it being objectively clear that Taiwan has violated China's interests and so justified the use of force, Beijing will decide, based on its own interpretation of the fuzzy lines it has delineated, whether Taipei has crossed them.


For China's leaders to err on the side of ambiguity makes a certain amount of sense. They have to react to a political environment—a democratic Taiwan—with which they are totally unfamiliar and that constantly changes. They cannot always gauge the significance of each of the myriad political initiatives that emerge on the island. Is it part of a campaign to advance the legal separation of the island from China forever, or is it just another appeal by politicians to their supporters? Ambiguity helps China's leaders maximize their room for maneuver in defining when there is a Taiwan problem and when there is not. It helps them retain the initiative. Because they fear surprises, because Taiwan can be a radioactive political issue, and because they sometimes try to enlist the U.S. government in bringing Taiwan leaders under control, ambiguity doesn't tie them down the way that specificity does.

But if deterrence is China's goal, too much ambiguity can be a dangerous thing. We doubt that China's leaders will use only the provision of the antisecession law cited earlier to decide whether to use force. China is not, after all, a nation of laws. True, the antisecession law was a deliberate effort to demonstrate to several audiences (in China, in Taiwan, and in the United States) that the Chinese government was serious about opposing separatism. But we do not think that China would be guided solely by those words. Still, the ambiguity of those words is a startling example of the open-ended and contingent basis on which China actually judges how to respond—forcefully or not—to a Taiwan provocation. It is rather akin to Justice Potter Stewart's classic definition of pornography, "I'll know it when I will see it." For China, "We'll know secession when we see it."

Magnifying China's very contingent approach to deterrence are three other factors. The first is Beijing's system for analyzing developments on Taiwan. Composed of a number of intelligence agencies and research institutes that have grown up over the past twenty-five years, this analytic apparatus has steadily improved in many areas. Yet it is still weak on the most dynamic features of Taiwan's democratic politics, and it is part of a decisionmaking structure that is still fairly centralized. There is a tendency, particularly under situations of stress, for higher levels to preempt lower levels and for policy to preempt analysis. The second is the arcane nature of some of the issues involved. The core of the China-Taiwan dispute is the legal connection between the island and the mainland and between the government in Taipei and the government in Beijing. China is not exactly at the forefront of constitutional law and so is not always well equipped to judge the significance or intent of developments on Taiwan. The default response is to be suspicious.

The third factor is a serious one. China does not talk much to Taiwan. If China had authoritative communications channels, it could clarify the meaning of its deterrence warnings and Taipei could clarify the significance of its political initiatives. But Beijing has tended to insist that Taiwan leaders allay its mistrust of their motives before creating communications channels, even for the sake of crisis prevention and crisis management. When Chen Shuibian took office, Beijing said that he had to accept some version of the "one-China principle" before it would resume political dialogue. Chen was familiar with PRC negotiating tactics and feared that if he accepted its principle he would be making major concessions before talks even began. So there is a pernicious vicious circle. Mistrust on both sides makes each reluctant to engage in communication, which is the only way to reduce mistrust and to mitigate the possibility of conflict—or to manage conflict once it has begun.

China's reliance on ambiguity in its conduct of deterrence and its refusal to communicate present Taiwan with challenges. Whoever is the island's president presumably wishes to defend Taiwan's interests and avoid war. Yet uncertainty remains as to those steps that should *not* be taken. If Taiwan were totally submissive to China, there would be no deterrence problem. Yet Taiwan does take positions that China opposes, and Taiwan's politics does generate proposals and actions that China regards as threatening. Taipei leaders seek to strengthen the island's sovereignty, and Beijing sees secession. In addition, Taiwan politics foster actions that make China nervous—and polls indicate that 72 percent of the Taiwan population would opt for independence if there were no danger of war with China, so that sentiment is likely to continue.[4] Politicians sometimes paint China as the enemy that would bring Taiwan under its domination. At a minimum, the Taiwan public wants the island to have a greater international role—through participation in international organizations, for example—and is offended when China blocks efforts to secure that role.

The most vivid and recent episode of Taiwan politics escalating cross-strait tensions was during the 2003–2004 Taiwan presidential campaign. Recall that Chen Shui-bian was trailing badly and was having trouble mobilizing his own political base, in part because his first-term agenda had not been sufficiently radical. Like George W. Bush in the United States, he made a strategic decision to concentrate on his base, and therefore made proposals to appeal to them. Among them was a long-standing yet dormant DPP proposal for a new constitution, to be approved by a referendum. Beijing quickly denounced the plan as the functional equivalent of a declaration of independence and reaffirmed its willingness to use force if the plan were carried out. It placed most of its bets on the United States, expecting that Washington would value its China relationship enough and need another conflict so little that it would rein Chen in. The Bush administration did criticize Chen, but it drew a different line than Beijing. It made clear that it would not oppose constitutional revision if Chen would do it according to established procedures and avoid changes that touched on China's sovereign rights (Beijing had been opposing revision of all kinds). After Chen's victory, he accepted Washington's advice, effectively reneging on his campaign commitments.

This was a time of white-knuckle anxiety. Although most observers agree that Chen Shui-bian was playing a reckless game (and that he was encouraged to do so by mixed American messages), to this day there is disagreement about where his high-wire act was leading. Had he been playing a clever triple game, with the ultimate goal of full, legal independence (as China and some Americans believed)? Did he believe, that is, that if he won and was able to carry out his plan, the Chinese did not have the military strength or the political will to actually use force and that Taiwan's friends in the United States were influential enough that George W. Bush would not dare block or punish him? Or was this a case of campaign politics all along? That is, did Chen intend to pump up his supporters, play the courageous hero standing up to the Communist enemy *and* American criticism, all the while planning to ditch his proposals if he won (and if he lost, it didn't matter)? The fact that the Bush administration issued stern and public warnings only a month before his inauguration indicate that it remained genuinely concerned about Chen's intentions. The fact that Chen in the end abandoned his campaign proposals suggests at least that he was amenable to last-minute American pressure and perhaps that his solidarity with his political base was tactical and temporary.[5]

Whatever the case, the episode demonstrates a chain reaction that occurred among campaign proposals on Taiwan, China's perception of those proposals as a fundamental threat, and Beijing's saber-rattling to get Chen to back down and to pressure Washington to make him do so. Lost in the shuffle of those tense times was a question. Did Chen Shui-bian's proposal for a new constitution to be approved by a referendum actually represent a fundamental challenge to China, or was this a misjudgment by China? The Bush administration did not openly accept Beijing's substantive legal case, but it clearly saw Chen as a troublemaker and was not in a mood to risk a conflict with China over the issue. But China had tolerated significant constitutional change on Taiwan before. There would be a point at which most lawyers would agree that something fundamental had changed. Chen had been reckless, to be sure. But for China to declare this something of a casus belli even before the election had been held and before the shape of the new document had emerged was reckless as well.

This discussion of China's strategy of deterrence leads us to a disturbing conclusion. Although the heart of deterrence is preserving peace by using the threat of force to shape an adversary's intentions, China will not and cannot state in advance what Taiwan actions would trigger a war. That is because it cannot in advance evaluate how threatening to China's interests future Taiwan initiatives might be. At the same time, Taiwan cannot know what actions may lead China's leaders to decide that force is justified. Moreover, the island's political dynamics can produce actions that China may decide, after the fact, are a threat to its interests. Perhaps Chinese leaders have overestimated the political threat that Taiwan poses to China's objective of unification, and perhaps Taiwan's leaders have underestimated the risk that their actions and China's threat perception pose. Consequently, deterrence as a means to prevent war is highly imperfect.

If we turn to coercion, our confidence in Chinese caution is not reinforced. Recall that the Pentagon has concluded that China is acquiring the sort of military capabilities consistent with a coercion strategy, not just deterrence. Not only is it trying to dissuade the island's leaders from moves toward separatism that China fears, it is also securing what it would need to quickly coerce Taiwan—both its leaders and the public—to submit to unification negotiations on its terms, negotiations that Taiwan wishes to avoid. In the case of deterrence, the trigger has been Taiwan's actions. In the case of coercion, the trigger could be Taiwan's actions. But it could be its inaction as well.

China has talked less about the coercion option. After all, it is on higher moral ground if it can put the blame on Taiwan for "separatism" and portray its military buildup as necessary to preserve peace and any use of force as necessary to restore the status quo ante. To discuss the circumstances under which it would take the initiative against Taiwan would cede that high ground. But it has not been completely silent. Recall that one of the conditions in the antisecession law for the use of force was that "possibilities for a peaceful reunification should be completely exhausted." This is very interesting because one reason why the chance for unification might disappear could simply be Taiwan's refusal to negotiate (a form of inaction). Indeed, in a previous statement of its conditions for the use of force, in February 2000 China explicitly mentioned a Taiwan refusal to agree on unification through negotiations.

✲      ✲      ✲

Again, the problem is one of perceptions. Who will decide when the possibility of unification has been exhausted? China, of course, based on its own subjective judgment. And if China has concluded that the possibility is nil, who is it likely to blame, itself or Taiwan? In fact, Beijing has a persistent habit of blaming its adversary for any impasse. China always views its offers as generous and the other's objections as narrow-minded and mean-spirited. Putting itself in the other's position, accepting that it may be at fault, and adjusting its position accordingly is not part of the Chinese playbook.

Of course, a likely reason why Taiwan might be reluctant to negotiate on unification is that China's terms on that issue are broadly unacceptable to Taiwan and fundamentally at odds with its own core principle, that its government is a sovereign entity. Conversely, Beijing has refused for fifteen years or more to give any consideration to that idea, and to acknowledge that its own proposal—one country, two systems—may be the reason why there has been no progress in resolving the dispute.[6]

This deadlock is more likely to occur, ironically, should the conservative "Blue" opposition to President Chen come to power in Taiwan. Even though that coalition would be more accommodating toward China on economic issues and on political style, it would likely not differ fundamentally from past positions on issues of sovereignty. Hence, Beijing's disappointment would likely be greater. If Beijing fears the action of Chen's "Green" coalition, it might react to the inaction of the Blue coalition.

So we have another situation where the two sides could ignore the dangers that lurk around them. In assessing why it has not achieved its political goals, China could easily blame Taiwan for a deadlock that is really in larger measure one of its own making. It might conclude that the problem is insoluble through negotiations and that coercive action is necessary, when in fact negotiations would succeed if it merely moderated its position. Taiwan, on the other hand, would fail to see the looming storm because it continues to argue its long-standing position, one that China has seemingly tolerated for years.

✣     ✣     ✣

In short, we worry that the leaders of China and Taiwan will find it hard to avoid the brink because they are unclear where the brink is.

China has had trouble assessing the intentions of Taiwan leaders and a tendency to overestimate their hostility. When Taiwan Green governments are in power (that is, the parties with a proindependence background, of which the DPP is the larger), Beijing fears the danger of separatism and sometimes exaggerates it. The PLA's deterrent grows, and with it the temptation to use it. If a Blue government came to power (the parties from a prounification background, mainly the KMT), there is a danger that Beijing would be disappointed because of excessive expectations. It might conclude that unification is impossible and coercion is necessary. Taiwan has the opposite problem: underestimating China's resolve to fight, along with assuming that it is more rational than it actually is. China might make the same mistake: minimizing Washington's resolve to defend Taiwan.

If it weren't bad enough that Beijing and Taipei were hazy about the location of their brink, two other factors make the situation a lot worse. First, the governments don't talk to each other, and, as we have noted, the public signals are ambiguous. China has insisted that Taiwan meet certain political preconditions before dialogue takes place. Taipei is unwilling to make the concessions that such preconditions entail. So any crisis prevention and crisis management that communication would bring are lost. Washington provides something of a substitute through its diplomacy with Beijing and Taipei. But it is a weak substitute. Second is domestic politics in Taiwan, China, and the United States. Populist forces in all three countries are pushing leaders toward the brink, whether they like it or not.

There are many reasons why war between China and Taiwan is unlikely. That is a good thing. But to say that war is unlikely is very different from saying it is impossible or even highly improbable. The script by which China and Taiwan stumble together off a cliff that neither really knew was there is easily written. All it takes is for Beijing to exaggerate Taipei's hostility, for Taipei to overestimate

Beijing's rationality and underestimate its resolve, for both to be confused about the intentions of the United States, and for leaders in both China and Taiwan to feel captive to nationalist publics. And once the guns start firing, the consequences would be catastrophic.

As we finish the manuscript of this book, in the fall of 2006, the trend lines on the Taiwan Strait seem to favor peace and stability. The more radical and more proindependence Green forces on Taiwan are weak, discredited, and in disarray. The Blue forces have regained their confidence and already have a charismatic presumptive candidate for the 2008 presidential election, Ma Ying-jeou, the mayor of Taipei and chairman of the Kuomintang. China appears to sense that time is on its side and has been more skillful in appealing to the Taiwan audience. When Mr. Ma wins, by this scenario, he will not engage in the kind of provocations of his predecessors.[7]


So the danger of war has disappeared, right?

Not at all. We would remain very cautious. First, there is some time to go before the next Taiwan presidential election, and at least in the pan-Green camp there is fear that the window of opportunity for achieving their goals is closing. Moreover, they think that China will want to present a good image to the world while hosting the 2008 Summer Olympics and so will be constrained from its usual intimidation. Actually, President Chen Shui-bian, the leader of the Green forces, cannot challenge China's fundamental interests without amending Taiwan's constitution. That is the only way that he can change the name of the country or change its territorial boundaries or announce a new state—the functional equivalents of a declaration of independence that would certainly prompt a forceful Chinese response. And according to the rules of constitutional revision, Chen cannot make any changes without a broad political consensus. He would need a three-fourths majority in the legislature; but the pan-Blue party has a slim majority there and is opposed in principle to the sort of constitutional changes that would anger China.[8]

So if the pan-Blue maintains that opposition, there will be no challenge to the status quo. But that is an interesting "if." In a sense, the 2008 campaign has already begun. President Chen is trying to place the pan-Blue and Mayor Ma on the defensive, and to force him to define himself in the eyes of Taiwan voters (Chen himself cannot run, but he is preparing the ground for his successor). Since Ma's family happens to hail from China, he can win the presidency only if he makes the case that he won't sell out the interests of the native Taiwanese. Chen may try to corner Ma and get him to prove his loyalty to Taiwan on the issue of constitutional change. Ma will face a tough choice: do what is right in principle (oppose provocative revision), or go along with what's politically safe, even if it risks offending China. It is worth recalling that what sent China into a semipanic in late 2003 was not that Chen proposed a new constitution but that the pan-Blue leaders abandoned their opposition to the idea because Chen had outmaneuvered them politically. Beijing will be watching like a hawk to gauge how firm the pan-Blue is in its opposition to Chen's tactics. If Ma folds on the issue of constitutional revision, look for another crisis.

Second, there is no guarantee that Ma Ying-jeou, if he is indeed the pan-Blue candidate, will win the election. He is currently favored, but he will face a campaign of attrition to discredit him. The effort may not succeed, but his victory is not guaranteed. If the as-yet-unnamed pan-Green candidate wins, China is likely to be even more vigilant for a challenge to its interests. Its tendency to misread Taiwan's actions will not have diminished. Its military power will only have grown.

Third, even if the pan-Blue regains power, it will not go too far to accommodate China. The cross-strait atmosphere would certainly improve and relations would become more predictable. Progress would likely occur on air and sea links so that passengers and cargo would be able to travel directly instead of through a third area, as is now the case. Ma Ying-jeou (if he indeed is the next president) would seek a long-term peace treaty between the two sides. But he also would adhere to the principle that the Republic of China (Taiwan's official name) is a sovereign state. It was that principle that caused the divergence between Beijing and Taipei in the early 1990s. That principle, which makes a fundamental point about Taiwan's legal identity, may become an obstacle to the peace treaty and economic links that Ma so desires. And it may foster impatience in Beijing over the long-term prospects for unification. If even the more accommodationist pan-Blue are going to assert Taiwan's sovereignty, some Chinese are likely to say, a settlement on our terms will never occur. The only way to achieve our goals, they will argue logically, is to engage in coercion. And as China's military power grows, so will the strength behind that logic.

And if Ma wins election in 2008 and is not able to make the progress he promises, he may disappoint the Taiwan electorate.


Consider the following speculative scenario:

The time is the year 2012. It is a special year because Taiwan, China, and the United States are picking leaders—Taiwan and the United States through popular elections in March and November, respectively, and China through selection by the Chinese Communist Party (CCP) elite. This conjunction of events, which brings politics to the fore in all three countries at the same time and complicates the management of external relationships, has never occurred before.

In the spring of 2012, Taiwan's Democratic Progressive Party (DPP) makes a comeback. The DPP had won the presidency in 2000 and 2004, with Chen Shui-bian as its candidate. The Kuomintang (or Nationalist Party), the DPP's archrival, had won in 2008 under the leadership of the young, good-looking, and media-savvy Ma Ying-jeou. For the past four years, President Ma's China policy has alienated much of the Taiwan public by pursuing an accommodationist policy toward China. To maximize Taiwan's economic benefits from the mainland, he has made political concessions that seem excessive. He has given the DPP a political issue, and it quickly taps into the feeling that Ma has appeased China and sold out Taiwan's interest. And unlike 2000, when Chen Shui-bian had run on a moderate platform, this time the DPP candidate—let us call him Chai—has come from the radical base of the party and run on a radical platform. He has argued that Taiwan needs to stand up to China rather than cowering, and that it needs to take a stand. The best way, he has proposed, is to write a new constitution for Taiwan and approve it through a plebiscite. China would bluff and bluster, he has said, but would soon back down. Nor would the United States object to this exercise in democracy.

And Mr. Chai then wins. Moreover, the DPP and other like-minded parties gain a significant majority in the legislature (called the Legislative Yuan [LY]), the KMT and its allies losing their majority. With that victory, Chai now actually has a hope of carrying out his agenda, since any constitutional amendment must first be passed by a supermajority in the legislature. He is in striking distance of achieving the long-held goal of the DPP faithful.

Meanwhile, across the Taiwan Strait, the Communist leadership watches with increasing alarm. For them, a DPP surge is their worst nightmare. For Taiwan to take any action that looks like a declaration of independence, which would separate the island permanently from China and close the door on unification, is a fundamental challenge. They had chosen, literally, not to force the issue, in the belief that the economic ties that had proliferated between the island and the mainland would bring political reconciliation and unification. Now Chai is upsetting their play-for-time strategy. He offers reassuring words about his intentions, but Beijing looks at his record and sees an independence diehard who cannot be trusted at all. Allowing Chai to even begin on his separatist agenda (as they see it) will only encourage him to grab for more. Before it is too late, China should act, with force if necessary. Chinese leaders are fond of telling American officials that a Taiwan breakaway is no different from the emergence of the Confederacy in 1861, and they have the right that Abraham Lincoln exercised to use whatever means necessary to restore national unity. In Chinese decisionmaking circles, military leaders, who have built up the power of the People's Liberation Army over the past two decades, are particularly vocal in warning of the threat that Chai poses and predicting that the time is coming when those capabilities should be used to protect China's interests. Preemption is not a monopoly of American strategists.

Beijing officials are also fond of telling Americans that any Chinese leader who loses Taiwan will not remain leader very long.

As it happens, domestic political considerations are particularly salient in the spring of 2012, for China is in the midst of picking a new generation of leaders. Hu Jintao and his colleagues have led

China since 2002 and have done well to sustain China's economic growth and expand its political influence in Asia and the rest of the world. But they have not completed the "sacred mission" of reunification, and now their prescribed term in office is ending. China, of course, does not hold elections, but new cohorts of leaders must be approved by the "selectorate" of the CCP. Candidates for the political bureau and its standing committee are subject to a thorough process of vetting that tests their competence and adherence to long-established party positions. No candidate, particularly the person slated to succeed Hu Jintao as party general secretary and state president, will survive this gauntlet by being soft on Taiwan. Indeed, those "campaigning" for higher office have every incentive to prove their "purity" and toughness by calling for a hard line against the Chai challenge. An alliance forms between civilian "rising stars" and military officers who have stars on their epaulets.

Politics also is very much at play in the United States. There are at least three ways (and probably more) in which American politics could plausibly increase the risks of a serious crisis.

First, general fatigue over the Iraq war and large budget deficits could make Americans more wary about playing a strong global role in defense of friends and allies. Or at least China might rate the situation that way.

Second, an ideological administration could decide to support Taiwan, including its push for independence. This would be particularly plausible if the new U.S. administration had taken a strongly anti-China stance in general due to the PRC's form of government and human rights violations, as well as bilateral trade tensions and disagreements over how to handle countries such as North Korea, Iran, and Sudan (not to mention Japan).

Third, the combination of a partially or wholly Republican Congress and a Democratic president in the United States also could spell trouble. The Republican Congress might continue the modern tradition of critiquing the Democratic president for purported weakness on matters of national security. Encouraged by a caucus of members sympathetic to Taiwan, it also might have kept the president on the defensive by proposing bills and resolutions that would strengthen U.S. relations with the island, particularly in the military field, and generally provoking Beijing. Sixty years before, Republicans had hurled accusations that the Truman administration had "lost China." Now, in 2012, it might take the stance that the current administration was about to lose Taiwan.

In the Chinese playbook, the first move in responding to any Taiwan provocation is to pressure Washington. The United States, Beijing claims, has a responsibility to restrain Taiwan, and Washington has tried to do so since the mid-1990s. Actually, both Democratic and Republican administrations have pursued an approach of "dual deterrence." But dual deterrence worked best in the Bush administration, when the Republican Congress remained passive, even when Bush criticized Chen Shui-bian. A Democratic chief executive constantly jockeying with a Republican Congress might not have that kind of flexibility. As a result, Beijing might get no satisfaction from its escalating appeals for U.S. intervention. And Chai could interpret American ambiguity as approval.

China does not speak only to the United States. It also issues a stern statement in advance of Chai's inauguration, which occurs on May 20. Beijing seeks to back Chai away from what it regards as his separatist project. It cites the antisecession law passed in March 2005 and restates its conditions for the use of "nonpeaceful means." It demands that Chai explicitly renounce his plan for constitutional revision in his inaugural address or bear the consequences for his actions. But this heavy-handed approach, fueled by intense succession politics in Beijing, backfires. Buoyed by the righteous indignation of his supporters over China's threats, the moral support of much of the United States, and his own sense of mission, he stands his ground. He will not give into Chinese bullying. He will not renounce his plan. Instead he announces the creation of a constitutional drafting commission that within sixty days will complete a draft of a new constitution for consideration by the legislature and the public. Privately, Chai believes that Beijing is bluffing, that what he proposes is not really a threat to China's fundamental interests or a transgression of the antisecession law's vague red lines. He also believes that Washington will get Beijing to back down, and to create the appearance of U.S. support, he engineers a congressional resolution that welcomes his inauguration.

The Communist leadership in Beijing is in turmoil. In the hot-house of Chinese decisionmaking, it is decided that Chai's program is the functional equivalent of a declaration of independence. There is little confidence that the opposition parties on Taiwan or the reasonable segment of the public will be a match for what they see as DPP demagoguery. Nor is the United States acting as a check. The nightmare has become a reality. The only way to meet this challenge is to threaten force and to use it if Chai does not back down.

# 6

# Adding Fuel to the Fire

War between China and Taiwan is a distinct possibility. Such a war could easily drag in the United States, pitting the world's only superpower against its main rising power and thus leading to the first serious conflict in history between nuclear weapons states.

It seems inconceivable, in this day and age, that the United States and China could really wind up in war. Their mutual interests in cooperating are so strong, their economies are so intertwined, the dangers of war are so enormous, and the number of other problems for them to worry about is so great that it would seem the height of foolishness for the two huge powers ever to come to blows.

There is much truth to this. Indeed, as we have argued in chapter three, most of the reasons why China and the United States could theoretically fight do not in the end hold water. But the Taiwan problem is different. Not only does it involve a third actor over which neither Beijing nor Washington has control. Not only does it involve a territory that China sees as an integral part of its own nation and that the United States sees as a long-standing, stalwart, and democratic friend. In addition, the way that a China-Taiwan crisis could begin and escalate would hold the inherent potential for escalation to direct superpower war. This chapter explains why. The next chapters get into the dynamics of what could happen if that war began, how it might be terminated before getting extremely serious—but also why it could be tough to control.

99

The overall message is sobering. Even if the chances of war between the United States and China are less than 25 percent—indeed, even if they are less than 10 percent—they are far from zero. And given the enormous consequences of any such war, in terms of immediate danger as well as lasting effects on the international system, every effort must be made to prevent it. World War I did not seem very likely to most world leaders in 1912 or 1913 either; certainly a horrible four-year struggle, followed two decades later by an even worse world war, was not predicted. We must avoid the mistakes of that era and take seriously the possibility of a war that, even if unlikely already, must be rendered more unlikely still.

In short, the reasons why that war could occur, are as follows:

- First, China really does consider Taiwan its own, and even as it has arguably adopted a more subtle and sophisticated approach to the Taiwan challenge in recent years, it has explicitly kept the threat of force on the table.[1]
- Second, China's military capabilities are growing fast even as Taiwan's begin to stagnate, meaning that Beijing could sense an opportunity—if it can keep the United States out of the fight.
- Third, Taiwan could push the sovereignty issue in a way that China interprets as the pursuit of full independence. While China would probably be wrong in reaching any such conclusion, perceptions could matter more than reality in such a situation.
- Fourth, while Washington's commitment to Taiwan is long-standing, it is also somewhat ambiguous, so leaders in China might convince themselves that the United States really would sit out a China-Taiwan war.

Also, in such a crisis, there is likely to be a period of testing. Both China and the United States are in the habit of deploying military forces to send messages, which means that in a crisis both might send forces near Taiwan—and hence near each other's militaries—with all the inherent risks of accidental or inadvertent uses of armed power that such proximity inherently entails. In shooting at Taiwan forces, China might strike American units by mistake—easy to do in the fog of war. And finally, as the historical example of the Cuban Missile Crisis (which we review here) reminds us, when superpowers put their prestige on the line in a crisis, they often have trouble backing down. Not only do they worry about the immediate stakes, but they also worry about broader damage to their reputations and how such damage could affect their standing in the global community.

China has the world's largest military by far. But its traditional strength of sheer numbers has never been enough to conquer Taiwan. Now China is recognizing that fact, and streamlining its still huge forces while also modernizing them. In short, trends are starting to work in its favor, at least in regard to the island of Taiwan fighting on its own.

China has moved ahead of Western powers—Japan, the United Kingdom, France—for the clear claim to third-greatest level of military spending in the world, trailing only the United States and Russia.

That is based on the most widely accepted estimates of its actual expenditures (roughly $70 billion to $105 billion in 2006, according to the Pentagon[2])—not its own misleadingly low official figures, which claim a total of about $35 billion.[3] Then secretary of defense Donald Rumsfeld called attention to this large and secretive defense budget in his June 2005 speech to an International Institute for Strategic Studies symposium in Singapore, in which he also challenged China to explain why it was investing so much in new defense capabilities even in the absence of a serious foreign threat.[4] Others see the Chinese investments as more natural, for a rising power with a growing economy and unresolved issues over Taiwan in particular.[5] But regardless, the trend is noteworthy.

Taiwan has a much smaller and considerably less expensive military—but it is still about tenth in the world in total defense spending, and its reserve forces are actually larger than those of China (though minimally trained). Taiwan's active-duty troops are generally better educated and better trained than China's, even though they have significant weaknesses themselves. Finally, while Taiwan's defense technology is of uneven quality, it certainly surpasses that of the PRC. For example, its foreign arms purchases in the 1990s exceeded those of China by about seven to one.[6] However, this gap is starting to close, as Taiwan's major arms purchase agreements in this decade have been slow to translate into actual contracts and even slower to result in weapons deliveries, while China has upped the pace of its own modernization, receiving some $11 billion in hardware from Russia (which supplies 95 percent of its arms imports) in this decade so far.[7]

China's military is far and away the world's biggest, with 2.255 million active-duty personnel in uniform.

Its inventories of major weaponry are also among the world's largest. The size of its nuclear arsenal, while a far cry from that of Russia or the United States, stacks up soundly against any other country's—and its force of twenty stationary long-range ICBMs is expected to double or even triple in size this decade, with the addition of mobile missiles (as well as improved submarine-launched long-range missiles also capable of striking the United States).[8]

Historically, however, China's sheer military brawn has not translated into a strong power projection capacity. Quantity, while admittedly important, has been much more impressive than quality, and the latter has left a great deal to be desired. China's armed forces have emphasized internal and border security more than foreign operations.

These conclusions have obvious implications for the Taiwan Strait. Even though Taiwan is only about a hundred miles from mainland China, the fact that it is separated by water further constrains the PRC's ability to project military power there. China clearly has advantages—the fact that one of its three main naval fleets focuses directly on Taiwan and that the other two are not far away, the fact that it has about a hundred dual-purpose airports within six hundred miles of Taiwan (with a total of about seven hundred combat aircraft deployed within range of Taiwan under normal conditions[9]), and the fact that its internal road and rail systems are getting much better.[10] All that said, few PRC troops could

### Basic Military Data (2006)

| Type of Military Capability | China | Taiwan | United States |
| --- | --- | --- | --- |
| Population (millions) | 1,306.3 | 22.9 | 295.7 |
| Active-duty military personnel | 2,255,000 | 290,000 | 1,515,000* |
| Reserve personnel | 800,000 | 1,657,000 | 956,000 |
| Active-duty army/marines | 1,610,000 | 200,000 | 783,000 |
| Active-duty air force | 400,000 | 45,000 | 355,000 |
| Active-duty navy | 255,000 | 45,000 | 377,000 |
| GDP (2005; billions) | $1,890 | $340 | $12,500 |
| Defense spending (2006; billions) | $100 | $8 | $535 |
| Heavy tanks | 7,600 | 925 | 8,000 |
| Armored fighting vehicles | 5,500 | 2,100 | 24,300 |
| Large artillery | 17,700 | 1,800 | 8,000 |
| Combat jets (number of advanced jets) | 2,800 (240) | 510 (420) | 3,900 (all) |
| Major warships (number of aircraft carriers) | 71 (0) | 32 (0) | 118 (11) |
| Attack submarines (number of advanced subs) | 57 (11) | 4 (2) | 58 (58) |
| Nuclear weapons | 300 | 0 | 9,000 |

*Sources:* International Institute for Strategic Studies, *The Military Balance 2006* (Oxfordshire, Eng.: Routledge Press, 2006), pp. 29–45, 264–269, and 292–294; and U.S. Department of Defense, *Annual Report to Congress: Military Power of the People's Republic of China, 2006* (Washington, D.C.: U.S. Department of Defense, 2006), pp. 44–50.

*The U.S. figures for active-duty military personnel include activated reservists.

deploy over water, given China's very limited amounts of military airlift and sealift. Its fifty or so amphibious ships could move about twelve thousand to as many as twenty thousand troops with their equipment, including up to five hundred armored vehicles. Airlift would be able to move another five thousand to ten thousand troops in the coming years, or perhaps somewhat more counting the possibility of helicopter transport as well.[11] But these are modest numbers given Taiwan's military strengths.

These shortfalls in transport and logistics have been magnified by China's other military weaknesses. Most weaponry is a far cry from state of the art, and capabilities in areas such as airborne command and control, reconnaissance, and electronic warfare have been weak. Training has left much to be desired, with little in the way of realistic or joint-service exercises.[12] The armed forces have not tended to attract China's best. Most soldiers are semiliterate peasants serving short tours of duty. The Chinese military's aspirations to conduct "local wars under high-technology conditions" remain aspirations more than realities.[13]

At least that's the way it has been, and to some extent the way things still are. But they are shifting fast—at least by comparison with the normal time horizons over which advanced militaries tend to be built (usually measured in decades). China instituted major reforms in the 1990s in doctrine, logistics, organization, and training.[14] And the results of these reforms have begun to appear. For example, China conducted two large-scale amphibious exercises in 2004 involving many thousands of troops (roughly division-size in scale) and another in September 2005, making for a total of eleven such exercises (with Taiwan as the presumed target of the mock assaults) this decade.[15] And there is again talk that China may be making a former Russian aircraft carrier operational (even though previous speculation about PRC aircraft carriers has been consistently wrong). If this really happened, it would not itself constitute a huge capability vis-à-vis the United States, but it would surely help solidify China's military stature in the region, and signal its interest in developing true power projection capabilities.[16] While the Pentagon talks of China's possible ambitions in becoming a more regional military power, and moving beyond Taiwan contingencies to prepare for possible battles over islands and seabed resources, it sees China's current ambitions as focused almost exclusively on territories China claims as its own. That said, Beijing has somewhat ambitious claims to numerous islands and seabed resources, so the fact that its current ambitions can be defined as "defensive" is not totally reassuring.[17]

Paradoxically, China's deep cuts in military strength have enabled it to devote more resources to enhancing the quality of smaller armed forces. Its active-duty personnel numbered almost 5 million in 1980, declined dramatically to 3 million a decade later, and have continued on that same downward path ever since—reaching about 2.5 million at the beginning of this decade and 2.25 million more recently. It is not every day that militaries improve by radically downsizing, but in China's case that is just what was called for and just what has happened. As military salaries in China nearly doubled over the past decade, much of the double-digit annual real growth in the PRC military budget since then has been consumed in paying people—not buying equipment or improving training. And the effort to maintain large forces has precluded an emphasis on excellence. Now a smaller force is focusing much more intently, for example, on creation of a competent noncommissioned officer corps.[18]

China is trying to implement a "revolution in military affairs with Chinese characteristics."[19] It also seeks to be able to fight and win "local wars under the conditions of informationalization."[20] Not all the increased funding has gone to salaries and other personnel costs. China has managed to improve its technology. Its domestic industries are improving, even if they still depend on foreign suppliers for many key inputs—though China has just obtained the ability to manufacture a high-performance turbofan engine. Its progress in commercial activities such as information technology and shipbuilding is finally being leveraged to improve defense products as well. And some institutional reforms in the defense industry also have taken place.[21]

China also profits from Russia's need for hard currency and the desperation of its arms industry to sell more weaponry. China has patched up relations with its northern neighbor enough, through border dispute resolutions and other such efforts, that Russia seems to feel few reservations about selling China virtually whatever it wants. High on the list in recent years have been the Su-27 and Su-30 advanced combat aircraft (whose numbers have grown from roughly fifty to almost two hundred in the past half decade); quiet diesel submarines such as the Kilo, which will increasingly carry advanced weapons such as Russia's SS-N-27 "Sizzler" antiship missile (with up to twelve Kilos arrived or on order[22]); advanced air defense systems such as the S-300/SA-20, with much greater range than its predecessors (as well as improved shorter-range systems); and modern destroyers (Sovremenny class) carrying sophisticated antiship cruise missiles. China's arms imports from Russia, averaging just over $1 billion a year in the 1990s, have as noted typically been twice as great this decade, with plans to acquire at least eight more major ships among other ambitions.[23]

More generally, China is trying to benefit from both foreign technology and its own to develop what Chinese scholars, taking a page out of their country's ancient history, call "assassin's mace" weapons. (Taiwan's ministry of defense uses another colorful and culturally appropriate phrase, referring to China's interest in "acupuncture warfare."[24]) Such systems would be designed to cleverly counter and neutralize American advantages in indirect ways. They also would try to mimic some of the new forms of warfare demonstrated by U.S. forces, and carefully studied by Chinese military experts, in the Iraq, Afghanistan, and Balkans wars. While current capabilities are generally modest, according to both U.S. and Taiwanese estimates, they might soon include accurate cruise missiles, counterspace systems, stealth, unmanned aerial vehicles, and information warfare.[25] Perhaps most notable is the number of mobile short-range ballistic missiles now based near Taiwan—about 750 by late 2005, according to the Pentagon, and growing at a rate of about 100 a year (the more modern versions being substantially more accurate than earlier types).[26] On balance, China's military capabilities have been improving faster than many expected at the turn of the century. In the words of George Washington University professor David Shambaugh, "the PLA has made a mini-leap forward over the past three or so years."[27]

Taiwan's armed forces have substantial strengths. Although much smaller than China's, they are backed by a very large reserve. And the rise of Taiwan's sophisticated electronics industries in recent decades has helped give the island a technological sophistication that has extended to its military as well. Among the manifestations of its high technology are a fairly good air force (including imported and domestic aircraft), as well as high-quality missiles such as the American-made AIM-120C air-to-air missile and numerous other systems.[28]

But there are big problems, too. Like the PLA, Taiwan's military is dependent on conscripts, meaning the quality of its forces is mediocre. Taiwan also has a very small submarine force of limited capability. That is largely a result of American policy, since Washington wanted to discourage Taiwan from attacking shipping headed for China. Taiwan's other antisubmarine warfare capabilities also were evaluated as poorly integrated and weak in a recent study by visiting American analysts.[29] The United States has tended to discourage Taiwan from developing tactically offensive systems such as surface-to-surface missiles, despite periodic Taiwanese interest in such weapons.[30] Taiwan's services often do not work very well together.

Taiwan also suffers from a big problem that China does not: as a result of Taiwan's domestic politics, its defense budget has declined since the 1990s even as China's continues an impressive growth.[31]

Indeed, a number of American officials and former officials have become increasingly critical of Taiwan in recent years for not making the investments that could allow it to meet more of its own self-defense requirements.[32]

That some of its weaknesses are classified, and hence unspecified in the open literature, does not make them less real. A great deal of U.S.-Taiwan collaboration has been under way to address a number of them in recent years, and some progress made as a result, but budgets, bureaucracies, and politics get in the way of many other efforts.[33] Even those recent modernization decisions that have been made will have to be put into effect in the coming years before doing Taiwan any good—and again, reduced budgets could interfere with the completion of such plans.[34]

On balance, while the military balance across the strait does not fundamentally advantage China, especially once the realities of geography and military water crossings are factored into the equation, it is moving in China's favor. Taiwan's historic edge in defense technology and a more advanced economy are being lost to a rapidly growing China with strong commercial ties to Russia and a smart plan to focus less on deploying a huge military and more on deploying a good one. Combine that with Taiwan's strangely lackadaisical attitude about defense modernization, and the story to date of the decade has been a military shift in China's favor that will continue given current trends.

✻        ✻        ✻

China might be willing to start a war against Taiwan, in light of these military trends. It might be even more inclined to do so if it thought it could keep the United States from intervening. And there is some real chance that China's leaders could form that dangerous perception.

China's leaders keep their estimates about America's intentions to themselves. We can only infer their calculus from various strands of evidence. One strand is the fact that the United States has not had a formal treaty commitment for the defense of Taiwan since 1980. Beijing insisted that Washington abandon that obligation as a condition for establishing diplomatic relations. But other aspects of American policy still suggest a defense commitment. The Taiwan Relations Act, which Congress passed in 1979, does not require the United States to go to war, but many American politicians believe it does.[35] Then there are statements of American presidents that suggest not quite explicitly that U.S. forces would fight for Taiwan. The most famous was this exchange between President George W. Bush and Charlie Gibson of ABC News on April 25, 2001:

> GIBSON: I'm curious if you, in your own mind, feel that if Taiwan were attacked by China, do we have an obligation to defend the Taiwanese?
>
> PRESIDENT BUSH: Yes, we do . . .
>
> GIBSON: And . . .
>
> PRESIDENT BUSH: And the Chinese must understand that. Yes, I would.
>
> GIBSON: With the full force of American military?
>
> PRESIDENT BUSH: Whatever it took to help Taiwan defend theirself.

To supplement these high-level statements, there is the ongoing U.S. approach of dual deterrence, which we described in chapter five. Washington warns China not to use force—and warns Taipei not to take political actions so threatening to Chinese interests that Beijing is provoked to take military action. The implication of those parallel warnings is that if China were to attack Taiwan without obvious provocation, the United States would most likely come to the island's defense.

A second strand is the pattern of Chinese acquisitions. Some of the advanced systems that the People's Liberation Army is getting from China could be used not to damage Taiwan's population or its armed forces but to keep the U.S. military out of the conflict. Why would the PLA be getting these systems if it did not believe that the United States was inclined to intervene? Moreover, it knows that the Pentagon is engaged in an ongoing modernization of forces in the western Pacific, largely intended to maintain its capability against China.

But U.S. statements and Chinese acquisitions can be read another way. Just as Washington seeks to convince China of its seriousness, so, too, Beijing reminds the United States of its resolve to "crush" any "Taiwan independence scheme," whatever the consequences for the country's economic development or international reputation.

That was probably one reason for China's passage of the antisecession law in March 2005: to show a willingness to use force. Similarly, China is acquiring capabilities to raise the cost of an American intervention to defend Taiwan. Effective and accurate antiship and land-attack cruise missiles could be examples of such weaponry. So could advanced fighter jets and more advanced submarines to fire the various missiles—as well as reconnaissance satellites to help target American assets such as aircraft carriers, and better communications systems to get any such targeting information to weapons-carrying platforms quickly.

A third strand is what might be called the perceived balance of interests. In official and unofficial discussions, Chinese scholars and leaders often make arguments such as these: (1) Taiwan matters more to us than to you Americans, (2) much of the rest of the world, except Japan, is ambivalent about supporting Taiwan or inclined to support China; and (3) the risks of war between two nuclear weapons states would be so great that whichever one of them has less interest in a conflict over a given issue will be strongly inclined to avoid the conflict.

Then there is the casualty issue. Chinese leaders may ultimately think that Americans' limited tolerance for casualties, as evidenced in Lebanon in 1983 and in Somalia in 1993, and to some extent even in the increasingly unpopular war in Iraq, would keep the United States out of a conflict over an island that in the end could not possibly matter as much to Americans as it does to them.[36] (They also might assume that America's military operations in Iraq would preclude a simultaneous U.S. response over Taiwan. That would be a mistake, because the latter scenario would emphasize navy and air force assets that are not being strained nearly as much as the Marines and army by operations in the Persian Gulf. Still, China could miscalculate.)

Chinese strategists also might observe that a war against China would be unlike the kind of combat to which Americans have become accustomed, against rogue states with populations of ten to twenty-five million and backward technology bases, in which outcomes are rarely in doubt even if costs and casualties may be. This would be a war between the two titans of the twenty-first-century world, with the potential for an extremely serious and bloody war. While the U.S. military probably would prevail in classic terms against China in any Taiwan war in the next one to two decades, the United States could lose many thousands of military personnel in the process—and perhaps even see its society threatened with nuclear strikes. In addition, the repercussions of such a war could restructure the international system for decades to come, ushering in a new type of cold war between the PRC and the United States together with at least some of the latter's close allies.

The reasons for U.S. intervention that China's leaders probably would ignore or have difficulty appreciating are intangibles.[37] One real reason for possible U.S. intervention is America's strong historic and moral bond to the island. Its people have depended on the United States for decades, and whatever the faults of their leaders, do not deserve to have their trust betrayed. Despite the problems of their democracy, it is still a democracy. More significant, it is hard to believe that the United States would ever stand by and watch Taiwan be conquered because of what this would say about the United States. This is not just because President Bush said he would do "whatever it took" to protect Taiwan—though those words matter.[38] It is also because almost everything in the American strategic psyche argues against appeasement or the abandonment of allies in tough times. Ever since World War II, American leaders, and most American voters, have been convinced that firmness is a critical element of successful national security policy. They are especially inclined to feel this way when a democratic friend is threatened by a nondemocratic enemy.

Standing by while a close friend was attacked could be dangerous policy, since it would weaken America's credibility more generally around the world. Among other implications, that could lead to more nuclear proliferation and quite possibly more wars.[39] Yet both these factors—a moral commitment to Taiwan and broader American credibility—could be underestimated in any Chinese calculation (in fact, they are often underappreciated by scholars and leaders from other regions when discussing Taiwan).

In the end, China could well speculate that the United States would have good reasons not to fight it over Taiwan, and so convince itself that war was an acceptable risk—or, at least, no more unacceptable than letting Taiwan get away without a fight. China also might think it would be less unacceptable to them than to us, meaning that America would find a way to stay out. And while it might not dispute the above assessment of America's military dominance, it also might think it had found the right "assassin's mace" to outwit the U.S. armed forces or find their Achilles' heel—or at least make Americans worry that they had, thereby deterring a U.S. intervention.

This situation is a prescription for danger. Everyone could tell themselves a story about how they could win—a situation that has often led to war historically. The fact that one or more is usually wrong in its calculations is largely irrelevant. At this stage of the process, perceptions count more than reality.[40] Depending on how badly they wanted to believe their own theories of victory, they could take action that increased the chances of a serious war. This may not be the situation today. But leadership changes, and political dynamics change. And if something sparks a serious crisis or an actual PRC-Taiwan conflict, cooler heads in places such as Beijing and Washington may not carry the day—especially as the situation develops a momentum of its own. Under such circumstances, war could even happen accidentally, and also would become harder to prevent than it is under normal circumstances right now.

In the tragic but not improbable scenario we imagine, China's leaders believe that Taiwan's president is challenging their interests more than he or she really is, and underestimate American resolve to support Taiwan. Taiwan's leaders may misread how Beijing will interpret their actions. At this point one of two things could happen. On the one hand, Beijing could decide to go straight to war on the basis of its flawed decisions; in the next chapter we explore how such a conflict might take place. On the other hand, there could well be an intermediate period of testing, where the two sides both prepare for battle *and* engage in diplomacy to avoid war and hope that some sort of mutual face-saving stand-down (ideally advantageous to themselves, of course) can be arranged. Such an effort by Beijing would be firmly in the tradition of the ancient Chinese general Sun Zi—who counseled that "generally in war the best policy is to take a state intact," and that "to win one hundred victories in one hundred battles is not the acme of skill. To subdue the enemy without fighting is the acme of skill."[41]

This time of three-way testing among China, Taiwan, and the United States is dangerous itself. Each side tests the resolve of the other, daring it to back down, and matching bluff with bluff. Neither wants to show weakness. Communication is difficult. Mutual mistrust is endemic, and retreat from the brink becomes difficult as a result. And what magnifies the danger by many times is that the mobilization of military forces and an escalating tempo of exercises become weapons in the political showdown (as well as a preparation for war).

Mobilization and exercises are, of course, standard responses when one country wants to threaten another, and give the threat some real teeth and some urgency.

They also are good ways to get ready to carry out an actual attack.

But they raise the risks of inadvertent war, since militaries in close proximity to each other can make mistakes. Sun Zi may have been able to brilliantly subdue the enemy without fighting, but few modern generals or political leaders have his uncanny knack for actually winning a war without engendering an all-out conflict.

The United States has used military exercises to send strategic messages several hundred times since World War II. On several occasions, China has been the intended audience and Taiwan the issue.[42]

The United States did so in the 1950s, when China threatened the islands of Jinmen and Mazu. As noted earlier, it did so again in 1996, after China fired missiles near Taiwan's shores; in that case, the United States sent two aircraft carriers toward Taiwan (though neither one physically entered the strait or directly approached the PRC shoreline).[43] China has gotten into the act itself, carrying out exercises near Taiwan in recent years that have involved up to tens of thousands of troops.[44] It has used advanced fighters such as the Russian Su-27, submarines, large warships such as the Sovremmeny class ships (also purchased from Russia), and substantial numbers of amphibious craft in the exercises.[45]

It is nearly inevitable that similar dynamics would resume over any major future crisis. The precedent has been established. Both sides view exercises as ways to show resolve. They are also an easy recourse, since they seem muscular yet low-risk. They are a "half pregnant" sort of approach—using military force for signaling but without firing shots.

Of course, this characteristic of exercises also makes them dangerous. Both sides can inch toward war without realizing it. They can be cocking their pistols metaphorically, but having become accustomed to taking such actions, they may feel safer than they really are. Leaders in Washington and Beijing would know full well that deliberately bringing armed forces into proximity with those of a potential adversary during a crisis is dangerous. That is why, over the years, both sides have worked to develop rules of the road and confidence-building measures to reduce the risks of inadvertent conflict during crises. (The United States has more experience in this area than China, but the latter has shown some initial interest as well—e.g., in the 1998 Military Maritime Accord signed by Secretary of Defense William Cohen and Defense Minister Chi Haotian.[46]) Yet their natural instincts in this sort of crisis would be to do exactly what they normally take pains to avoid doing.

In war games and crisis simulations of the type sometimes done by former government officials and scholars, these kinds of reflexive deployments are more or less automatic. Officials would generally try to keep their forces away from the other side's, to avoid incidents such as the 2001 EP-3 episode in which Chinese aircraft challenged an American spy plane, resulting in a landing of the U.S. plane under duress on Hainan Island and the death of one Chinese pilot. For example, former secretary of defense Bill Perry has written that he did not want to send American carriers into the immediate proximity of Chinese ships and planes in the 1996 deployment—even though he did want to get close enough to make a statement.[47] But that said, as the EP-3 incident underscored, reconnaissance is a normal activity of major militaries. So if the United States and China both deployed forces into the region around Taiwan, each also would want to know what the other was up to. Spy satellites could help answer the question, especially for the United States, but both sides also would want tactical intelligence of a more precise variety from airplanes and from ships and submarines as well. Thus, while the risks would be relatively limited in any mutual deployment of Chinese and American forces to the vicinity of Taiwan, there would be at least some risks even at this stage of things.

What types of military assets might be used in any exercise or maneuver? For the United States, its main capabilities would begin with air and naval forces normally based in the western Pacific. They probably would come in large part from Japan. Any elements of the Hawaii-based Pacific Fleet that happened to be nearby could contribute as well. Forces in Guam would be reasonably well positioned, too. Some U.S. forces in South Korea also might deploy near Taiwan, though it is not clear that Seoul would allow them to use bases on South Korean territory for combat operations.

### American Military Forces in the Asia-Pacific Theater, 2006°

| Location | Distance to Taiwan (miles) | Total | Army | Navy | Air Force | Marines |
|---|---|---|---|---|---|---|
| Alaska | 5,000 (Anchorage) | 17,300 | 7,600 | 100 | 9,600 | 20 |
| Hawaii | 4,700 (Honolulu) | 34,200 | 17,100 | 7,400 | 4,900 | 4,800 |
| Guam | 1,500 | 3,200 | 40 | 1,400 | 1,800 | 5 |
| Japan | 1,300 (Tokyo) | 34,900 | 1,800 | 4,500 | 14,100 | 14,500 |
| Korea | 1,000 (Seoul) | 30,000 | 20,000 | 300 | 9,100 | 300 |
| Other countries (mostly Australia, Singapore, Thailand, Philippines) | NA | 700 | 100 | 200 | 200 | 200 |
| Afloat | NA | 12,300 | 0 | 12,100 | 0 | 200 |
| *Total* | NA | 137,400 | 51,700 | 26,000 | 39,700 | 20,000 |

Sources: U.S. Department of Defense, "Active Duty Military Personnel Strengths by Regional Area and by Country (309A), March 31, 2005," available at Web1.whs.osd.mil; International Institute for Strategic Studies, *The Military Balance 2006* (Routledge: 2006); and personal communication from Bernard Cole, National Defense University, Washington, D.C., February 15, 2006.

° Numbers are generally rounded to the nearest hundred. Most ships travel 500 to 750 miles a day, with loading and unloading typically requiring several days as well. The air force has approximately 96 combat aircraft in Alaska, 15 in Hawaii, 84 in Japan, 84 in South Korea, and roughly a dozen in Guam. The navy has some 22 submarines and 9 major surface combatants in Hawaii. It also stations an aircraft carrier, 9 surface combatants, and 3 prepositioning ships with equipment aboard (enough for a brigade of Marines) in Japan. The army has a brigade in Alaska, 2 in Hawaii, and 1 in South Korea; the Marine Corps has the equivalent of 2 brigades in Okinawa, Japan, and 1 more in Hawaii.

Depending on the nature of the provocation and the scale of China's deployments, the United States might leave it roughly at that, sending a subset of the forces shown in the preceding table. However, if China was mobilizing large fractions of its force, an American president might feel the need to begin to address the "tyranny of distance" represented by the Pacific Ocean—and start sending at least some additional assets towards Taiwan as well.

Naval reinforcements could come from Hawaii within a week. More assets could deploy from bases on the West Coast of the continental United States, and perhaps also the Persian Gulf, within about two weeks. Substantial numbers of land-based combat aircraft from Hawaii, Alaska, and the lower forty-eight could reinforce those based in Okinawa and Guam within days. However, finding places to station them could quickly become a problem, since Japan and Guam would be the only likely locations for basing the planes. Okinawa alone has more than a dozen airfields, but it is not clear how many would be made available to the U.S. military; normally, America's only major operational bases there are Kadena and Futenma.[48] (Okinawa is the only place in the region within reasonable tactical combat range of Taiwan—assuming that the United States had not deployed planes directly on Taiwan.) Adding these types of reinforcements would be faster than deploying ground forces, as in the Iraq wars. Indeed, most needed forces probably could be deployed to the immediate vicinity of Taiwan within a month of a decision to do so. By that point the United States could, if it wished and its regional allies assented, have well over 100,000 personnel and perhaps closer to 200,000. These numbers might well include four to six aircraft carriers; several hundred more land-based combat aircraft; dozens of support aircraft for command and control, reconnaissance, electronic warfare, and antisubmarine operations; and up to 20 attack submarines.[49]

Clearly, China's ability to deploy forces of whatever size and type it preferred would be constrained far less by geography and allies, and far more by its military's proficiency in mounting large operations. Certainly the available military capacity is enormous. For example, its navy of about 250,000 active-duty sailors, who operate among other things 69 submarines and 63 major warships, is divided into three main fleets. At least one of those—the East Sea Fleet—could be devoted virtually in its entirety to any Taiwan operation. Its South Sea and North Sea fleets surely could contribute as well if desired. China's air force of 400,000 personnel, featuring some 2,500 combat aircraft, has many dozens of available airfields within reasonable range of Taiwan and could muster a large fraction of its total capability there. Limitations on aerial refueling, as well as command and control, might severely constrain operations. But just for starters, there are about 700 combat aircraft within unrefueled range of Taiwan at all times.[50] Finally, of its huge army of more than 1.5 million soldiers, several tens of thousands could prepare to load onto ships or airplanes as part of any exercise. Most probably would come from the Nanjing Military Region, one of seven in China's ground forces, though the Guangzhou Military Region has contributed to exercises around Taiwan in the past as well.[51] The bulk of the army could not credibly prepare to deploy to Taiwan, unless loading onto commercial shipping. It is for that reason, among others, that we conclude in the next chapter that an amphibious assault of Taiwan probably would fail. But China would have a great deal of capability to bring to bear nonetheless, and many military options as a result.[52]

Even without a deliberate decision to strike by Beijing or Washington, however, putting some of the most potent military capabilities on Earth within direct firing range of each other would itself be a risk. Massive mobilizations of major armies have often been the immediate prelude to war, with the actions of the major European powers in 1914 the classic example.[53] More than two million men under arms were mobilized in the summer of 1914; World War I was, of course, the result.[54]

Wars do not usually begin as complete accidents. And such mobilizations are not themselves usually the causes. Countries often harbor illusions about what wars will be like, and expect them to be shorter and easier than is often the case. Again, to take the World War I case, most expected troops to be "home before the leaves fall."[55] But few conflicts actually begin without a deliberate decision.[56] In that sense, the deployments of Chinese and American forces near each other might not itself seem hugely worrisome.

Unfortunately, this element of safety would itself be dangerous. Knowing that wars do not generally begin by accident, Beijing and Washington could decide to conduct such deployments without viewing these steps as preludes to war. That would put their forces into position for rapid escalation should something then trigger a battle that neither had intended nor even considered particularly plausible.

Compounding the danger of this time of testing, recall that Taiwan, which ostensibly created the crisis (at least in Beijing's mind), would not be completely passive. Its armed forces would be on high alert and operating in proximity to Chinese forces. The Taiwan military has not fired a shot in anger since 1958, and the PLA has not done so since the 1980s. Neither has the kind of command and control that the U.S. military possesses. In this hair-trigger situation, if a ship or fighter of one side strays over the ambiguous middle line of the Taiwan Strait, the other is likely to read the worst into the action.

Politically, anxiety over war would be at a fever pitch and especially on Taiwan. The island's democratic system and hyperactive media would guarantee that every new twist in the crisis would be analyzed and overinterpreted. Political leaders would debate endlessly how to respond to China's threats (with toughness or accommodation?). The Taiwan president would want to show resolve, including stating and restating the principle that "the Republic of China is an independent, sovereign state." That formulation is irritating to Beijing in the best of times.[57] In a crisis, its reaffirmation would be like waving a red flag in front of a bull. The more radical of the island's Green political forces might call for a declaration of independence. Many more people could call for holding an "emergency referendum" on a whole range of issues that China would find very provocative.

The United States, of course, would seek to restrain both Taiwan and China in this very tense environment, and it might succeed for the most part. But U.S. ability would be constrained by a variety of factors. First, leaders in all three lands would be operating in political contexts in which moderation would be read as weakness. Second, communication mechanisms around the U.S.-China-Taiwan triangle are not strong. According to the rules established when Washington broke diplomatic relations with Taiwan, senior American officials never meet with the island's presidents. Besides denying them the face that Asian culture leads them to seek, it makes it hard to check signals in a crisis. Subordinates have to carry presidential messages. Between China and Taiwan, as we noted in the previous chapter, the Beijing government has shut down communications when it mistrusted the intentions of Taiwan's leaders. That makes it very hard to prevent crises, and even harder to manage them once they start. And between Washington and Beijing, Chinese leaders tend to hunker down in times of trouble. The hotline established for the American and Chinese president to talk at just this time does not get used, and not for lack of American attempts. China's decision making is often slow and very consensual, and its president is unwilling to pick up the receiver unless he knows what to say.

Third—and this is fairly speculative because there is no experience to go on—there is a distinct possibility that once a Taiwan crisis begins and takes on a military character, the Chinese military will take over decisionmaking within the regime. At that point PRC diplomats could be taking their orders, in effect, from the generals, not from the senior civilian leaders. That could confound Washington's diplomatic efforts to contain the crisis.

Finally, the drivers here are the subjective perceptions of leaders in Beijing and Taipei in situations of high stress and aggravated by populist politics, especially in Taiwan. The dangers of escalation are profound. For example, China might try to use just enough force to affect Taiwan's behavior in the desired way, but not so much—*China believed*—that large-scale war or American military intervention became inevitable. For example, the PRC might be tempted to try the same kind of limited strikes it conducted back in 1995 and 1996, when it fired missiles across the strait that landed near Taiwan. Only this time, China might actually try to hit something. Its leaders might reason that a very small but nonetheless real attack could signal serious resolve without itself engendering an all-out conflict. Yet such a limited Chinese use of force would probably not get Taiwan to back down. Although there is some danger that Taiwan would take an independent action that would escalate the crisis even further (firing cruise missiles at mainland targets?), Washington would likely use its influence with Taipei to block such deliberate action. The problem lies elsewhere. Limited missile firings may well harden political attitudes in Taiwan and the United States.

They could reduce leaders' room for maneuver and raise their need to show resolve in the face of Chinese pressure.

As China tried to tighten the political screws through gradual escalation, Americans could become accidental casualties. There are large numbers of Americans living in both China and Taiwan. A limited use of force against the island would not discriminate the nationality of the people it hit. On the mainland, the government would not necessarily be able to control nationalist sentiment against American residents even if it wanted to.


Historical examples shed some light on how naval and air forces in close proximity can make for very dangerous situations. In 1967, during the Arab-Israeli war, Israel attacked an American reconnaissance ship, the USS *Liberty*, and killed some thirty-four U.S. sailors, extremely carelessly but almost surely by accident.[58] The Soviets were natural suspects; thankfully the United States did not respond forcefully against them before learning the truth. In 1970, during another Mideast crisis, Soviet and U.S. ships came into close proximity of each other, at which point the Soviets prepared surface-to-air missile batteries for launch and pretended to fire them at nearby American aircraft. Fortunately, this was recognized as bluffing at the time, and no shots were exchanged. In 1984, a Soviet submarine bumped into the U.S. aircraft carrier *Kitty Hawk*, another unintentional encounter. Thankfully no one was hurt, and the strategic context made it relatively easy to discern that no hostile intent was involved.[59] That was hardly the only submarine accident involving multiple ships in the recent past; in 2001, a surfacing American submarine ran into a Japanese fishing vessel near Hawaii, killing 9 Japanese, including several young students. In 1988 the USS *Vincennes* mistakenly shot down an Iranian civilian airliner during tense times in the Persian Gulf, killing 290 (a year before, the USS *Stark* had been severely damaged by Iraqi fire in the same vicinity, resulting in 37 fatalities).

These cases illustrate several points. First, even the world's best militaries make mistakes at sea. Second, even good friends can inadvertently shoot at each other (as in the *Liberty* episode). Third,

when near each other during a crisis, competitive militaries will sometimes thump their chests in regard to the other, to convey resolve—
either by deliberate orders from their capitals or sometimes at the
direction of local commanders. At times this can involve preparation of weapons for actual use, and the beginnings of firing sequences.
In truly tense times such actions can be incendiary.

Before delving into the details of the Taiwan scenario, a historical
analogy may help reinforce the above worries and illuminate the
risks involved over Taiwan. Despite numerous differences, the 1962
Cuban Missile Crisis may be the best case for comparison. The sim-
ilarities are notable—a small island effectively allied with a distant
superpower, just off the coast of another superpower, with which it
has poor relations. Both of the superpowers in question are nuclear-
armed. There is a serious risk that the nearby superpower will
attack the island in a manner the distant superpower would find
unacceptable. Finally, while the two superpowers may agree that
the importance of the island is not enough to justify a nuclear
exchange, they still could wind up fighting over it, hoping the other
side would blink first.

In one sense, the Taiwan situation is much more comforting
than was Cuba in 1962, since Beijing and Washington have far better relations today than Moscow and Washington did in 1962. (Beijing and Taipei also have better relations today than did Havana and
Washington, though that could change.) But in another sense, the
Taiwan situation is more complicated. It is a three-party interaction,
in which Taipei is an important independent actor—whereas Castro
neither caused nor had the ability to cause the Cuban Missile Crisis.

The history of the Cuban Missile Crisis in a nutshell is as follows. In the late summer of 1962, the Soviet Union, in an effort to
compensate for lagging behind the United States in the strategic
nuclear competition, began to deploy medium-range ballistic missiles capable of hitting the United States to Cuba. It shipped forty-
two of an intended deployment of eighty. It apparently did not get
around to also deploying nuclear warheads for the missiles (though
it may have deployed several short-range nuclear warheads in

position to help defend the island against invading U.S. troops if necessary). In addition, the Soviets deployed about forty thousand conventional forces, not only to operate and defend the missiles but also to constitute a tripwire against any possible American invasion.

American intelligence spotted the initial efforts to deploy the Soviet missiles, foiling the Soviet plan to deploy them and then present the world with a fait accompli. President Kennedy quickly decided that the Soviet plan was unacceptable, blockaded the island to prevent further deployments of weaponry, prepared an air strike force and an invasion capability of some 150,000 troops in the southeastern United States, demanded that the Soviets remove the missiles and any warheads already there, and threatened that the United States would do so by force if the Soviets did not. After securing a face-saving American pledge not to invade Cuba, and an informal promise to withdraw nuclear-tipped U.S. missiles in Turkey as well, Premier Nikita Khrushchev obliged.[60]

How close did the world come to nuclear war? Although McGeorge Bundy, President Kennedy's national security adviser, did not think that the United States and the Soviet Union had come quite to the nuclear brink, others disagreed, with President Kennedy himself estimating the chances of some type of war between one in three and one in two. Certainly American military commanders thought the chances of war at least that great; they advocated the air strike, and only Kennedy's good judgment led to use of the quarantine and a tough but pragmatic negotiating strategy (including the threat of an eventual air strike) instead.[61] Had war erupted, there was obviously a danger that the Soviets would fire nuclear weapons at any invading U.S. forces in Cuba (apparently Soviet commanders were given the authority to use the short-range weapons at their discretion, though Moscow kept the reins over the missiles in Cuba that could hit the United States).[62] They also might have fired the medium-range missiles at the United States once the warheads were deployed on them. That action could easily have then provoked all-out American retaliation against Soviet strategic forces, general thermonuclear war being the likely result.[63]

Even though the crisis was resolved successfully, a few sobering points are in order. Accidents or inadvertent uses of weapons could have themselves led to nuclear war, given the tensions of the time. Or small actions, such as the Soviet downing of a U-2 plane over Cuba in this period, could have been met with escalation. If the Soviet Union had challenged the quarantine and if American ships had fired on Soviet assets, there is no telling what might have happened. If Soviet premier Khrushchev had tried to play for time, or negotiate tougher, the United States might have run out of patience and carried out its air strikes—which would not have profited from precision-guided weaponry and could easily have missed some of their targets, allowing Soviet retaliation.

Moreover, the Cuban Missile Crisis was over a relatively symbolic issue, the strategic nuclear balance. By contrast, while U.S.-China relations today are much better on the whole than were U.S.-Soviet relations at the time of the missile crisis, Taiwan is a core territorial issue in Chinese eyes. Preventing its independence, in Chinese eyes, is necessary to ensure the PRC's national sovereignty and cohesion. In American eyes, preventing its takeover is critical for protecting a valued democracy and for demonstrating U.S. global credibility to stand by its friends. That credibility is important for deterrence, for nonproliferation policy (since more countries will want the bomb if they cannot count on America to protect them), and thus for the entire architecture of the international security system. For both sides, the stakes over Taiwan are very high.

# 7

# China Might Think
# It Would Win

War between the United States and China over Taiwan really could happen—that is the disturbing message of the previous chapter. But sliding into conflict in a high-stakes game of chicken is only the first of several ways by which hostilities could begin. China could decide that its bluff had been called and that it had no choice but to fight. Or it could skip the bluffing stage and go straight to war. There are tactical arguments either way.

However war began, wouldn't it be brought to a quick end—either by America's military dominance, or the two countries' shared interests in avoiding the risk of a huge war and even nuclear escalation together with their mutual desire to keep trading and otherwise cooperating with each other?

The answer is—perhaps. In fact, the dynamics of a war over Taiwan would be complex, and could go in many different directions. The world's main superpower, with two-thirds of the planet's capacity for projecting military power and a defense budget equal to that of the rest of the international community combined, would face up against the world's largest country and most impressive rising power over an issue that China considers perhaps its most important national security problem.[1] Any battles would be focused in a zone of conflict more than five thousand miles from the U.S. mainland but just a hundred miles from PRC shores. In other words, each side in any war would have impressive advantages very different from the other's.

In theory, China could try to seize Taiwan through an amphibious assault like some of the great campaigns of World War II in Normandy and the Pacific. That invasion scenario is the most dire. It is also the hardest to pull off, as we explain in the appendix, in a military sense. In addition, it is also the riskiest should it fail. It strikes us as very unlikely that leaders in Beijing would ever attempt it.

However, China's options would not end with invasion, especially if it was prepared to accept something short of Taiwan's unconditional surrender in any future war.

If it caused Taiwan sufficient pain or economic loss, it might convince Taipei to accept an outcome that met China's political requirements. Thinking this way, China might try missile strikes, a naval blockade, computer attacks—or some combination of the above.


That type of scenario is very worrying. Even though a U.S.-Taiwan victory would be likely, Taiwan could pay a very great price before it would be assured. So could China, especially if it attempted an outright invasion. Indeed, so might American armed forces; it is entirely conceivable that battle could lead to the sinking of several ships, including an aircraft carrier or two. Even Japan could take a serious hit; U.S. military bases on Japan would be likely targets of Chinese missile attacks. And the vulnerability of large military targets to Chinese attack will grow substantially in the coming years, as the PRC masters precision-strike technologies and deploys them in much greater numbers. Long before it could ever aspire to military parity with America, or even to the possibility of crossing the strait and seizing Taiwan, China will surely be able to destroy many more fixed land targets than it can today. Its antiship capabilities will improve as well, especially in close-in waters. So will its air defenses against any plane that approaches Chinese airspace. It even may develop a substantially improved capacity to target aircraft carriers deployed well east of Taiwan, most likely through use of submarines (or unmanned submersibles).

And that is the good military news. The above assumes a conventional war that does not escalate much beyond the immediate Taiwan theater. Given the stakes involved, it is not clear that China would accept defeat—taking solace that it had at least demonstrated its willingness to fight for its territorial integrity, and making Taiwan pay a price for whatever action Beijing felt had caused the crisis. No; China might actually feel a very strong need actually to win. That probably would be true for its leaders before any war; their thinking could actually harden and intensify as the realities of war brought out their nationalistic feelings and their resolve to prevail. After all, few leaders start wars just to see how they might go, quickly reconsidering if they get off to a bad start.

What this means is that China might escalate.

It might begin a war hoping a combination of better precision-strike capabilities, America's policy of ambiguity toward its role in any future China-Taiwan war, and American casualty aversion would keep the United States out or convince it not to fight hard.

But if Beijing misread the situation, it might not accept defeat at U.S. hands. It could seek to threaten and punish Japan even beyond attacks against U.S. bases on Okinawa. Or it could enlarge the scope of conflict in a different sense. It might back down from a major interstate war, but instead promise continued harassment attacks—missile strikes, state-sponsored terrorism against government facilities, cyberwar, the occasional sinking of a ship headed to Taiwan—as long as the government in Taipei refused to negotiate unification on China's terms.

Heaven forbid, China also could threaten nuclear attacks—probably not against Taiwanese, Japanese, or American cities, but perhaps against American ships or U.S. ports and airfields in the region or back home. It might also detonate a nuclear weapon high in the atmosphere east of Taiwan, where it would kill few if any people but fry all unprotected electronics for hundreds of miles in any direction. Exploded at the right altitude, it might cause maximum damage to Taiwan and nearby American forces and only modest damage to China's own territory. And while America enjoys a huge numerical advantage in offensive and defensive nuclear forces over China, it will remain highly doubtful that the United States could stop the PRC from successfully carrying out such limited nuclear strikes.

None of this means that a war would be Armageddon. Quite possibly, perhaps even probably, Beijing and Washington would figure out a way to stop it before escalation got out of hand. Or China would recognize that a defeat on the conventional battlefield, especially if accompanied by a bit of face-saving, was preferable to starting the world's first real nuclear war. But the stakes are so high, the dangers so great, the potential protagonists so strong, that we would be foolish to assume a happy resolution of any conflict between these two huge powers and among these three militaries.

Earlier we explained the possibility, low perhaps but real all the same, that China might misinterpret a relatively benign Taiwan action as a challenge to its fundamental interest and go to the brink. Taiwan might have pushed the issue too far in the first place by assuming greater Chinese tolerance for such actions than was warranted. China might doubt America's commitment to Taiwan, based as it is on somewhat ambiguous commitments short of a treaty. Having decided to go to the brink to coerce Taiwan to back down, and with its "face" on the line, Beijing could then be fully prepared to use force if its threats did not work. The United States would have not only a moral commitment to a long-standing and democratic friend, but also credibility issues of its own. China's military action would challenge its self-defined role as the guarantor of peace and security in East Asia, even when China asserted (as it surely would) that this was not an international issue at all, just unfinished business from a civil war it had every right to handle without interference. From Washington's perspective, however, every other Asian nation would view the U.S. response to a Taiwan crisis as a litmus test of its future leadership. Reckless bullying would not do, but nor would passivity in the face of Chinese aggression.

This may sound preposterous. How could either the United States or China go to war over an island the size of two New England states or a minor Chinese province? They are huge economic partners, and Taiwan is an economic asset to each. China and the

United States are also, of course, both nuclear-armed superpowers. Taiwan may be important, but few could conclude that it was worth enough for either country to bring about Armageddon to gain the political outcome it wanted.

The explanation, of course, is that countries often miscalculate. They misread the actions of their adversaries and exaggerate the threat those actions pose. Or they assume that they can make the other side blink first by being tough. Either way, they may convince themselves that war will not escalate, or that they will win handily and quickly.

Regarding Taiwan, both the United States and China could convince themselves that there was a tactically reasonable way to use force in limited doses that might not involve such great risks. The problem, of course, is that they could be wrong. Moreover, China might believe that, after PRC forces attacked Taiwan, the United States might stay out or be kept out by the People's Liberation Army's increasingly sophisticated assets.

Our greatest worry is not, as noted, about the invasion scenario. Even if it succeeded, Taiwan could be so badly damaged in the process that the economic effects would be quite negative for a "reunified" China. The international community would be particularly likely to punish China severely after witnessing the carnage it would have caused with such an attack.

Most fundamentally of all, it is doubtful that China could pull it off. Historically, countries succeeding in amphibious assault have enjoyed air dominance, the ability to establish local superiority as they initially came ashore, and the capacity to reinforce their initial lodgment more quickly than the defender can strengthen his. Successful attackers, from the United States in World War II and Korea to the British in the Falklands, have virtually always had at least two of these advantages. Attackers lacking two of them, from the British at Gallipolli, Turkey, in World War I to the allies at Anzio, Italy, in World War II to the Cuban rebels at the Bay of Pigs, have typically lost. (Indeed, they have often lost when lacking just one such advantage.) China would probably have no such advantages today. It would have a chance of achieving air supremacy, or at least some degree of air superiority, if it pulled off a picture-perfect first strike against unsuspecting Taiwanese air force units. But its amphibious and airborne capacities would certainly be inadequate to achieve dominance in ground forces at the point of attack. Moreover, in the era of precision-strike weaponry and twenty-four-hour all-weather reconnaissance (in which Taiwan's assets would be backed up by America's), the vulnerability of amphibious shipping to attack has only increased. So China would probably need more of an edge today than invaders have in the past, rather than less.

But China could try to use military force in a more limited way to pressure Taipei to accept terms for political association highly favorable to Beijing. In contrast to an invasion, these are options for China that really might be successful, even if it continues to fall far short of the kinds of military capabilities possessed by the United States.[2]

There are probably two main options for China in this regard: naval blockade and missile strikes.

The missile strike scenario is credible for several reasons. First, China has already done it, in 1995 and 1996, though it aimed at waters near Taiwan rather than the island itself. Second, China has been greatly building up its stock of missiles in the southeastern part of the country near Taiwan. Third, Beijing knows that neither Taiwan, nor for that matter the United States, can reliably intercept a large number of missiles aimed at the island. Nor could either Taiwan or the United States, given modern technology, plausibly find all the missile launchers and destroy them preemptively.

From their current positions, China has a stock of some 750 M-9 and M-11 missiles that can reach Taiwan, and the number is increasing by about 100 per year, according to the Defense Intelligence Agency.[3] And Taiwan is clearly worried about them; its defense ministry speaks somewhat breathlessly of a possible "multidimensional non-linear saturated missile" strike.[4]

The missiles could be used in a number of ways, going well beyond what happened in the mid-1990s. They could be aimed at remote farmland or mountains, to minimize the risk of casualties (if only a few missiles were used, in a strictly symbolic way against such sites, it is plausible that no one would be killed, though, of course, China could not be sure in advance). They could be aimed very close to land such that they would be visible to residents when their warheads exploded. They could be aimed in the waters just outside ports, or even within harbors, implicitly threatening Taiwan's economy but again without being likely to cause many casualties. If the crisis intensified, successive missile strikes might be aimed closer to shore and closer to cities, with a greater risk of casualties but still little likelihood of causing massive loss of life. Missiles also could be directed at military installations if a stronger message were desired but China still wished to avoid civilian casualties.

There are, however, limits to the advantages of the missiles option. Most of China's ballistic missiles are not yet very accurate, with expected miss distances of a hundred meters or more.[5] The above types of strikes, while perhaps unlikely to cause many casualties, also would be unlikely to achieve much direct and lasting military or even economic effects. And escalation would be problematic for China. Using them against cities would be seen as a brutal, terroristic act that could do more to unify the people of Taiwan—and perhaps the world—against China than to achieve Beijing's war aims. At least that has often been the historical norm when cities have been bombarded in the modern era, be it by airplanes in World War II or ballistic missiles in the Iraq-Iran and Persian Gulf wars.[6] For these reasons, missile strikes might be a logical way for China to begin any use of force, but it would probably need a backup option in case they failed.[7]

Of course, the physical damage might be less important than the psychological damage.

Recall that in 1995 and 1996 the PRC fired a few missiles with dummy warheads that did not come near the Taiwan landmass but effectively collapsed the Taiwan stock market and the value of the island's currency. The Taiwan government used its financial resources to prop up the currency (at some cost).[8]

But this was an exercise that everyone knew would end on a certain day. What would be the psychological and economic effects on the populace and on politicians of a more systematic and open-ended campaign?

Cruise missiles can be much more accurate, and China is obtaining them, too. It may have two hundred or more with sufficient range to find targets in Taiwan by 2007. The warheads on these missiles may be smaller, and their likelihood of being shot down much greater, but this threat may be on balance somewhat more militarily meaningful. Still, perspective is needed; the United States has frequently used cruise missiles in modern war, and often used more than two hundred in a given conflict, but has never come close to achieving wide-scale military objectives with such missiles alone. In modern wars it has typically had to deliver many thousands of precision bombs to achieve its goals.[9]

That is where a naval blockade could appeal to China. It could be "leaky" and still effective at directly threatening Taiwan's economy. To do so, it need not physically stop all ship voyages into and out of Taiwan.

It would simply need to deter enough ships from risking the journey that Taiwan's economy would suffer badly. The goal would be to squeeze the island economically to a point of capitulation.

This solution could seem quite elegant from Beijing's point of view—it could involve only modest loss of life, little or no damage to Taiwan itself, more terror than harm suffered by the people of Taiwan, and the ability to back off the attack if the United States seemed ready to intervene (or if the world community slapped major trade sanctions on China in response).

It is doubtful that China could truly cut Taiwan off from the outside world with such a "leaky" blockade. However, if willing to take losses, it certainly could exact attrition from commercial vessels trading with Taiwan as well as Taiwanese military forces trying to break the blockade. Even with such a leaky blockade, China could sink enough commercial ships to scare others off, and do so over an extended period. Should it convince most commercial shippers not to risk trips to Taiwan, it could effectively begin to strangle the island. If it reached that point (i.e., absent external intervention),

Beijing would then be in a position to exploit its military advantage to secure its political objectives: some sort of unification on Chinese terms.

A Chinese blockade could take a number of forms, including simply a demand that ships headed to Taiwan first stop in China for "inspection" if their owners also wanted to keep doing business in the PRC. Militarily speaking, the least risky and most natural approach would simply attempt to introduce a significant risk factor into all maritime voyages into and out of Taiwan by occasionally sinking a cargo ship with submarines or with mines laid in Taiwan's harbors. Submarines would seem China's weapon of choice, because using airplanes and surface ships would put more of its own forces at risk, especially since it could not realistically hope to eliminate Taipei's air force with a preemptive attack (though airpower might be used in a hit-and-run raid, especially as an initial strike before Taiwan's defenses were fully alerted). A blockade using planes and surface ships also would be rather straightforward for the United States to defeat quickly.

To be sure, a blockade would be challenging and dangerous for China. Perhaps the greatest worry for Beijing would be its likely inability to distinguish one country's merchant ship from another's. In other words, it could wind up sinking ships from neutral countries or even from friendly ones. It could not realistically target just Taiwan-flagged carriers, for example, since its submarines probably do not have sufficiently sensitive sonar to identify one vessel from another through underwater acoustic means (Even if the sonar were sufficiently sensitive, the PRC probably does not have a comprehensive database on the sonar signatures of the world's commercial ships, so it would not know which noise signal to associate with which ship.)

But if Beijing announced to the world that those shipping toward Taiwan were aiding and abetting its enemy, and gave fair warning, it might consider itself to have done enough to warrant attack against any vessel not heeding its demands. Moreover, it might offer countries the option of first docking in a PRC port for inspection (e.g., if it decided to allow humanitarian goods through or ships from certain friendly countries but not others) and then being escorted safely to Taiwan. As a final measure, it might also keep search and rescue crews on standby so it could try to save the crews from any ships it sank within a reasonable distance of the Chinese coast. None of these measures would be perfect, but together they could allow Beijing to claim it had taken every reasonable step to reduce threats to innocent crews. Finally, since this strategy might require it to sink only a few ships to achieve the desired aims, even in a worst-case scenario it might believe it was threatening the lives of only a hundred to two hundred commercial seamen. Given the perceived stakes involved, Beijing could well consider this a reasonable risk.

China might couple such a blockade with a preemptive air and special-forces attack—but perhaps just a limited one focused on Taiwanese submarine-hunting ships and airplanes, as well as some key port infrastructure. An all-out commando, air, or missile attack could defeat the purpose of a coercive strategy by hardening Taiwanese will and ensuring an American military response. In addition to using airpower and special forces, China might find it appealing to employ its missile force to complement the blockade. Perhaps several could be launched at a supertanker moored at a berth fairly distant from a city center, for example, with the attack timed at night to minimize the likelihood that passersby would be hurt.

Cyberattacks might play a secondary, supporting role to any blockade as well. China might be tempted to try computer attacks because they would also, in a nonlethal manner, target Taiwan's economy. Though cyberattacks have yet be used successfully in a military situation, China has created a cyberwar unit in its armed forces. Taiwan should assume that cyberattacks would accompany any other Chinese use of force against it and prepare accordingly.[10] Similarly, China may rightly believe that some aspects of the U.S. military logistics and transportation capability depend heavily on vulnerable computer systems. That said, given that computer systems worldwide are routinely being attacked, and that they are generally reparable, and that at least the most important U.S. military computer systems are reasonably well protected, it is dubious that a cyberattack by itself could be decisive in any future crisis.[11]

❈        ❈        ❈

In blockading Taiwan, China would be taking advantage of three main facts. First, Taiwan has only a small coastline and a small number of ports—forcing ship traffic to take predictable routes. Second, it is quite vulnerable to blockade because it has few natural resources, extreme energy dependence, and no other way to import or export than via sea or air. Taiwan's foreign trade accounts for two-thirds of its GDP.[12] Finally, Taiwan has few submarines or long-range attack aircraft to conduct a countervailing blockade of its own.[13] Ships headed to or from China could avoid most of Taiwan's military assets simply by sailing far around the island.

Two other types of limited attacks are sometimes discussed in regard to Taiwan, but they strike us as relatively unlikely even if not dismissable out of hand. First, China might be tempted to detonate a single nuclear weapon high in the atmosphere east of Taiwan as well—not to kill people, but to fry electronics. If done right, such a nuclear burst might damage unprotected electronics on the island while doing minimal direct damage to Taiwanese citizens. Taiwan should ensure that its big infrastructure could survive such attacks, but they are probably not all that likely, since China would have to cross the nuclear threshold to carry them out (non-nuclear EMP strikes are possible in theory but require many more weapons delivered quite precisely, since the strength of conventional EMP bursts is far far less). Doing so would likely cost China whatever moral high ground it thought the world might otherwise accord it in the conflict. This tactic also would increase the odds of immediate U.S. military intervention—and quite possibly an immediate decision from Washington to recognize and support Taiwan's independence. China could well lose substantial amounts of its own electronics in the southeastern part of the mainland as a result (and also could destroy electronics in countries such as the Philippines and Japan).[14]

Second, China could try to use special forces to assassinate Taiwan's government and install a friendly regime. To succeed, many things would have to break China's way. The PRC would have to infiltrate enough special forces—at least hundreds, presumably—to be able to capture or kill a dozen or more senior leaders on the island. Taiwan's protection forces would have to fall down on the job. Taiwan's leadership succession plan would have to be flimsy enough that, with a few top leaders dead or out of touch, no one else could stand in to take their place. The Taiwan people and armed forces would have to acquiesce to this external coup. And the international community would have to be willing to accept the outcome of a puppet regime in Taiwan; China would presumably not carry out this plan if it expected to suffer major and lasting trade sanctions as a result, for example. Should this type of brutal, thuggish attempt to replace Taiwan's government fail, moreover, there is every possibility that Taiwan's people would then move unabashedly toward independence—and that Washington along with the rest of the world might well support them in the venture. In short, this would be an extremely high-risk option with very limited prospects for success. (Taiwan could make China's prospects even worse by further clarifying its succession arrangements should top leadership be killed, so that some legitimate leader would remain legally in power and functionally in control of the nation's military regardless—and it should probably do so.) Given their limited understanding of democracy, Chinese leaders might misread the situation and try such an operation anyway, if desperate. But chances are high that even they would recognize the likely futility of this style of attack.

By contrast, China's blockade options look rather promising—even after considering how Taiwan might respond. Taiwan could redirect ships to ports on Taiwan's eastern shores as much as possible, forcing the PRC to attempt attacks in the open ocean far from Chinese territory.[15] However, if Taiwan tried to do so, it would give up use of its Kaohsiung Harbor, which is one of the largest ports in the world and accounts for almost three-fourths of Taiwan's trade, as well as harbor facilities near Taichung, which account for another 10 percent of Taiwan's trade.[16] Other ports probably could handle somewhat more traffic than they do today, but Taiwan's harbors are already busy, and it is implausible that they could sustain anything close to current levels of trade without Kaohsiung and Taichung. Taiwan also could adjust by rationing use of fuel and certain foods, stockpiling manufactured goods with long shelf lives to export once the blockade was lifted, and giving preferential treatment to its highest-revenue exports and most crucial imports. It also could offload some ships anchored near shore using small barges, easing the constraint posed by the limited harbor capacity on its eastern shore.[17]

But as with Britain in World War II, its ability to endure a long blockade is not certain.[18]

Most of China's submarines do not have antiship cruise missiles or great underwater endurance. However, the PRC submarine force is steadily improving. Even today, Chinese subs have adequate ranges on a single tank of fuel—typically almost ten thousand miles—to stay deployed east of Taiwan for substantial periods. Although their ability to coordinate with each other and reconnaissance aircraft is limited, that might not matter greatly for the purposes of a "leaky" blockade. Even if picking up commercial ships individually by sonar or by sight, such submarines could maintain patrols over a large fraction of the sea approaches to Taiwan. It could take Taiwan weeks to find the better PRC submarines, particularly if China used them in hit-and-run modes.[19]

Taiwan could use its surface fleet to set up and accompany convoys of merchant ships. It would be harder to do this for ships approaching Taiwan that for those leaving, however, since those that approach come from many different places—and if they assembled east of Taiwan to wait for escorts they would be vulnerable at that point. An additional complication is that Chinese submarines lucky enough to be lying quietly in wait in the right places would tend to hear approaching convoys before they were themselves detected, making it likely that they could often get off the first shot—if not the first couple—before being at risk themselves. (This capacity also will get much better as China improves its space reconnaissance capabilities, allowing it to detect convoys as they form.)

Submarines could threaten Taiwan's shipping in another way—by planting mines near its harbors. Each Chinese submarine can carry two dozen to three dozen mines, so half of its entire submarine fleet could carry hundreds. If half the fleet was able to deploy mines near Taiwan without being sunk, China would be able to deploy nearly as many mines as Iraq did—with considerable effect—against the U.S.-led coalition in 1990–1991 (when U.S. forces were discouraged from mounting an amphibious assault, in part out of worry over the damage that mines could cause).[20] China surely has, and will acquire, more sophisticated mines than Iraq possessed, moreover, including "smart mines" that would be difficult for minehunters to find or neutralize.[21] Moreover, Taiwan's minesweeping ships are limited in number and mediocre in quality and condition (even U.S. countermine capabilities would probably be severely stressed by a Chinese mining operation).[22] It is likely that China could exact a price with its mines, perhaps causing attrition rates of a couple percent each time ships tried to enter or leave Taiwan's ports, by analogy with the U.S. Persian Gulf experience and other previous conflicts. That by itself could be enough to give many shipping companies pause about continuing to do business in Taiwan, helping achieve exactly the economic effect that China probably would be after.

Taiwan could likely defeat a Chinese invasion attempt without material help, but it probably could not endure and finally break a blockade by itself—at least not without major and lasting damage to its economy.

While it would not have to react immediately, the United States might well have to accept the main burden of breaking the blockade eventually, unless prepared to see Taiwan successfully coerced by the PRC.

The basic idea for the United States probably would be to deploy enough forces to the western Pacific to credibly threaten the following type of operation. The United States would set up a safe shipping lane east of Taiwan. In addition, it would have to heavily protect ships during the most dangerous part of their journeys when they were near the island. To carry that mission out, the United States, together with Taiwan, would need to establish air superiority throughout a large part of the region, protect ships against Chinese submarine attack, and cope with the threat of mines near Taiwan's ports.

As we spell out this scenario further, it should be noted that our analysis is somewhat speculative. It is not based on any detailed knowledge of U.S. war plans. Rather it comes from more general knowledge of military operations, our assessments of the state of military technology, and the open literature on the U.S., Chinese, and Taiwanese militaries. Some of the specifics may be imprecise, or hard to predict in advance of an actual scenario even for those with intimate knowledge of war plans. That said, the following should be a fairly accurate illustration of the kind of operations that war over Taiwan could well entail.

Given the realities of physics and the limits of modern technology, the most challenging part of an overall U.S.-led operation to break a PRC blockade of Taiwan probably would be the antisubmarine warfare (ASW) element. Missile defense also would be quite challenging. But as noted above, given current PRC capabilities and those likely in the coming years, Chinese missiles may have limited capacity to inflict targeted damage on specific military and economic assets.

The ASW effort could have multiple aspects. The United States would surely be tempted to deploy its own attack submarines as close as possible to China—certainly in the Taiwan Strait, maybe just outside PRC ports. This approach would provide American submarines with a good prospect of destroying PRC subs at their source, before they were in a position to fire on commercial shipping (or U.S. aircraft carriers) in more distant waters. However, this type of ASW would be extremely delicate strategically, especially if it involved attacks in Chinese territorial waters, as we discuss more below.

Whatever happened near Chinese shores, there would surely be additional layers of American ASW farther out to sea. The convoys sailing to and from Taiwan would need protection. American ships, primarily ASW frigates, would accompany convoys of merchant ships as they sailed in from the open ocean waters east of Taiwan. These convoys might form a thousand miles or more east of Taiwan, and enjoy armed protection from that point onward as they traveled to the island and later, as they departed. The frigates would use sonar to listen for approaching submarines, and for the sound of any torpedoes being fired.

Additional surface ships as well as P-3 maritime control aircraft flying from bases in Japan or perhaps even Taiwan would be dedicated to various special purposes near Taiwan itself. And some additional assets would deploy to places where Chinese subs might be expected to transit, or where sonar was known to propagate particularly well, to hunt for submarines in a more offensive mode.

In all, the United States probably would deploy dozens of surface combatants and airplanes such as P-3s to the region for this mission. Some would help protect U.S. aircraft carriers, of which at least four would likely deploy east of Taiwan to establish air superiority in the event of any conflict. As noted, others would provide additional protection to merchant ships or mine warfare vessels as they operated near Taiwan's shores. U.S. minehunters and minesweepers would, of course, operate near Taiwan's ports and the main approaches to those ports. Land-based or ship-based helicopters might assist them. So might robotic submersibles deployed from ships near shore.

U.S. aircraft carrier battle groups would operate east of Taiwan. They might function as pairs (to allow for continuous twenty-four-hour operations and to provide insurance against battle damage). One pair might be stationed relatively near the island to provide air superiority over and around Taiwan. Another pair could operate well east of the island. In part, this would serve as backup to those near Taiwan. In addition, this would provide control of the airspace over the open ocean east of Taiwan. Doing so would help defend against any Chinese attack (most likely by longer-range bombers) that managed to avoid the first pair of carriers and Taiwan's air force. It is certainly possible that a third pair would be used as well—perhaps to operate in a more offensive mode, looking for PRC aircraft as soon as they left their bases and attacking them as soon as they reached international airspace (or even earlier).

In addition, several squadrons of U.S. Air Force or U.S. Navy aircraft might be deployed to land bases in the region. The most logical places would be Okinawa and perhaps Taiwan itself. These planes would require hardened shelters (of which there are not enough in the region at present, for the increased number of planes that would be required in a conflict), effective air defense, and logistics support. These planes could include combat jets, electronic warfare planes, reconnaissance platforms, and other capabilities. Bombers and some other planes would surely operate from Guam as well.

If the United States went ahead with the blockade-breaking operation, it could simply announce its intentions and begin to establish air and sea patrols in the region and escort merchant ships to Taiwan—leaving it to China to initiate hostilities.

This would probably then become the last clear chance to avoid a direct U.S.-China war.


If China then used its submarines in attacks on shipping, or if direct hostilities began in another way, the United States would almost surely begin to actively search for and fire on Chinese submarines as a matter of normal operations. Any Chinese submarine wishing to fire at a merchant ship or aircraft carrier would then first have to run quite a gamut. It would have to evade submarine detection as it left port, avoid any open-water search missions that the United States and Taiwan established, and then somehow penetrate the defensive ASW perimeter of whatever convoy it was attacking as it approached its target. To survive the overall engagement and return to port it would, of course, then need to successfully negotiate all of this in the other direction.

During the Cold War, the effectiveness of ASW operations was commonly assessed at 5 to 15 percent per "barrier" (Cold War barriers were more linear and literal perimeters than would be likely here, but the fact remains that Chinese subs would have to survive perhaps three types of pursuers at three different parts of their journey to or from home base.) By those odds, the typical Chinese sub would do well to survive for two full missions from base.[23] But it might succeed in getting off several shots against valuable surface ships before meeting its own demise.

U.S. losses could be significant.

Chinese submarines could just as easily fire at American ships as at commercial vessels in the two or so missions the typical PRC vessel might survive before being destroyed. The typical Chinese submarine probably would be able to fire several torpedoes in its battlefield lifetime, of which one or more on average might find its target.

A particularly skillful (and lucky) Chinese pilot also might penetrate a carrier's air defenses and manage a strike against it. Certainly, Argentine aircraft did against the British during the 1982 Falklands War, with a less capable air force than China now fields. American carrier defenses are much better than those of their British counterparts, but the risk would remain. In the event of a catastrophic attack against a carrier, causing its sinking, U.S. losses could even reach into the low thousands.[24]

Moreover, in the age of precision long-range missiles, China would not necessarily need to penetrate the U.S. carrier defenses. Either a ship or an aircraft might launch a longer-range missile salvo—perhaps after a Chinese fishing vessel with military personnel aboard holding GPS range finders and satellite phones managed to locate a U.S. ship and call in its coordinates.[25] In addition, over time China could develop satellite capabilities to help it target a U.S. aircraft carrier. Perhaps it would even learn how to deploy significant numbers of small, unmanned underwater vehicles armed with antiship cruise missiles that could be given targeting information by those satellites. While America would still have substantial assets to draw on to replenish combat losses, it is entirely possible that several thousand U.S. military personnel could perish even in a conflict that remained tactically limited to breaking a Chinese blockade of Taiwan.[26]

# 8

# Spiraling Out of Control

Would China and the United States really fight each other in this situation? Even once the Chinese had attacked Taiwan, even as America had deployed forces to the region itself, logic would seem to suggest that both would find ways to avoid shooting at each other.

That is to be hoped, of course. But as we explained in previous chapters, even if American diplomats might seek to keep the crisis at a moderately low level, China might not be interested in talking to them or to Taiwan. Moreover, once a military crisis begins, civilians in all capitals often feel pressure from generals. In that regard, the incentive to attack first and attack vigorously also would be keenly felt on both sides.

There always has been a premium on striking first in war—and on striking hard.

Attackers have, according to U.S. Army databases, won more than 60 percent of the wars in modern history.[1] Tactically, countries exploiting surprise often gain advantages that make their forces about twice as effective as they would be otherwise, in the opening hours or days of battle. Sometimes, as with Israel in 1967, they can effectively win the war with their surprise attacks.[2]

These trends have only intensified in the modern era. Especially since the invention of the aircraft carrier, the goal in naval warfare has been to bring enemy ships under fire from the greatest distance possible while keeping one's own ships out of range of the adversary's weapons. In other words, one tries to shoot at the enemy while one's own forces are still out of harm's way, given the incredible lethality of antiship weapons and the high value of the targets at which they are aimed. The vulnerability of ships to aerial attack, already substantial, was greatly exacerbated with the arrival of cruise missiles, which can be fired from a distance and which are quite difficult to intercept in flight. Two British ships were sunk by French Exocet missiles in the 1982 Falklands War.[3] It was also an Exocet, fired by an Iraqi aircraft, that struck the USS *Stark* in 1987.[4] Torpedoes also have become much more sophisticated. Often they can follow the wakes of ships, and also can be equipped with sophisticated guidance systems to make it hard to throw them off course.

The vulnerabilities of U.S. ships to attack are amplified in shallow, littoral waters. In the open oceans, the U.S. Navy generally can detect enemy ships or aircraft long before they are close enough to strike. But in shallow waters, shore-launched antiship missiles are a threat, as are weapons fired from aircraft or ships that dart out from a country's coastal regions. A similar conclusion applies to the threat from submarines and from torpedoes. In the open oceans, the U.S. military can rely on sonar (from aircraft, fixed underwater arrays known as SOSUS, and ships) to get a good sense of the approach of enemy submarines. Sonar is relatively predictable in deep waters; moreover, any ship approaching a U.S. vessel would have to travel a great distance to reach it in such a location, offering multiple opportunities for detection. By contrast, shallow waters are complex sonar environments, where sound waves bounce back and forth in multiple and unpredictable directions. This makes ambush a real worry, especially for the mine warfare vessels and surface ships that would have to escort commercial vessels all the way into Taiwan's ports.[5]

To be sure, the U.S. Navy would not deploy most of its assets near China all at once. But China still might think that a quick strike that sank a carrier and killed hundreds or thousands of Americans would cause Washington to waver in its future commitment to the defense of Taiwan. As China expert Michael Swaine has argued, in past wars Chinese leaders often have escalated dramatically in the hope that the shock effect of such tactics would intimidate or overwhelm an enemy.[6]

Since Operation Desert Storm in 1991, many have talked about a modern "revolution in military affairs" or RMA (though the concept dates back to the Russian general Ogarkov in the 1970s). Although definitions of the RMA vary, the main point is that precision weapons, linked to modern sensor, computer, and communications systems, have made offensive strikes far more effective than ever before. This is not always true. In complex terrain or bad weather, for example, many types of precision-strike weapons do not work as well, as the United States recently relearned in the 1999 Kosovo War (though some progress has since been made in this area).[7] In counterinsurgency, it is still quite difficult to find the enemy amid civilian populations, as the United States has been experiencing in Iraq since 2003. But in open area warfare, such as that generally surrounding the waters and seas of Taiwan (or the deserts of the Arabian peninsula), the RMA hypothesis is mostly right.[8] What this means is that even more than before, the side shooting first will have enormous advantages.

Not all surprise attacks need rely primarily on high technology. Indeed, as noted earlier, it is critical that Taiwan continue to improve procedures to ensure the survival of political and military leadership even if top officials are assassinated by Chinese special forces. The latter type of contingency would be extremely risky for China, but it could yield dramatic benefits—and even a clean win— if Taiwan did not have viable procedures for retaining a solid chain of command. To reduce the chances that China will either try such an attack, or cause Taiwan's capitulation if it dares to try, Taiwan must continue to work on this aspect of its leadership survivability (just as the United States did during the Cold War, when there were acute worries about nuclear first strikes).

Although U.S. armed forces first showed the potential of the RMA, trends in warfare pose as many risks for U.S. armed forces as they do opportunities. For example, as defense scholar Andrew Krepinevich has argued for years, fixed military bases on land—like those the United States uses on Okinawa, not to mention the facilities of the Taiwanese military—are becoming more vulnerable. And a country such as China, with the resources and technology to develop better cruise missiles and related weapons, is exactly the type of country that will be able to threaten such bases.[9]

Technology trends are putting U.S. ships at risk, too. Hypersonic antiship cruise missiles are becoming more common and are extremely difficult to defend against, even for high-performance U.S. Navy ships with advanced Aegis radar systems. The ranges of the cruise missiles are now reaching or exceeding 150 miles. Advanced torpedoes also could be a threat if Chinese submarines gained information on the whereabouts of American carriers and could launch at them from roughly ten to thirty miles' distance. China already is buying such weapons from Russia. Moreover, to make these weapons more effective, China can be expected to try to improve its targeting and communications systems, too. For example, it is putting into orbit more satellites capable of detecting large objects on oceans.[10] With the information from satellites, guidance systems on the cruise missiles could then guide them to the vicinity of their targets, where terminal seekers on the missiles themselves could finish the navigation job. China also might predeploy substantial numbers of floating minisensors in the waterways east of Taiwan, perhaps camouflaged on driftwood or submerged just below the ocean surface. They could listen for ships and then relay any relevant information through a communications network back to land. Although China probably has not developed these sorts of targeting capabilities yet, modern computers and sensors are putting such things within theoretical reach of even second-tier high-technology powers.[11]

Age-old military verities, together with modern technological trends, would undoubtedly make American military commanders see great value in striking hard at PRC forces early in a conflict. That would be the best way to deny China the ability to carry out sustained strikes against U.S. forces and the bases on which they would heavily depend. The United States has enough respect for China's growing military capability that the United States surely would have powerful reasons to want to attack hard and aggressively early in any fight, rather than assume that gradual escalation would automatically work to American advantage. As the Pentagon's 2006 strategy document put it, "Of the major and emerging powers, China has the greatest potential to compete militarily with the United States and field disruptive military technologies that could over time offset traditional U.S. military advantages absent U.S. counter strategies."[12]

Moreover, according to respected intelligence expert William Arkin, during the Bush administration the United States has formalized its planning for possible war against China. Previous Pacific Command thinking about possible conflict against the PRC was only general, being described under the heading of CONPLAN (for conceptual plan). But since 2001, the ideas have been formalized into more concrete and detailed operations plan for war (OPLANS—specifically, in this case, OPLAN 5077-04). This classified plan reportedly includes a wide range of military options, including attacks against targets on the Chinese mainland and even, under some extreme circumstances, nuclear exchanges.[13]

Similarly, Chinese leaders would likely believe that their best chance to drive America out of the conflict would be to hit it hard and early, taking out a ship or two and shocking the American public so much that the U.S. president sought a way to limit losses and pull back. That would almost surely be an incorrect reading of the nature of the American political psyche; when the stakes are high and their forces are directly attacked, Americans have historically increased their resolve. But Chinese leaders might misjudge the United States—or might hope that their only real chance of winning was to hope that Americans proved less than steely against a nuclear-armed budding superpower. They might look to the 1983 Lebanon example or the 1993 Somalia experience and convince themselves that the right punch might knock the United States out early. Although U.S. Navy assets would be on high alert in any blockade scenario, such a strategy might even catch American commanders at least slightly off guard. Again, many military arguments would argue strongly for a robust early strike.[14]

Of course, these military arguments would not necessarily carry the day. Just as President Kennedy rejected the advice of the Joint Chiefs of Staff to strike early in the Cuban Missile Crisis, leaders in

Washington and Beijing would have even stronger incentives to try to avoid superpower war—or, failing that, to contain it at the lowest level of danger and damage—than to pursue a clear military victory. (Indeed, some American military officers might be among those counseling that broader strategic arguments favoring restraint were more important than military tactical concerns favoring quick escalation—though it is hard to know in advance.)

It is possible that early in a conflict, American commanders might be severely restricted by the president. The initial rules of engagement might direct them to protect only Taiwan, and themselves, from imminent attack—not to go on the tactical offensive. For example, they might be prohibited from attacking PRC planes and ships that had not yet crossed the midway line between the PRC and Taiwan. Or they might be forbidden from carrying out any attacks on Chinese territory or within its territorial waters (which extend twelve miles from land).

Such guidelines surely would lower the risks of escalating war, relative to unrestricted rules of combat, but they hardly would guarantee stability. For example, even with such restrictions, American commanders would have powerful incentives to set up submarine ambushes near PRC territory (perhaps at exactly twelve miles' distance from land) to try to destroy Chinese submarines as they left or entered port. They also would have reason to be suspicious of Chinese commercial ships, since such vessels could easily be outfitted to carry torpedoes or cruise missiles or mines. American commanders might therefore demand that the Chinese ships avoid a large region around Taiwan or be subject to attack. If these types of measures quickly led to several ships being sunk on one side or the other, tactics that were intended to signal restraint might not seem so restrained to the country that had just lost hundreds of its personnel and hundreds of millions of dollars' worth of ships.

Moreover, for the United States in particular, there would be a serious strategic incentive to escalate quickly, above and beyond arguments about military self-defense. That is because time would seem to be China's natural ally in a Taiwan contingency.

The PRC could strike a few ships, produce an economic shock to the island's economy, and then delay subsequent attacks for months while it let the island's political system stew over its choices. Although Taiwan could begin to resupply itself after the Chinese attacks stopped, the island's economy and psychology would only partially recover in the short term. For American forces, maintaining a blockade-busting and mine-clearing effort over months would be onerous. Meanwhile, China could just wait. If U.S. ships and aircraft eventually went home and China attacked again, a pattern unfavorable to the United States would have emerged. It would have shades of the way Saddam "jerked the U.S. chain" in the 1990s, causing minicrises over weapons inspections, only to back off when U.S. and U.K. forces were deployed to coerce his compliance. Not wanting to play this game with China, the United States would have incentives to do more than just play defense. What little has trickled out of the Pentagon about its classified war plans confirms our instincts—that at least implicitly, they have generally anticipated rapid escalation in the event of war over Taiwan. Some of this may have been changing recently, at least somewhat, but it is impossible to know for sure from the outside.

A number of major powers are near China and Taiwan. Several have formal security partnerships with either the United States or China. What would their likely roles be in any war, whether in regard to sending combat forces themselves or to providing indirect military assistance such as base access?

Japan would be the most important country in this scenario. Japan would hardly desire a fight with China, but it would probably at least allow the United States use of critical military facilities on Okinawa, given its strong ties to the United States and Taiwan (not to mention worsening relations with China of late). Although Tokyo's permission cannot be taken for granted, U.S.-Japan alliance statements have increasingly placed Taiwan within their scope of concern and attention in recent years.[15]

Knowing this, China might threaten airfields on Okinawa. Such attacks would be hard pressed to shut down air operations for long.

But they could interfere with flights at a critical moment. They also might destroy a number of American aircraft. China might further hope that such attacks, in addition to their direct military effects, would convince Japanese leaders to rethink their role in the war. China might even get an added measure of support from a Chinese population that has become increasingly angry at Japan in recent years and might welcome the chance for at least a small measure of revenge against their former occupier (even if many Okinawans do not see themselves exactly as Japanese).

Again, China probably would be wrong. Given its concern about the growth of Chinese power and recent tensions, and its recent increases in nationalism, a more likely Japanese reaction would be to reaffirm its support for America and perhaps even join the war itself. And if Japan did so, its help could be very important. Its navy is quite impressive. Designed largely to help protect the Pacific sea lanes against possible Soviet attack during the Cold War, it retains extensive antisubmarine warfare, missile defense, and air defense capabilities (featuring eighty P-3 antisubmarine aircraft, nine frigates, sixteen submarines, and forty-five destroyers with air defense as well as antisubmarine capacities).[16]

No other regional actors would likely loom large in military terms. South Korea's leader, President Roh Moo-Hyun, has suggested that his country would have no role in a Taiwan conflict.[17] South Koreans live too close to China for most to want to get involved in this dispute, and then live with the consequences thereafter. In fact, President Roh has made it clear that he sees Korea's future role in the regional security environment as that of a balancer, and that he would oppose any American presumption that it could use bases in Korea for purposes beyond the peninsula without Seoul's full participation in decisionmaking.[18] But since U.S. forces probably would not need bases in South Korea to carry out combat operations, Seoul would not have the military levers to ratchet down a potential war.

Despite recent improvements in U.S.-Philippine security relations, it is not obvious that Manila would allow American forces to operate out of Luzon Island in any war. Philippine leaders also seem to prefer a certain distance from the United States. They decided to terminate U.S. military basing rights in the early 1990s. More recently, despite the fact that the Philippines and the United States are still allies, and that they have cooperated in fighting Muslim insurgents within the Philippines itself, Manila also has provided only minimal military help in Iraq. It also has been enjoying improved relations with China relative to the norms of the 1990s.[19] The Philippines might well help in the end—certainly Beijing could not rule out the possibility—but Washington could not count on it. If the Philippines did provide base access, the suitability of its facilities for large-scale combat operations would be open to some doubt given the fact that U.S.-Philippine military cooperation has diminished so much over the past fifteen years. The Philippines are a wild card but seem unlikely to be a major player.

The help of Australia, along with Britain perhaps America's most steadfast ally over the past hundred years or so, would be in some doubt given its increasingly strong diplomatic and economic ties with China.[20] China has displaced the United States as Australia's number two trade partner, largely by purchasing minerals. The PRC also has committed to buy $1 billion of natural gas a year from Australia for the next quarter century. It was for reasons such as these that in a 2005 poll, 72 percent of Australians agreed with the statement of their foreign minister, Alexander Downer, that Washington should not automatically assume Australian military support in the event of a Taiwan conflict.[21] That said, the U.S.-Australian alliance is fundamentally a strong one with deep historical roots. Canberra would be reluctant to abandon its long-standing ally in tough times.[22] But whether it fought alongside the United States or not, Australia would not swing the military balance in a major way. Its 10 frigates could help in the antisubmarine mission but represent a modest-sized force. And its 150 land-based combat aircraft, while capable, would not add much. The United States would itself already have far more airplanes than it could fit on regional bases.[23] Canberra might be able to play an honest broker role diplomatically, but would not have the military power to be a decisive determinant of force balances in a future war over Taiwan.

Singapore and Thailand are too far away to be of much help in providing bases. Like other ASEAN states, their militaries are focused on territorial and coastal defense and thus are far too limited in power-projection capability to send more than token forces (in the unlikely event they wished to).[24] India, while in ways a rival of China, is not focused on the Taiwan issue as the focal point of the rivalry and seems extremely unlikely ever to do so.[25] But none of these countries would be crucial for American forces, so none would have the power to stop a conflict through denial of military assets.

The United States and Taiwan would almost surely not have to worry about anyone else helping China militarily. China's only semiformal military alliance is with North Korea, a country hardly in a position to pick an unnecessary fight with the United States.[26] The Shanghai Cooperation organization, of which China is a founding member, was designed primarily to settle border disputes with Russia when created in 2001. It hardly constitutes a military alliance. (It now also includes Kyrgyzstan, Tajikistan, Kazakhstan, and Uzbekistan.)[27] The Shanghai group has recently tried to exercise some influence as a strategic counterweight to the United States, calling on the United States to formulate a plan to move out of bases in Uzbekistan and Kyrgyzstan eventually. But that is a far cry from active military cooperation.[28] Of the Shanghai group, besides China, only Russia has significant deployable military power. It has recently increased its defense cooperation with China. Notably, it conducted military exercises with China along their Pacific coasts in August 2005. The exercises involved about ten thousand troops (mostly Chinese) as well as amphibious ships and combat aircraft. But Russia cannot afford a fight with the United States itself. Nor does Russia care enough about the Taiwan issue to put its own forces on the line there. Much more likely, the exercises were designed to signal Washington that its foreign policy causes other powers concerns—and also to solidify a security relationship that, while far from an alliance, does net Russia very large revenues through arms sales to the PRC.[29] But, of course, for a fight over an island just a hundred miles from its shores that it saw as a key part of its territory, China would hardly be restrained by a lack of active allied help.

❊    ❊    ❊

Assuming a war between China and the United States begins, and then starts to escalate in some of the ways mentioned above, there would seem to be two most plausible outcomes of the conventional conflict. One is that the two sides could fight vigorously, with a U.S. victory the very likely outcome. The other is that the Chinese would stand down from the military conflict and the two sides would work out diplomatically some sort of *modus vivendi*—probably different from the current status quo, perhaps guaranteed by the United States, and probably to China's temporary disadvantage. The first might seem appealing to an American, but it would be in fact highly dangerous. It would raise the biggest question of all, whether China should accept defeat or escalate, perhaps with nuclear weapons.

Whether China would ever do so is difficult to determine. On the one hand, Chinese leaders would have to be very reluctant to make nuclear threats or seriously consider carrying them out. The dangers would be too great; the possibility of an actual nuclear exchange too real; China's prospects of prevailing in any such exchange against a country with twenty-five times more nuclear weapons too dubious. In addition, China retains a policy of nuclear no first use. And its traditions are in line with that doctrine as well. Even as brutal a leader as Mao, who ruled over China when it got the bomb in 1964, tended to be cautious when thinking about nuclear weapons and their role in international security.[30] Almost certainly, China would not quickly escalate to nuclear weapons, or even consider its nuclear arsenal a viable way to keep the United States out of any war over Taiwan in the first place.[31] But what it would do if losing is much harder to ascertain.[32]

On the other hand, nuclear-armed countries with inferior conventional forces have a certain logical reason for considering—or at least threatening—nuclear weapons use in the event of war over interests they consider critical to their security. The best historical example of this is the United States itself, which had a doctrine allowing for possible nuclear first use to defend overseas allies against possible Soviet attack.[33] Of course, such doctrines are designed primarily for deterrence. But if and when deterrence fails, the same country that sought to use nuclear threats to prevent war may attempt to use limited nuclear attacks to compensate for its conventional inferiority—even if it could not, militarily speaking, "win" a nuclear war. The situation would be more akin to a game of chicken than a traditional battle, even after shooting had begun. As Columbia University professor and nuclear strategist Robert Jervis writes about such situations, "Resolve and judgments of the other's resolve are as crucial to warfighting as to deterrence."[34] So China might try to show resolve by firing off a nuke or two, at carefully chosen targets (probably not large cities at first), and hoping that doing so would convince Washington to accept a negotiated, compromise solution that protected the PRC's core interests.

In thinking about this issue, Chinese leaders could consult dusty histories of Cold War crises in Europe. But they also could consult their own memories. They remember, collectively if not personally in all cases, that the United States made direct nuclear threats against their country in the 1950s over Taiwan. It also made somewhat more subtle threats against China over Korea and even Vietnam.[35] (In fact, the memory of such threats is one reason why China will strive hard to make sure it always has a second-strike capability against the United States, including a means to counter any American missile defense system that would threaten to deny them their nuclear deterrent.[36]) This is not to argue that Washington was right to make those threats. As Richard Betts writes convincingly about Taiwan, "the use of nuclear threats in the straits crises of the 1950s was reckless and undesirable even then, given the disproportionality of risks to stakes, as critics at the time argued, and should have been avoided."[37] That the United States may well have been wrong in issuing such threats is largely immaterial, however; they were made.[38] As such, they now form part of the collective historical memory of the U.S.-PRC relationship in general and the Taiwan conflict in particular. They also constitute an example China might be sorely tempted to follow when it perceives its own vital interests to be at stake.

The United States had the advantage of a nuclear monopoly in regard to China in the 1950s, making the situation very different. But as students of nuclear strategy know, in any nuclear face-off, the side with more at stake may be willing to take the greater risks. That fact alone can be an advantage that compensates for numerical inferiority. Indeed, even after it had lost outright nuclear superiority, the United States still made nuclear threats in 1973 and 1980. It put its forces on alert during the October War in the Middle East in the first case, to deter Soviet intervention. And in the second case, it made clear it had nuclear first-use options in the Persian Gulf should the Soviet Union continue from Afghanistan to invade Iran.[39] It is not necessary to be able to dominate conflict at every rung of a hypothetical "nuclear escalation ladder," to use a concept developed by the famous strategist Herman Kahn in the 1960s. Rather, as another famous strategist, Thomas Schelling, convincingly argued at about the same time, simply being willing to inject the risk of a nuclear conflict into a situation provides a country with a certain leverage—albeit at the very high price of risking nuclear war. Any nuclear conflict that actually did occur would be so uncertain in its dynamics that it would be impossible for the better-armed country to be sure of a favorable outcome.[40] And, of course, even a few weapons detonated on one's own soil would constitute a catastrophe of historic proportions, "win" or "lose."

Once nuclear threats began to be made, there would be all sorts of risks. In the Cold War, U.S. and Soviet commanders sometimes undertook risky or careless behavior with nuclear-armed assets, or thought they were about to be attacked even when that was not the case. Under hair-trigger circumstances, mistakes can quickly have enormous implications.[41] In addition to the fact that tactical commanders would be jittery, so would political leaders. They would realize that in the event of war they could quickly perish themselves, increasing the pressures to strike first.[42]

For those who still doubt that China could ever contemplate nuclear escalation during a Taiwan conflict, the words of two of China's generals can be instructive. They have suggested that China might indeed be willing to run nuclear risks, and make nuclear threats, over the Taiwan issue. In their eyes, China has both a disproportionately large interest in winning a war over that island, and conventional military inferiority vis-à-vis the United States that could make nuclear escalation necessary. In July 2005, Major

General Zhu Chenghu, a dean at China's national defense university, said that China might have to use nuclear weapons first in
response to an American deployment of conventional forces near
Taiwan, given the U.S. advantage in the latter category of military
capability. He suggested that more than a hundred American cities
could be hit with nuclear bombs as a result. This statement smacked
somewhat of (suicidal) bluster, partly because China's arsenal
includes only about twenty long-range single-warhead ICBMs at
present (and even under future projections, would contain perhaps
several dozen long-range weapons by 2015, though it is possible
that China could go higher than that).[43] His outlandish comments
were rebutted, but only several days later, by China's minister of
foreign affairs, who reiterated the country's official no-first-use policy, and Zhu later received an administrative punishment.[44] A
decade before, as we related at the beginning of this book, a senior
Chinese office general, probably General Xiong Guangkai, asserted
to former Clinton administration official Chas Freeman in the fall
of 1995 that "you [the United States] care more about Los Angeles
than you do about Taipei." That could be taken as an implicit threat
to the United States that China might use nuclear weapons in any
war over Taiwan.[45]

Other Chinese generals have quarreled with these hawkish views.
But then again, some pro-Western Chinese civilian analysts have
noted that in the event of a conventional war over Taiwan that China
was losing, it is entirely plausible that Beijing would contemplate
nuclear escalation.[46]

So China might deliberately decide to raise the nuclear specter as a
matter of policy. But there are other, more accidental or inadvertent
ways that nuclear war could occur.

For example, American armed forces might use *conventional*
weapons to deliberately target China's *nuclear* forces (at the same
time American forces activated missile defense systems in the theater and in the United States to be able to intercept whatever PRC
nuclear capability might survive the initial attack). Such a non-
nuclear attack would nonetheless have direct nuclear implications

for China, which then could feel strong incentives to threaten to use whatever nuclear forces survived the American attack before losing them in a follow-up strike.

The United States also might destroy Chinese ships carrying nuclear weaponry (most notably its long-range ballistic missile submarine, as well as vessels carrying shorter-range systems that could be used against U.S. forces in the region or Japan). And it might target military command and control headquarters with conventional as well as nuclear missiles. The United States might do all of this deliberately, or it might do so inadvertently as it targeted Chinese conventional capabilities.[47] Knowing how these dynamics could play out in advance, Chinese leaders might transfer some greater degree of nuclear release authority to local commanders in the event of a conventional conflict. Beijing might transfer enough physical control, and leave local commanders with sufficiently ambiguous instructions, that the latter might take matters into their own hands—especially if they were cut off from national command centers for an extended period.[48]

All-out intentional nuclear war from any of these possible causes would, of course, be insane. But a nuclear war would not have to begin with strikes on cities, and it probably would not. That is reassuring in one sense. But it is frightening in another, for it makes the notion of nuclear war slightly less apocalyptic—and thus slightly less unthinkable. U.S. nuclear war plans have a good deal of flexibility, with the ability to attack a handful of crucial key targets such as major ports, or dozens of military assets of second-tier importance such as airfields and major depots. Chinese plans presumably do, or at least could, as well.[49] For example, China could target Okinawan military airfields, Guam, Pearl Harbor, and any U.S. aircraft carriers near Taiwan that it could roughly localize. Perhaps it also would attack remote Taiwanese airfields—and Americans might be killed in such attacks, too, if small teams of military technical assistants had been deployed to Taiwan by then. If it was prepared to use dozens, not just a handful, of nuclear weapons, China could mount a fairly comprehensive attack that also took aim at U.S. military depots, a range of major and minor airfields, and reconnaissance and command centers throughout the Asia-Pacific theater. Such attacks would still be extremely lethal, of course, but would likely kill thousands or tens of thousands of civilians rather than millions. And they could have significant, even if not decisive, military implications for the conventional battle near Taiwan. In other words, while it would surely recognize the gravity of such strikes, Beijing might under conditions of extreme duress consider them—especially if the alternative was seen as losing the war as well as Taiwan.

The most likely initial Chinese attack option would probably be very limited. Its purpose would perhaps be less military than psychological—signaling to Washington how seriously China took the situation, and implicitly raising the possibility of further escalation. While Chinese leaders would know that they could not "win" an exchange of nuclear blows with the United States in any literal military sense, they might try to shock Washington into accepting a type of war-termination negotiation process that allowed China to achieve its most important objectives.

Of course, Washington probably would not back down in such a situation. Rather than negotiate, it could escalate. It is doubtful that any American leader would resort to all-out nuclear attacks in response to a Chinese nuclear strike. However, an American attack using a mix of conventional and nuclear weapons against all locatable PRC nuclear forces as well as their military command centers—or at least those outside of center cities—would be entirely plausible, and consistent with many nuclear concepts that American strategists have developed over recent decades.[50] Knowing this in advance, Chinese leaders could well have placed any nuclear forces they did not use in an initial attack on hair-trigger alert, ready to be launched quickly at the first sign of such an American reprisal. The situation would be highly combustible—perhaps even more dangerous, by this point, than the Cuban Missile Crisis ever became four decades ago.

China's most promising way to threaten Taiwan militarily over the next decade is with a blockade, primarily using its submarine force, and perhaps complemented by a modest number of missile strikes.

Such a blockade, if effective, might not be enough to ensure Taiwan's capitulation, but it could put Beijing in a good position to coerce Taipei into accepting terms for unification on political terms highly favorable to China.

Were the PRC to undertake a blockade, U.S. help might be needed to break it. Technically and tactically speaking, the U.S. Navy could almost surely do so—now, and well into the future. But whether China could accept such an outcome is unclear. Indeed, it might well consider escalation, perhaps attacking U.S. bases in Japan or even threatening strategic attacks that could involve nuclear weapons against the American homeland. Thankfully, such a war is not likely; we do not mean to fearmonger. But nor is it out of the question. If there is a great-power war in the twenty-first century, our crystal ball says that it will be between the United States and China over Taiwan, with a very serious potential for a horrible escalatory process. Even if the chances of war are not high in an absolute sense, they are still far too high for comfort. A U.S.-PRC war could be one of the worst events in human history and would certainly be calamitous for the century's prognosis. Everything must be done to reduce the chances that it could ever happen, and to minimize the risks of escalation if it does. We now turn to these crucial issues.

# 9

# From Standoff to Stand-down

This book is not meant to be alarmist. Most hypothetical causes of war between the United States and China turn out, upon inspection, to have little or no basis. The two countries will not duke it out simply to settle the question of who will "run the world" in the twenty-first century. Conquering territory or controlling other countries is no longer a sensible notion in international politics, and nuclear weapons add further deterrence. Both China and America need each other for economic prosperity; China's leaders in particular rely on the U.S. market and American technology and investment to preserve domestic stability and keep themselves in power. They have made the correct and pragmatic judgment that exporting goods into a globalized economy is a better way to advance their country's interests than exporting revolution and attempting to overturn the international system. Historical tensions with America's ally Japan are a worry, and smooth relations with Japan are as a result unlikely, but it would take a huge breakdown in politics and policymaking in both China and Japan to make war a possibility over an issue such as mutual dislike, or even disputed seabed resources.

Taiwan is another matter—an island that China sees as core to its sense of self and to its national cohesion, and also an issue in which a third party introduces unpredictable dynamics into the equation that Washington and Beijing cannot themselves directly

161

control. It is the most credible possible cause of war between the twenty-first century's two great superpowers.

Even on this matter, there is no cause for despair. We think that policymakers have generally handled the Taiwan and China problem reasonably well over the past quarter century, and expect that they will continue to do so. It appears that after flirting with more provocative ideas in late 2003 and early 2004, President Chen of Taiwan is internally constrained from pursuing anything that Beijing would regard as independence. And China, while passing the antisecession law that explicitly threatened force in March 2005, also has underscored its willingness to be patient in pursuing the long-term challenge of reunification and is content for now with pursuing the goal of blocking independence. All this is to the good.

But even if not alarmist, our message is designed to focus the reader's mind—and to cause some constructive level of anxiety. Just a modest possibility of U.S.-China war, with the potential to escalate to all-out conflict or even nuclear exchanges, should be enough to make Americans sit up and take note.

A U.S.-China war over Taiwan is indeed the most likely way in which the United States could wind up in a nuclear war in the twenty-first century. That is reason enough for every citizen to understand the dangers, the stakes, and the policy options.

For policymakers, they need to continue to focus on two main sets of concerns—how to do whatever we can to avoid a crisis over Taiwan in the first place, and how to quickly contain any major crisis or shooting war that begins despite our best efforts to prevent it. A good deal of effort has already gone into the first question, though there is still more to be done. A great deal of room for improvement exists on the second matter.

Past American policy on preventing, or quickly controlling, crises over Taiwan has been generally sound. But two broad arguments need to be articulated nonetheless. First, the theory behind past policy needs to be better understood by more policymakers—so that Congress will not push to give Taiwan more license and leeway than prudence would dictate, and so that future American administrations can be well prepared as they formulate China and Taiwan policy in the critical early months they are in power (a period when mistakes often are made). Second, some modest yet important changes are needed in American policy. While maintaining traditional firmness toward China over possible uses of force, Washington also needs to help Taiwanese politicians appreciate the danger of making provocative comments on the campaign trail. Such statements are sometimes harder to walk away from, in a democracy, than Taiwan leaders with their limited experience in such matters may appreciate.

But the core of U.S. policy is basically correct. The last two American administrations—one Democratic and the other Republican—have learned that the best way to manage cross-strait relations and avoid a crisis is to practice dual deterrence.

Washington warns Beijing not to use force against Taiwan but reassures the PRC that it does not support the island's independence. At the same time, Washington warns Taipei to avoid political steps that might provoke Beijing to use force but simultaneously assures Taipei that its freedom will not be sacrificed. Implied in this combination of warnings and assurances is the threat to use force to resist an unjustified Chinese attack against Taiwan and the threat to not come to the island's aid if it is unnecessarily reckless. Depending on a party's behavior at any given time, the United States may emphasize warnings over assurances or vice versa.

Obviously, the United States must exercise a lot of judgment here. Where does it draw the line between Taiwan political steps that all parties concerned should tolerate and those that are not reasonable? To put it differently, among the actions of the island's leaders, which are (a) truly separatist (and thus seriously provocative); (b) superficially provocative, really just designed to secure domestic political and electoral advantage; and (c) in a gray area in between? How Washington defines the situation will determine the exercise of dual deterrence and whether to stress warnings or reassurance toward each side. Of course, leaders in both Beijing and Taipei will try to get the United States to accept their own version of reality.

Just as obviously, communication is an essential component of this diplomatic approach. In each new set of circumstances, Washington must interpret the general formula of dual deterrence for both Beijing and Taipei. Taiwan's contacts with the United States are particularly important, since its political initiatives are often the triggers of tension and crisis, but its track record of communication has not always been the best. Often Taipei announces its steps first and explains later, even though there is some small probability—at least in American eyes—that its actions might trigger a conflict and the deployment of American forces. Yet neither can Beijing be ignored, for its decision-making system is relatively closed, and it often reads more into Taipei's actions than is meant. For its part, the United States must speak with one voice. If Taiwan sees one part of the U.S. government giving it a green light and another is signaling yellow or red, it is likely going to respond to the signal it prefers.

We have stressed above all the danger that conflict would begin because of misperception and miscalculation. China and Taiwan would teeter off the brink because they do not know where the edge of the brink is. As in the past, Taipei might try to protect its sovereignty and Beijing instead would see a drive for independence. Their brinkmanship would not necessarily be a wholly innocent matter of course. It could very well be because either Taiwan leaders might think they could get away with separatist recklessness, or because Chinese leaders believed they would pay no price for bullying a democracy. The United States would then be drawn into the fight, either by deliberate choice to defend Taiwan or because its forces were operating close to China's during a period of bluffing and testing.

This provokes a question: should the United States do more to shape how Beijing and Taipei see each other? We believe it should.

With respect to China, we think that Washington should challenge the Chinese view that Taiwan's claim of sovereignty is ipso facto evidence of an intention to strive for de jure independence and total separation from China. True, Beijing has reason to fear the claims that some people on Taiwan assert—that the best outcome is a Republic of Taiwan—and the United States needs to stay vigilant to make sure this view does not gain momentum unopposed. For the most part, however, Taiwan ideas of the island's sovereignty are compatible with certain kinds of unification. They are just contrary to Beijing's preferred formula of one country, two systems.

But for Beijing to brand those more benign, unification-friendly sovereignty ideas as separatist is to make a difficult situation dangerous. For the United States not to contest China's definition of the situation on this issue is to suggest, at least in Beijing's mind, that we implicitly accept it. Washington should not necessarily adopt Taiwan's position when it comes to sovereignty. Washington can, however, still be firm in pointing out the logical inconsistency of Beijing's position. Notwithstanding common PRC views, Taiwan's rejection of one country, two systems does not mean that it is rejecting all kinds of unification. And when Chinese charges that Taiwan actions are separatist are unjustified on the merits, the United States should quickly challenge those allegations. Such refutations do not have to be public, but China will be clearer about the location of the brink if it knows that *we* know where it is.[1] In those cases where Washington is certain that Taiwan politicians are engaged in provocative rhetoric merely for domestic political purposes and have no intention of acting on it, we should reassure Beijing on that point.

With respect to Taiwan, the United States needs to do three things. First, it needs to have a hardheaded discussion about the nature of decisionmaking in China. Taiwan officials often assume that Beijing is more rational on this subject than it actually is and that it can distinguish actions that the island's politicians take for political gain and those that reflect policy intentions. In fact, in dealing with Taiwan, China's leaders are prone to emotionalism, and Taiwan officials must take the possibility of Chinese miscalculation into account as they consider their own initiatives. Second, Washington should encourage Taiwan leaders to hold out the possibility of certain kinds of unification, to give China confidence that a peaceful settlement is possible. Obviously this is a two-way street. Taiwan is less likely to reassure Beijing on its ultimate goal—unification—unless China signals Taipei that it is prepared to be flexible on its issue, sovereignty. Just as a vicious circle of misunderstanding about Taiwan's relationship to China can lead to war, a virtuous circle of growing understanding can stabilize the peace.

Third, Washington should insist that there must be no surprises when it comes to Taiwan political initiatives that affect China's political interests. The United States has suffered a series of those surprises since 1999, and they have frayed a security relationship that should be based on good communication. That does not mean that Taiwan has to act according to China's dictates, but Taiwan should keep informed the government of the country on which it relies for protection against Chinese military power.

One very obvious way to reduce the probability of misperception and miscalculation is for China and Taiwan to talk to each other in an official manner. Such a channel would be a useful mechanism for crisis prevention, if not for stabilization or resolution of the dispute. Representatives of the heads of the Beijing and Taipei governments have not talked publicly since 1999 or privately since 1995. Since 2000, Beijing has insisted that before public dialogue can begin, Taipei must pledge its adherence to some version of the "one-China principle." China does not trust the intentions of Taiwan's leaders so, understandably, China asks that Taipei offer reassurances that its intentions are not separatist before any discussions begin. Taiwan has equal or greater mistrust of China's intentions and worries that by accepting China's principle it also will be accepting how Beijing defines that principle and making major concessions in the process (Taipei's fears probably are well founded). Taiwan is willing to treat "one China" as an issue, not a precondition.

Washington's view is that the only way to reduce mutual mistrust is to talk. It believes that precisely because each side doubts the other's intentions, they should engage. So the United States advocates dialogue without preconditions (in effect, it has sided with Taiwan), and it has sometimes encouraged the two sides diplomatically to begin talking. This provokes the question, should the United States go further than reducing the possibility of conflict through dual deterrence and mildly encouraging direct China-Taiwan dialogue? Should the United States intervene more directly as a mediator?

We believe that the United States should tread very carefully before trying to bring the two sides together. The benefits of conflict prevention would be high, but the prospects and costs of failure also would be high. First, a go-between or mediator must enjoy the trust of the two parties to be effective, but neither Beijing nor Taipei has that kind of confidence in Washington. Each would like the United States to dictate its solution to the other or to block the other from behaving badly but is not ready for it to be a true honest broker. Indeed, in 1982 Taiwan secured a pledge from the United States that it would not be a mediator, and still values that commitment. China fundamentally regards the Taiwan Strait issue as an internal affair. To allow American mediation would be inconsistent with that long-held principle. Second, Taiwan still has substantial political support in the U.S. Congress. Any administration would be reluctant to engage in mediation knowing that the ally of one party to the dispute was looking over its shoulder. Even if Taipei were willing at the outset to allow American mediation, the administration would likely fear that Taiwan and its congressional allies would get cold feet halfway through. Finally, the United States is in a real sense a party to this dispute because it provides advanced weaponry to Taiwan and to some degree guarantees the island's security. Those roles would sooner or later become key issues in the negotiation. How at that stage to maintain the confidence of the two parties—the sine qua non of a mediator—would become exceedingly difficult and probably impossible.

This is why the United States has for decades taken the position that the Taiwan Strait issue should be resolved peacefully by the two parties themselves. Even if Beijing and Taipei were to overcome past positions and mistrust of the United States and invite Washington to serve as a mediator, any administration would still probably be very reluctant. Nor is it clear that there is much that Washington can add in terms of substantive ideas or political will that the two parties cannot or will not have to provide themselves.

Under the current circumstances and given U.S. interests, Washington still should consider an extension of its current role, as an added means of conflict avoidance. That is to try to serve as a quiet catalyst for the resumption of authoritative cross-strait communication, certainly private contacts and public dialogue if possible. The key to this effort would be reducing some of the mutual misunderstanding, a process that the two sides would then continue on their own. There is no guarantee that they would accept Washington's playing such a catalytic role. Beijing may feel that trends in Taiwan politics allow it to play for time with few risks. But the effort is still worth exploring.


Despite the best efforts of many, there is a chance that all of the above types of efforts may fail. In fact, this book is predicated on the assumption that a crisis not only could occur, but that the situation could become considerably graver than witnessed in 1995–1996.

Chinese shows of force near Taiwan would themselves be nerve-racking. But the danger would grow most acutely if China or the United States fired shots at the other (or if China struck Americans inadvertently while targeting Taiwan). Therefore, the key would be to resolve any crisis before the big powers started to trade direct blows—just as the United States and the Soviet Union managed to avoid firing at each other during the Cuban Missile Crisis, various Mideast wars, and conflicts from Czechoslovakia and Hungary to Korea and Vietnam to Afghanistan. Some might argue that China and the United States could, relatively safely, contain a small conflict, just as India and Pakistan did over the Kargil region in 1999, or as China and the Soviet Union managed in their 1969 border battle. But these clashes were essentially border disputes, and in that sense naturally limited in scope. By contrast, a U.S.-PRC war over Taiwan would not be so inherently constrained, and would have a great potential for rapid escalation once the shooting began. It is easy to identify the escalatory firebreaks that should be respected, and just as easy to explain why they are likely to be breached—absent major efforts by the parties involved to understand their significance in advance (hence a chief purpose of this book) and attempt to respect them in the event of an actual crisis.

The best chance to keep the peace, of course, would be before any shooting occurred. Thus the first opportunity for military restraint, once a political crisis was well under way, would presumably fall to Beijing.

Ideally, China would consider nonmilitary options in response to a provocation, real or perceived, from Taiwan. In fact, should a crisis occur that seemed to be solely of Taiwan's doing, the best response for Beijing would be simply to ignore it, depending instead on the pledges of its friends in the United States, Japan, and elsewhere to restore the status quo ante. If Taiwan truly declared a change in the political status quo but the world's major powers refuse to treat it as such and worked hard to reverse whatever action caused the crisis, China's worries about genuine secession should be mitigated. But our argument in previous chapters is that the situation is unlikely to be so clear-cut. The provocation will be in the eye of the provoked (China). Moreover, the Taiwan issue is quite potent in Chinese politics, both within the Communist elite and within a nascent public opinion. It would be hard for Beijing to sit quietly by and let the United States and Japan, which together many Chinese regard as sources of the problem rather than the solution, walk things back. Action, not inaction, would likely be the Chinese default response.

At this stage of the crisis, if ignoring the perceived provocation did not suffice in Chinese eyes, Beijing might consider three other diplomatic strategies. First, it could intensively lobby Washington to rein in Taipei. The United States has responded to this before in less serious situations, as when President Bush stood with a visiting Chinese official in December 2003 and warned Taiwan against a "unilateral change in the status quo." What the United States does in any future situation depends on whether it buys Beijing's argument that Taipei really has crossed *the United States'* red line, not China's.

If Washington did accept Beijing's argument, then the next question would be whether Taipei could be stopped and how to do it. That would depend on whether the provocation had already been made and, if so, could be reversed, or was in prospect and could be prevented. Because the fundamental issue between China and Taiwan is the legal relationship between the two, the Taiwan provocation that would create the risk of war would hypothetically involve some sort of constitutional revision concerning that legal relationship. Constitutional revision on Taiwan is not something that can happen in the dead of night. It requires both action in the legislature and a popular referendum. There would be some warning that amendments were going to be considered. Hence the U.S. government, should it decide that Taiwan was about to make an unacceptable change in the status quo, would have time, if it chose to do so, to pressure Taiwan's leaders to abandon the initiative.

In this situation, the United States could warn Taiwan's politicians that if the proposal were adopted, Washington would not recognize the action and would not assume any responsibility for the consequences—including military consequences—that would ensue. (That, of course, is the implication of the dual deterrence policy, that Washington will not defend Taipei if it makes an unacceptable provocation of Beijing—though it is possible that Taiwan's leaders would conclude that America would eventually come to their defense regardless of what Washington said before a war.) China would have to have confidence that Taiwan's politicians and people were sufficiently pragmatic to respond positively to an American appeal, if it came to that. Taking this position would not harm America's global reputation, because if we decide that Taiwan acted provocatively, no one else is going to disagree.

If China could not get the United States to accept its definition of the situation, then it would have to meet the challenge on its own. Since 1995, Beijing has depended on Washington to act as its surrogate in blocking what it calls the forces of "Taiwan independence." (Beijing also has hoped that the opposition "pan-Blue" forces will be a check, but we assume for purposes of this particular discussion that they are too weak to be a major factor.) But Washington has not necessarily agreed with China on how it perceives Taiwan's goals. The United States has been willing to encourage restraint on Taipei up to a point. But we cannot rule out the possibility that China and America may part company on where Taiwan is going and what Washington should do about it.

China does have some other diplomatic options. It could ask the U.N. Security Council to stand against Taiwan's position. But this would require Washington's explicit cooperation, since the United States wields a veto at the Security Council. Beijing could appeal to other regional actors to disapprove of Taiwan's actions, and the public disapproval of Australia, the Republic of Korea, and the nations of Southeast Asia might well make Taiwan think twice. Still, the key actor is the United States (and to a lesser but real extent, Japan). If the United States backs China, then Taiwan is completely isolated. If it sides with Taipei, then the position of other countries will have only modest impact.

If all of the above failed, Beijing might consider stern but non-military responses such as a moratorium on economic interactions between China and Taiwan. Even a temporary trade embargo would be preferable to war. Such economic coercion, proportionately conceived and maintained over a sufficient time, would exert pressure on Taiwan decisionmakers to change course. If Beijing had already marshaled some type of international coalition to apply diplomatic pressure on Taiwan earlier in the crisis, as discussed above, that same coalition might hypothetically be available to consider a broader economic response as well.

Of course, this option has pitfalls for China, too. Taiwan companies provide China with investment, management know-how, jobs for millions of Chinese workers, access to key international markets, and allies in Taiwan's domestic politics (the business community). Mounting an economic embargo would threaten political stability in some parts of China and some of its export earnings. And creating a larger coalition to apply economic pressure on Taiwan collectively would be quite difficult. It would be very hard to gain Washington's support, since the U.S. Taiwan Relations Act identifies economic embargoes against Taiwan as a "threat to peace and security of the Western Pacific and of grave concern to the United States." In other words, the "peaceful" option would not be seen as quite so peaceful or innocent, would carry huge costs, and might well not work. The strong Chinese feelings about the Taiwan issue and the passage of the antisecession law in 2005, which authorized the use of force under certain circumstances, reinforce the judgment that Bejing might not be content with a purely economic response.

If China tried to bully other countries into joining any boycott or embargo, it probably would further increase the risk of strong American opposition. Perhaps it could convince a country such as Iran or even Russia to stop trade with Taiwan, partly by threatening to withhold trade with those countries itself. But China depends so heavily on the outside world economically—for raw materials from the Persian

Gulf, Russia, and Australia, for markets in the United States, Japan, and Europe—that China would have to worry that any muscular economic coercion strategy would lead to reprisals against itself.

But could Washington really organize such a reprisal? Might it be too dependent on China to afford such a head-to-head economic confrontation? There are two questions here. First, do we depend greatly on China for our economic prosperity? The answer clearly is yes. Second, do we depend more on China than it does on us—and is that dependence so great that our economy and our war machine simply could not function if China played economic hardball with us? The answer is so far no, and American policy should strive to keep things that way lest we develop an economic Achilles' heel that could render our military advantages irrelevant.

At present the United States and other countries do not depend heavily on China for absolutely critical materials. Generally, they do depend on China for a wide range of consumer products. As far as the United States is concerned, Chinese factories both manufacture countless goods that fill the shelves of Wal-Mart and other depart-ment stores and assemble notebook computers, display units, mobile phones, and DVD players. In 2005 America imported almost $250 billion dollars in Chinese goods, which is equivalent to about 2 percent of our GDP.[2]

To close U.S. markets to such a large volume of goods to get China to back down in a Taiwan crisis would entail an enormous economic risk. How long would it take American and other companies to find alternative suppliers for the goods embargoed? Until replacements were found, shortages would be disruptive for companies and con-sumers alike. Inflation would be a certainty as prices would rise to check demand. Even though consumption of most items imported from China might be deferred, are there some intermediate goods (e.g., switches and routers) for which China has become the sole supplier or at least the predominant supplier? Politically, some Amer-ican companies that are significantly committed to the China market probably would try to use their influence to block imposition of an economic embargo for these types of reasons. Finally, if the United

States sought to impose an economic embargo on Chinese goods, would China sell some or all of its stock of U.S. securities, thus triggering a rise in interest rates and a recession?

Clearly, a more formal economic analysis is needed to determine exactly what level of American dependence is too much and how much leverage it would have in a crisis. Overall, our dependence on China is probably not as critical as, say, the world's dependence on Saudi Arabia for oil, given the nature of most of the goods we buy from the PRC. And as for T-bills, any Chinese effort to sell them would drive down their price, costing the PRC lots of money as it also sought to drive up our interest rates. But our economy would suffer greatly in the event of economic warfare, and there could be a couple of key strategic vulnerabilities not yet widely appreciated (the Committee on Foreign Investments in the United States tracks only Chinese assets here, as the name suggests, not our overall economic dependence on China).

Taking stock of this situation, we recommend a more concerted U.S. government effort to track America's technology and economic dependence on China. Its main goal would be to provide policymakers with the information necessary to avoid development of critical U.S. vulnerabilities to any possible attempts by Beijing at economic coercion—and to reduce any such vulnerabilities that we may have, unwittingly, already created.[3]

It should be recalled that China itself would be running economic and political risks by engaging in economic warfare. Its economic relationship with the United States is one of mutual dependency. China's political stability rests on the employment of workers (more than a hundred million) who produce goods for the American market. China's growth of the past couple of decades has been driven by an export-oriented coastal sector, with the United States as its most important single market. Without that sector, China's growth would virtually stop; if major U.S. allies in Europe as well as Japan also severely curtailed their economic interaction with China, depression would surely result.

Ideally, Washington should do what it can to preserve trade sanctions as an option and to create in Chinese minds the impression that the option exists—even if it would be a painful and difficult one for

America to employ—and that the United States and its allies could win an economic showdown. The United States also needs to make sure that it does not develop a vulnerability to a Chinese act of economic warfare that could trump any U.S. military advantage. This issue will require extreme attentiveness in coming years. The United States—while continuing to expand its economic interaction with the PRC—will have to pay attention to the overall magnitude of its dependencies as well as specific strategic sectors of interaction.

If China did not choose an economic embargo, or could not make it effective, it might then contemplate some kind of military force. Obviously, although even symbolic missile strikes such as those in 1995–1996 are undesirable, they are preferable to more coercive attacks. They are demonstrations of force rather than the use of force. Yet we believe that China may not view this option as the centerpiece of its military strategy, for a couple of reasons. First, it has been used before. Taiwan has been desensitized from such demonstrations of force, so Beijing is likely to believe that more robust action is necessary.

Second, the "offense" that would produce a future military conflict, if conflict comes, would be a far more serious provocation than the one that prompted the firing of missiles in 1995 and 1996—Lee Teng-hui's visit to the United States. Although a future challenge would probably also be ambiguous, it would likely have more of a legal and irreversible character. Taipei probably would not be so reckless as to formally declare independence (for the simple reason that it understands that America's willingness to come to its defense would then be in serious doubt regardless of the nature of the military scenario). Still, more than loose words could be involved. It is difficult to speculate on specifics. But again, one possibility is significant revision of the Taiwan constitution embodied in a new document. That is an act that some in Taiwan would regard as a robust assertion of sovereignty, even the creation of a new state ("a second republic"), and one that China might interpret as the functional equivalent of de jure independence. What would probably be important for the United States is the substance of the exercise

rather than how some on Taiwan interpreted the action symbolically. For Washington, improving the island's democratic system of
government would probably be acceptable. Changing its legal identity vis-à-vis China would not.

Depending on circumstances, Chinese missile strikes against targets on land may then be attempted. But the current Chinese ballistic missile force lacks the accuracy for the kinds of attacks that would
be highly effective against military or economic targets. Moreover,
while missile strikes against land targets could create an element of
terror in Taiwan, that terror could inspire resolve and patriotism from
the island's citizens rather than any desire for capitulation.

As argued earlier, we believe that China's leaders are likely to
wind up imposing a naval blockade, quite possibly supplemented by
missile and cyber attacks, as the best match of their country's
strengths and Taiwan's weaknesses. In carrying out such a blockade,
Beijing's hope would be that the stranglehold on Taiwan's economic
lifeline would be so effective and its blow to civilian morale so devastating that the island would sue for peace. Moreover, a blockade
would not entail destruction of lives and property (except perhaps a
small number of ships; indeed, China might even rescue their
crews). All Taiwan would have to do to restore prosperity would be
to submit to China's political demands.

In the face of China's blockade of Taiwan, the ball would then
be in the American and Taiwanese courts. We believe that for reasons of international credibility and domestic politics, it would be
difficult, if not impossible, for Washington to stand by and watch
Taiwan fall to China or even to be severely coerced into a highly
unfavorable political settlement.

If Washington did not consider China's response to the situation
justifiable or proportionate to the initial Taiwan "offense," stern
measures would surely be considered. If the effect of China's
actions on Taiwan was principally economic, the United States
might try to respond in kind. It could seek to condemn China's
actions at the United Nations, even though Security Council resolutions would be out of the question, given Beijing's veto. The United
States could appeal to the broader community of Western and democratic nations, including not only those in Europe but also Korea,

India, Japan, and Australia, to oppose China's actions and signal that trade sanctions might follow. The United States also could ask oil suppliers to join in the coalition.

It is difficult in advance to know which kinds of diplomatic contacts and urgent missions might work best under various crisis and conflict scenarios. But there would be a few key possible players who might travel to relevant capitals; meet in the open or quietly with some combination of Taiwanese, Chinese, and American leaders; and otherwise try to rescue the world from the threat of a devastating conflict. (Top American officials rarely meet with those from Taiwan under normal conditions, but these circumstances would be much different; in any event, midlevel U.S. officials could certainly meet with Taiwanese leaders.) There would also be a few good historical models to bear in mind.

For example, the good offices of the U.N. secretary-general and of the European Union (EU) might be brought into the mix—perhaps to try to convince Taipei to modify whatever action had helped produce the crisis, depending on the nature of that action, and surely to pressure Beijing to relent in its use of force. This approach might follow the model of how Finnish president Martti Ahtisaari, representing the EU, helped negotiate the end of the Kosovo War with Milosevic—essentially presenting a gentler face, though not a neutral one, to Milosevic as Ahtisaari delivered NATO's demands (once Russia had essentially been convinced to support them as well).[4] In this case, however, the approach might be less promising since there is a widespread perception (especially in Taiwan) that the EU and the United Nations are favorably disposed toward China and not capable of playing the role of truly neutral arbiters. We raise the possibility not to suggest that it will work in a given situation, but simply to imagine what tool kit of diplomatic options might be available—and worth at least considering—in a crisis. In fact, perhaps more likely than United Nations or EU diplomacy would be regional mediation. Although institutional mechanisms are underdeveloped in Asia, and thus any approach would likely be ad hoc and improvisational, it is entirely possible that neutrally positioned countries such as India and Singapore could be more effective mediators than distant players would be.

The role of foreign ministers, and the American secretary of state, could be critical. If the opening to China in the 1970s warranted secret travels by such high-ranking officials, surely this type of crisis would, too. Emergency meetings at a halfway point in Russia or Alaska could be used to reaffirm stern warnings. For example, the United States could impress upon China that it could not stand by and watch Taiwan be conquered. (Depending on specifics, the United States also might send a private and even a secret mission to Taiwan to ask leaders there to do whatever they could to mitigate the crisis and definitely not make the situation worse. They should coordinate closely with the United States militarily and show restraint politically. For example, they should rein in any impulses of their own or the public to hold referenda to express righteous indignation over China's actions, because that might only exacerbate China's suspicions about Taiwan's motives.[5]) Such meetings also could be used to tender quiet offers, modeled in part after President Kennedy's quiet assurances to the Soviet Union during the Cuban Missile Crisis that U.S. missiles would soon be withdrawn from Turkey even if it was not acceptable to make their withdrawal part of an explicit deal. Drawing on another idea that came out of the Cuban Missile Crisis—when Kennedy was considering privately asking U.N. secretary-general U Thant to request that Kennedy withdraw the missiles from Turkey—American and Chinese leaders also might quietly ask for U.N. assistance here. The secretary-general might make parallel public demands on them— demands they might not like, and might not have been able to negotiate on their own for fear of losing face, but that they might nonetheless be willing to tolerate as long as the other side lived up to its obligations.[6]

Paradoxically, the military role can be quite important in diplomatic terms itself. U.S.-China military relations remain limited. However, since the days of Secretary of Defense William Perry in the first term of the Clinton presidency, they have received some attention. In the modern era, Pacific Command commanders also have worked to establish contacts with China; they also may have worked harder than before to sensitize U.S. civilian leaders to the details and the dangers of war plans against China. These facts point to several key possible roles for uniformed military and civilian defense leadership in both major countries, as well as in Taiwan. First, they can act as checks on civilian impulses to hasty action by reminding leaders of the ensuing dangers; counterintuitively, perhaps, military leaders might be more cautious than political leaders in some instances. Second, they can talk directly with each other—to explain what they are doing with their forces and lend their personal assurances that aggressive actions are not imminent (if that is the case). Of course, no such words can be totally believable in tense situations. But military leaders who have built up relationships with the other side (i.e., in the cases of China and the United States—not Taiwan, since China does not allow peacetime interactions between PRC and Taiwan military officers) may be able to defuse tensions that will surely mount if and when military forces are deployed near each other. This dynamic depends on the strength of the relationships in question, of course, so there should not be any assumption that it would resolve a crisis. But it could help. Third, in a much different spirit, military leaders also can underscore to the other side the seriousness of their country's intent and, especially in America's case, their confidence in its military capabilities. This message may be needed if, in a given crisis, the other side's leaders seem insufficiently attentive to the risks involved—or too inclined to wish that their potential adversary will back down rather than fight.[7]

If these diplomatic measures failed, the United States could then seek to impose broad-ranging sanctions. As the crisis wore on, China also could be told that sanctions would intensify with time—not only in their breadth, but also in their longevity, with the implication being that they might not be immediately lifted once the crisis was over.

But, of course, all that could fail, or take too long given the degree of Chinese pressure on Taiwan and the associated risks of Taiwan capitulation—leaving American military action as the only remaining recourse. In this situation, the United States would seek to physically break the embargo. As discussed in chapter seven, it would likely use ships and planes to establish convoy escorts for commercial ships heading to and from Taiwan, to try to sustain the economy as much as possible—and thereby also sustain Taiwan's will to resist.

It is worth underscoring that even a scenario stopping at roughly this point—after initial Chinese military action of some type, leading to American deployments but perhaps no direct combat between the two huge powers—would be most detrimental to the lasting interests of all concerned. Taiwan in particular would have to expect that its future economic collaboration with China would be seriously compromised, and given its strong dependence on the PRC, that would be a very high price to pay. Of course, things could still get far worse, as described below. But even a crisis that never produced direct U.S.-China hostilities, and allowed those two countries to repair most of their relationship in the aftermath, could hurt Taiwan a great deal.

Of course, decisions about possible military response would have to be made beyond Taipei and Washington as well. No country would face any more difficult choices than Japan. Should it stay out altogether, or more likely allow the United States use of its military bases, or even involve its self-defense forces in military operations? Although it is impossible to predict in the abstract how Japan would be involved in a Taiwan contingency, any direct use of its armed forces would be the country's most extensive military role since World War II. Even though Taiwan enjoys much sympathy among the Japanese public, any decision by Tokyo to deploy its force in this kind of conflict would be profoundly divisive and put substantial strain on the U.S.-Japan alliance. It also may expose Japan, whose relationship with China has grown increasingly hostile in recent years, to military attack, probably in the form of ballistic missiles—not to mention missile and torpedo attacks on any ships and planes Japan devoted to the possible blockade-busting and missile-defense missions.

A Chinese blockade also poses a couple of choices for Taiwan, in addition to the huge burden of holding on until the American rescue materializes. The first is military. Should Taiwan use its limited capability (mainly surface-to-surface missiles) to hit targets on the

Chinese mainland? Acquired mainly as a deterrent, these weapons, if used, would be liable to provoke a quick escalation by the People's Liberation Army that would outweigh any value they may have had in complicating its blockade. At some point it would be natural to expect Taiwan to act in its own self-defense. But if China had shown initial restraint in its use of force, Taiwan would be best advised to hold off on any such missile firings, at least for a time. The second choice would be political. Should Taiwan's civilian leaders give in to pressure from some domestic political forces to declare independence immediately, even though such an action would inflame an already tense situation? In both instances, the United States would likely be arguing that Taiwan should respect these firebreaks.

American intervention to resist China's blockade and to protect Taiwan then puts the onus on China to escalate and fire the first shot at a U.S. ship. Any Chinese submarines located by American sonar could be tracked with the clear message that they would be fired upon if they themselves fired. U.S. commanders also could call PRC military leaders to alert them to this situation, though the 2001 experience of American commanders failing to get through after the EP-3 episode is not encouraging here. Taiwan's economic plight would be at least partially alleviated. And China would be given the "last clear chance" to avoid a larger conflict, to use Thomas Schelling's phrase. This type of action would be logical and reasonable. Washington could take assertive action but still show restraint.

However, this approach could plausibly last only as long as no shots were fired at American forces by PRC assets. Once they were, any Chinese submarine in the combat theater would have to be treated as an imminent threat; the same would go for airborne aircraft or ships deployed from port. (In theory, China's Sunburn missiles might hit ships near Taiwan, even from their home ports. But it is dubious that they could find and track their targets from that distance—and also questionable that they could avoid being tracked and shot down themselves by American missile defenses.) At this moment, the United States would confront excruciating decisions about how far to escalate. The trade-off between ensuring tactical safety for its deployed forces, on the one hand, and running the risk of strategic escalation, on the other, would have to be weighed. The key issue would be where to draw the lines of the combat theater. Some commanders would likely argue for treating any Chinese ship or plane within tactical radius of Taiwan as a threat—and propose bombing airfields as well as ports on mainland China. Some might, even at this early stage, advocate preemptive conventional attacks against Chinese nuclear forces, in the hope that they could be taken out of the picture early in a crisis to reduce the risk of their being employed later, and to improve the odds that Beijing would back down from the hostilities quickly. Indeed, there is a good chance that U.S. war plans for dealing with a Taiwan contingency have included such rapidly escalatory options throughout much of the modern era.

A better approach would be to show somewhat more restraint. Defining the zone of combat along the midpoint between Taiwan and China, or at least avoiding any attacks in China's territorial waters and within its territory, would allow for robust self-protection measures while avoiding the politically fateful step of direct attacks on China's territory, with all of the latter's potential for very serious escalation. Not only would this approach avoid the symbolically dangerous step of directly attacking the Chinese mainland, it also would reduce the chances that China's ballistic missile submarine would be destroyed in port. This in turn would reduce the danger of nuclear brinkmanship, with all of its associated dangers, because Beijing would be less likely to adopt a "use them or lose them" mentality. In fact, even though the circumstances would be very different, in this situation the United States should emulate then secretary of state James Baker's reassuring conversations about Soviet nuclear weapons during the turbulent period in 1991 when the Soviet Union broke apart.[8] In this case, in addition to discussing matters of nuclear safety and security promptly and quickly, greater reassurances also would be appropriate. In particular, the United States should state that under no circumstances would it initiate use of nuclear weapons against China, even if hostilities became severe and prolonged, and state further that it expected Beijing to offer a similar pledge.

For the sake of clarity and emphasis, it is worth driving home the main guidelines that should inform Chinese and American leaders if they found themselves in the early stages of a military conflict. Specifically, they should keep the following firebreaks or red lines in mind:

- Not to expand the geographic scope of any U.S.-PRC fight beyond Taiwan's immediate vicinity, with a particular effort to avoid attacks on mainland China, Japan, and Guam (or the territorial waters surrounding them).
- Not to escalate to general conventional war (with possible attacks on command and control sites or other facilities near Beijing, Honolulu, San Diego, and so on).
- Not to fire (even conventionally) upon the other major power's nuclear forces.
- Not to ready nuclear weapons for use.
- Not to use nuclear weapons in any way, even against ships or isolated land bases or (via high-altitude bursts) against electronics.

Yet as our analysis of previous firebreaks has made clear, it is easy to state them, but one side or the other often has reasons to ignore them. Just as clearly, and as the Cuban Missile Crisis demonstrated, adversaries (and allies) must have some degree of communication and coordination if they are to avoid crossing over key escalatory thresholds.

The United States would very likely prevail unambiguously in a conventional conflict, even if it followed the above relevant constraints on its actions. It could lose aircraft or even a few ships in the ensuing battle, but it would almost undoubtedly gain control of the air and the ocean surfaces, and over time it would eliminate PRC submarines—especially those that fired at American forces, thereby revealing the submarines' locations. There is some doubt about American losses, but not much doubt about the outcome.

If this basic conclusion is correct, the next key decision—and the one we conclude on here—would fall to China. To be blunt, could it accept and make the best of defeat? Or would it look for some other way to win, crossing over the firebreaks we cite above, even at the risk of nuclear war? In contemplating its choices, China would be well advised to recognize that accepting defeat would not mean unconditional surrender.

To be sure, diplomats would be working overtime to craft a package that would permit China to salvage enough face to make conventional military defeat preferable to escalation. They would know that the sooner the shooting stopped, the easier it would be to restore the foundation of shared interests among China, Taiwan, and the United States that objectively exist. The longer conflict continued, on the other hand, the more hardwired and enduring hostility would be. The details of any settlement would depend, of course, on how the conflict started, which side had suffered the greatest damage, and which had the military upper hand. For example, had Taiwan been truly provocative, or had China manufactured a crisis?

Despite the efforts of diplomats to construct a rational settlement to end the conflict, other forces would be at play. In all three capitals, strong voices would harbor deep mistrust concerning the intentions of one or both of the other two parties as a reason not to agree. Public opinion in Taiwan and the United States could well argue for a hard negotiating stand against China, whereas Chinese citizens would likely oppose any concessions to the American "imperialists" and the Taiwan "separatists." What to Americans and Taiwanese might appear to be face-saving formulas could be too little, too late for politically besieged Chinese Communist leaders whose country had already suffered serious damage. Under such circumstances, they would face enormous pressure not to accept defeat, given the stakes at hand.

Some PRC leaders would then surely feel enormous pressure to consider escalation. At that point they might contemplate a high-altitude nuclear detonation east of Taiwan to create an electromagnetic pulse (EMP)—with the hope that it would incapacitate U.S. military forces below, as well as unsheltered Taiwanese equipment with vulnerable electronics. China also might fire nuclear weapons at an American aircraft carrier task force, several perhaps being shot at once to blanket a given region in which the U.S. ships were known to be. A nuclear weapon might even be used against the

Kadena air base on Okinawa, Japan. Any mobile ICBMs that China had built by then could be deployed away from their fixed bases, to protect them from American strikes and to send a message that they might soon be used.

Any of these Chinese actions would be extremely dangerous and should be avoided under all circumstances. Some could be tactically tempting. Most of all, an EMP burst, which would kill few if any people directly, might well be partially effective in incapacitating American and Taiwanese forces. Even though the United States would likely reciprocate, the overall effect would probably be to level the playing field between the U.S. and Chinese militaries. However, the economic implications of such an exchange would be so great as to be nearly equivalent to total war. Nor should China assume that all American military systems would be vulnerable to such attacks, designed, as many were, in the Cold War, when nuclear conflict was seen as a real possibility. Assets such as cruise-missile-capable submarines would survive; so would many bombers (which could be shielded in the United States once this type of exchange began). And after such a blow, the United States would at a minimum surely respond at the conventional level with whatever it had available; any previous talk of restraint would quickly dissipate in the corridors of the Pentagon and the White House. And with the nuclear genie out of the bottle, there is no reason to be confident that the escalation would halt exactly where China had intended.

Thus there are compelling arguments for controlling escalation all around. That is good news. But decisionmakers would have to be careful not to let a virtue become a liability. Knowing that there were multiple ways in which the escalatory process might be halted, at various stages along the escalation ladder, leaders might be tempted to throw caution to the wind and engage in brinkmanship at any given moment—believing that someone would still show restraint before the situation got out of hand. They might be right. Then again, they might not be.


The danger of any major crisis over Taiwan directly pitting Chinese and American armed forces against each other is real, and thus horrifying. If war resulted, escalation pressures would be enormous. It would be the first significant war between nuclear weapons states in world history. And the nuclear arsenals of the two sides could, as unreasonable and illogical as it sounds, come into play. Nuclear exchanges could even result. At a time when the threat of super-power nuclear war has become much less vivid in the public eye due to the end of the Cold War, a Taiwan crisis could—ironically enough—quickly create the most serious nuclear risk since the Cuban Missile Crisis.

This conclusion is not intended to be melodramatic. Even in the event of war, the risk of nuclear conflagration would be much less than fifty-fifty, since both sides would surely recognize the dangers. But crises have dynamics all their own. What neither side would see as desirable could nonetheless occur as the fog of war impeded accurate and timely information flows and clouded leaders' judgments—and as the loss of lives raised the stakes to the point where neither Beijing nor Washington could easily back down. In addition, the war plans of the two sides could create momentum of their own. Although details are classified (and always changing in any event), in the past these war plans apparently have called for hastier escalation than political leaders generally appreciate. This may have changed of late, and certainly recent American commanders in the region have been sensitive to the need to build positive relationships with China and to avoid assuming that any conflict would quickly escalate. But predisposition to restraint may not easily survive direct combat with a major military power; arguments in favor of rapid escalation will be powerful, whether or not they carry the day.

Leaders in Taiwan, China, and the United States need to think these issues through thoroughly in advance—for the sake of their war plans, their diplomacy, and their politics. They must figure out how to avoid escalation in any serious crisis or war that begins—for once the three parties get to that point, avoiding all-out U.S.-China war is more important than other realistic concerns. Indeed, it is so paramount in importance that Taipei, Beijing, and Washington must avoid the temptation to manufacture crises or play politics with the independence and sovereignty issues.

Among other implications, this set of conclusions argues for as much in the way of military-military dialogues as can productively be undertaken. They are worthwhile even if the Chinese side is less forthcoming about its thinking than the American side is.

In addition, governments need to face directly the types of scenarios discussed in this book. There has been some limited discussion of how to contain a Taiwan crisis, should one happen, but it has occurred mainly at the level of scholars who may or may not reflect the views of the American, Chinese, and Taiwan governments. Such exchanges should continue, and in fact expand, but they are not enough. That governments would not discuss an issue as sensitive as escalation control is understandable since, first, it is an admission that a war is possible, and second, any conversation would entail the kind of clarity about decisionmaking that civilian leaders and generals usually are loath to reveal. Yet we believe two things: one, that the costs of a U.S.-China conflict over Taiwan that did escalate would be severe; and two, that Washington and Beijing are unlikely to be able to learn how to do conflict containment in the middle of a crisis. Despite all the constraints, therefore, we believe it would be prudent for the two governments to authorize a dialogue in which knowledgeable officials, speaking in their "personal capacities" only (admittedly a bit of an oxymoron, but still a useful diplomatic device at times), engage in a conceptual discussion on the mysteries of escalation control in the nuclear age. They should then report back to their government colleagues for whatever value those conversations might have in the future.

This Taiwan problem could cause war, even nuclear war. That would be tragic. It also would be, even by the standards of international politics and international warmaking, quite foolish. This would be a war that no party can afford and that no party needs to risk. It is avoidable, and it must be avoided. For the sake of the world's future, it is essential that more key leaders in Taipei, Washington, and Beijing recognize this key reality and act on it at all times. Some already have. Many have not. It is time for that to change.

# Appendix

## Why China Could Not
## Seize Taiwan

Some analysts at the Pentagon worry greatly about a possible Chinese invasion of Taiwan.[1] As a 2004 Department of Defense report puts it, "The PLA most likely would encounter great difficulty conducting such a sophisticated campaign throughout the remainder of the decade. Nevertheless, the campaign could succeed—barring third-party intervention—if Beijing were willing to accept the political, economic, diplomatic, and military costs that an invasion would produce."[2] The tone of the 2005 report is not quite as dire, underscoring the complexity of an amphibious assault, but the Pentagon still seems anxious about this type of scenario.[3]

However, that conclusion is highly suspect. China does not have the basic key elements for a successful invasion, and is unlikely to obtain them in coming years. To succeed, an invader has generally first needed air superiority, and preferably outright air dominance or supremacy (China might be able to get the edge in the air, but it would have a hard time grounding or destroying the bulk of Taiwan's air force). Second, the attacker has used a combination of maneuver, surprise, and brute strength to land troops in a place where they locally outnumber defenders in manpower and firepower. Third, the attacker then must strengthen its initial lodgment faster than the defender can bring additional troops and equipment to bear at the same location. If an attacker can do most or all of these things, it has a good chance of establishing and then breaking out of an initial lodgment. As the following historical table shows, attackers can succeed without enjoying all three advantages. But in the cases considered here, they did not succeed without at least two of them. China could not attain any in all likelihood, with the possible exception of a measure of advantage in the air—not now and not in the coming next few years, unless Taiwan makes huge military mistakes that should be avoidable.

In modern times, amphibious assault forces have other problems, too. They need to worry about antiship missiles that could be launched from the defender's airplanes, ships, or shore batteries. Helicopters or airplanes used in the assault must deal with the threats not just of antiaircraft artillery but also of surface-to-air missiles. Given these trends in weaponry, amphibious assaults against fixed defensive positions are if anything becoming harder. The U.S. Marine Corps, recognizing these developments, has in the modern era placed a premium on maneuver and speed rather than traditional frontal attack.[4]

For the present and the foreseeable future, China has a chance of achieving some level of air superiority in any future war involving Taiwan, but not a good chance of achieving true air dominance. It has virtually no prospect of achieving either initial force advantages or sustained force advantages at the point of attack. In other words, at most it might partially

## Ingredients in Successful Amphibious Assaults

| Case/Attacker | Air Superiority | Initial Superiority in Troops/Firepower at Point of Attack | Reinforcement/ Buildup Advantage at Point of Attack |
|---|---|---|---|
| *Historical Successes* | | | |
| Okinawa, 1944/U.S. | yes | yes | yes |
| Normandy, 1944/U.S., allies | yes | yes | yes |
| Inchon, Korea 1950/U.S. | yes | yes | yes |
| Falklands, 1982/U.K.* | no | yes | yes |
| *Failed Attempts* | | | |
| Anzio, 1943/U.S. and U.K.* | yes | yes | no |
| Gallipoli, 1915/U.K., allies | no | yes | no |
| Bay of Pigs, 1961/Cubans | no | marginal | no |
| *Possible Chinese Attack on Taiwan* | | | |
| Taiwan Strait, 2000/PRC | doubtful | no | no |
| Taiwan Strait, 2010/PRC | doubtful | no | no |

*British forces were outnumbered on East Falkland Island, but they managed to build up their lodgment successfully and move out from it without opposition, satisfying the requirement listed here. At Anzio, although the forces there ultimately contributed to the Allied victory in Italy in the spring of 1944, their initial objective of making a quick and decisive difference in the war during the previous winter was clearly not met; thus the operation is classified here as a failure.

achieve one of the three criteria described above. That is almost certainly not good enough.

## Initial PRC Attacks with Missiles and Aircraft

China would almost surely have to try to surprise Taiwan with a major strike against ports and airfields. Otherwise, Taiwanese ships and airplanes could turn the shores near Taiwan into a shooting gallery as PRC amphibious ships and transport aircraft tried to approach. A successful surprise attack also would profit from the fact that it would take the United States several days—probably the better part of a week—to begin to deploy even air forces in substantial numbers to the region. If it employed this tactic, China could not start loading and sailing most of its ships toward Taiwan until after the missile and air strikes began, for fear of tipping off Taiwanese and U.S. intelligence about its intentions. In fact, the PRC would do extremely well simply to prepare its air and missile forces for the attack without having those preparations noticed.

China has a large ballistic-missile force and a large air force that could be used, among other missions, to attack airfields and planes on those airfields. The missiles are numerous, perhaps now totaling 750 in southeastern China near Taiwan. While China's ballistic missiles (as well as its cruise missiles) are rather inaccurate,[5] that will change in the coming years.[6] As for planes, China has about 100 airports within 600 miles of Taiwan, with a grand total of perhaps 700 military aircraft of all types at the 20 airports dedicated to such planes in peacetime.[7]

Between its missile force and its attack jets, China will increasingly be able to shut down Taiwan's airfields in the coming years. (Two dozen to three dozen planes might be needed to shut down a given runway, or a somewhat lesser number in combination with China's more accurate missiles.[8]) Taiwan would immediately begin to repair its damaged airfields after any attack. China could undertake subsequent attack sorties, of course. However, Taiwan's antiaircraft artillery and SAMs would then be at a high state of vigilance. Chinese planes might well suffer losses of 5 to 10 percent of their planes on each subsequent sortie, even if able to use standoff precision-guided munitions that allowed them to stay out of the immediate environs of the airfields.

China could directly attack Taiwanese aircraft on the ground. If Taiwan's military were caught napping, with jets exposed on runways, it could lose a great deal of its air force. But that should not happen. Taiwan has hardened shelters for many of its fighters.[9] Over time, China's precision-strike capabilities will improve. Taiwan will have to keep up by improving protection (as well as runway repair capabilities, radar, and air defenses) for its aircraft and also its fuel distribution systems.[10]

All told, while it might gain some edge, China could not achieve clear air dominance and thus would fail to satisfy fully the first criterion for most successful amphibious assaults as shown above. There is always a chance that luck, and a good battle plan, could favor China and give it a substantial advantage in the air. Given the complexity of the scenario, as well as the fact that neither China nor Taiwan has seriously conducted air warfare since the 1950s, it is, as noted airpower expert Ken Allen recently put it, "virtually impossible today to predict which side will be able to control the airspace over the Taiwan Strait in a future conflict."[11]

Of Taiwan's 600 or so combat aircraft, about half (those in shelters) would likely survive even a well-coordinated, large-scale Chinese surprise attack. Most of Taiwan's airborne control aircraft might be lost, and remaining combat jets might be reduced to flying only a sortie a day, at least in the war's first day or two, given damage to runways (and the possible, though unlikely, use of chemical weapons by the PRC). However, the surviving Taiwanese planes, at least 100 of which would likely be capable of ground attack, would generally have little trouble finding Chinese ships as they approached Taiwanese shores. Assuming two munitions per aircraft, 100 Taiwanese aircraft each flying a sortie might sink 5 to 20 ships a day in the subsequent amphibious phase of the conflict.[12]

Taiwan would lose airplanes to Chinese fighters, but only gradually, given the poor quality of those PRC aircraft and their command and control support. Since Taiwan's attack aircraft could fly low and concentrate their efforts in the eastern part of the strait, near Taiwan's coasts, China's ground radar and control centers would contribute little to the battle. Thus many Taiwanese aircraft would have a good chance to sneak through PRC fighter cover and carry out attacks, using antiship missiles or even dumb bombs against the poorly defended Chinese ships, and air-to-air missiles against transport aircraft. Taiwanese aircraft probably would suffer no more than 5 percent attrition per sortie, meaning that a given plane could fly many missions before being shot down.[13]

## A PRC Amphibious Assault

China can transport 10,000 to 15,000 troops with some heavy armor by amphibious lift. This number has not increased in this decade, according to the International Institute for Strategic Studies in London.[14]

Assume for the moment that China could deploy all of these ships to a single point on Taiwan's shores at once. Such a force would not be large given the defenses that the Taiwanese military could marshal in response. Taiwan, with 200,000 active-duty ground troops, 1.5 million more ground-force reservists, and a coastal perimeter of about 1,500 kilometers, could deploy roughly 1,000 defenders per kilometer of coastline along all its shores if it wished. So over any given stretch of 10 to 15 kilometers, a fully mobilized Taiwanese defense force would be able to deploy as many troops as China could deploy there with all its amphibious fleet. (An attacker would need to seize a shoreline of roughly that length, to create areas safe from enemy artillery.[15])

By contrast, on D-Day allied forces outnumbered German strength in Normandy by more than two to one within such tactical distances. As suggested in the table earlier in this chapter, successful invaders have generally managed to achieve initial force superiority at the point of attack as well.[16] China almost definitely could not. (Nor could China make up for a slow start later. Taiwan, enjoying the advantages of internal lines of communication, could send its very numerous reinforcements to an attacked area far faster than China could send ships back home, reload them, and return.)

The above assumed density of defenses presupposes no advance knowledge by Taiwan about where the PRC intended to come ashore. In reality, unless completely blinded and paralyzed by China's preemptive attacks against airfields, ships, shore-based radar, other monitoring assets, and command centers, Taiwan would see where ships sailed and be able to react with at least some notice. (It is also very likely that even if it did not immediately send combat forces, the United States would be willing to provide Taiwan with satellite or aircraft intelligence on the concentration of China's attack effort. The United States and Taiwan now have a military hotline, allowing for the possibility that the U.S. global surveillance system could plug holes in Taiwan's own capabilities or replace them after a PRC attack.[17]) Although the strait is typically only 100 miles wide, Taiwan itself is about 300 miles long, so ships traveling 20 knots would need more than half a day to sail its full length, and could not credibly threaten all parts of the island at once. In addition, amphibious assault troops cannot come ashore just anywhere. Only about 20 percent of the world's coastlines are considered suitable for amphibious assault. On Taiwan's shores, the percentage is even less, given the prevalence of mudflats on the west coast and cliffs on the east.

As a practical matter, then, Taiwan would not need to mobilize all its reservists to achieve force parity in places most likely to suffer the initial PRC attack. If Taiwan could mobilize even 20 percent of its reservists in the days that China would require to assemble and load its amphibious armada and then cross the strait, Taiwan could achieve force parity with China along key beachlines. Taiwan also has at least two airborne brigades that it could use to react rapidly where China attacked.[18] So China would be unlikely to establish even a local, temporary advantage along the section of beach where it elected to try coming ashore. Thus China does not possess the ability to generate the second element of most successful amphibious attacks as shown in the table earlier in this chapter.

The above analysis has ignored combat losses. In reality, such losses would be enormous, both in the initial assault and in subsequent reinforcement operations. Many of the troops crossing the strait in China's amphibious ships would never make it to land. As one way of getting a very rough quantitative grip on the problem, consider that the British lost 5 ships to missiles and aircraft and had another 12 damaged, out of a 100-ship task force, in the Falklands War—and that they did not generally have to approach any closer than 400 miles from the Argentine mainland during the conflict. That amounts to an effective attrition rate of 5 to 15 percent during blue-water operations—against an outclassed Argentine military that owned only about 250 aircraft.[19]

PRC losses would surely be greater against a foe whose airfields they would have to approach directly, whose air forces would likely retain at least 300 planes even after a highly effective Chinese preemptive attack against airfields, and whose antiship missile capabilities substantially exceed Argentina's in 1982. Taiwan possesses significant numbers of antiship missiles such as the Harpoon and its own Hsiung Feng. There are weaknesses in Taiwan's capabilities for resisting invasion; its air force has focused primarily on air-to-air attack, not antiship operations, and the United States has resisted providing Taiwan with certain attack capabilities out of fear they might be used provocatively. But despite these limitations, Taiwan's panoply of capabilities is considerable, and would be potent even at night or in bad weather. All told, the PRC would likely lose at least 20 percent of its forces just in approaching Taiwan's coasts and fighting ashore.[20]

### Estimated Daily Troop Reinforcement Rates
### (for days 3–10 after "D-Day," at a specific site on Taiwan)

| Means of Transport | China | Taiwan |
|---|---|---|
| Amphibious lift | 4,000 | 0 |
| Other sealift | 3,000 | 0 |
| Airlift | 1,000 | 0 |
| Internal land lines/roads | 0 | 50,000 |
| *Daily total* | 8,000 | 50,000 |

What if the PRC used chemical weapons in this part of its attack? If it could fire chemical munitions from its ship-based guns, it might be able to deliver enough ordnance to cover a battlefield several kilometers on a dimension within several minutes. China would presumably want to use a nonpersistent agent, such as sarin, so its troops could occupy the area within a short time without having to wear protective gear. The effects of the weapons on Taiwan's defenders would depend heavily on whether they had gas masks handy, the accuracy of Chinese naval gunfire, weather conditions, and the speed with which Taiwan could threaten the PRC ships doing the damage.[21] Historical experiences with chemical weapons suggest that China should not expect these weapons to radically change the course of battle in any event. Even in World War I, when protective gear was rudimentary, chemical weapons caused less than 10 percent of all deaths; in the Iran-Iraq war, the figure has been estimated at less than 5 percent.[22] China would need to worry that if its timing and delivery were not good, its own mobile and exposed troops could suffer larger numbers of casualties than the dug-in defenders.[23] Using chemical weapons also could invite Taiwanese retaliation in kind against China's relatively concentrated and exposed forces on and near the island.[24] All told, this approach would improve China's odds of getting an initial foothold on Taiwan slightly. However, it would not change the fact that Taiwan could build up reinforcements far faster than the PRC could subsequently.

Some have raised the possibility that the PRC could use its fishing fleet to put tens if not hundreds of thousands of troops quickly ashore on Taiwan. There are several important reasons not to take this threat particularly seriously, however. First, the ships could not carry many landing craft or much armored equipment. Second, Taiwanese shore-based coastal defense guns and artillery, as well as Taiwanese aircraft, small coastal patrol craft, and mines, might well make mincemeat of many of the unarmored ships, which would have to approach very close to shore for the disembarking soldiers not to subsequently drown.[25] Third, given the distances involved, it would be impossible to coordinate the assault very well; the ships would inevitably arrive on Taiwan's shores in ragged, staggered formations that would deny PRC troops the benefits of massed attack.[26]

A more serious worry, for an analyst looking out five to twenty years, is the possibility that at some point China will choose to build a major amphibious armada so that it has lots of the right kinds of ships to attempt such a forced landing. There is no doubt that this development would make the PRC threat more daunting. But any ship trying to cross the strait in the age of twenty-four-hour all-weather surveillance would still be at extreme risk. China never could be capricious about losing large fractions of its military in an ocean crossing (even if in theory it could build enough ships to compensate for the number likely to be sunk). In addition, the effects of such a buildup would be partially mitigated by the warning it would provide. Even if the United States did not take major steps in response, such as clarifying its commitment to Taiwan's defense or stationing more forces in the region, Taiwan could respond. For example, Taiwan could purchase much larger numbers of antiship weapons, stationing many directly on beaches in advance (akin to how Japanese and German forces prepared defenses in World War II). Taiwan also could predeploy minefields in waters near its most assaultable beaches that could be electronically activated when needed. These steps have not been vigorously pursued to date because the threat of invasion is not particularly great, but they could certainly be put into effect—more quickly than China could build dozens of large amphibious ships, provided the political will existed—if circumstances changed.

China could try to augment the role of amphibious ships with airborne operations. It currently can airlift two to three brigades of paratroopers, and, of course, the number could grow over time. China may already be adding a capacity to carry several thousand more light forces with the purchase of thirty Il-76 Russian transport aircraft.[27]

However, PRC paratroopers (or troop-carrying helicopters) over Taiwan would be at great risk from Taiwanese fighters, surface-to-air missiles, and antiaircraft artillery. Paratroopers in fixed-wing transports are particularly vulnerable in situations in which the attacking force does not completely dominate the skies and in which the defender has good ground-based air defenses.[28] Even if China somehow managed tactical surprise with its first sortie of airlift, thus keeping initial losses to a minimum—a highly dubious proposition—efforts to reinforce and resupply them would have to cope with alerted Taiwanese air defenses. Taiwan has well over 100 surface-to-air missile batteries with ranges of tens of kilometers—more than enough to have some coverage near all of its 20 to 30 large airfields and 5 major ports (the kinds of places where relatively immobile paratroopers might do the most good, seizing assets that could then be used to deploy PRC reinforcements). In addition to its air force, Taiwan also has hundreds of antiaircraft guns and many smaller surface-to-air missile batteries that use high-quality modified Sidewinder and Sparrow missiles. Even in the extraordinary event that China gained temporary control of a Taiwanese airfield, it could not build up its initial lodgment very fast, and its troops would likely be quickly overrun.[29]

A somewhat less reassuring implication of these quantitative assessments is that China might be capable of seizing Mazu or Jinmen, the small islands near the PRC coast that were the object of Chinese artillery attacks in the 1950s and that remain under Taiwanese control to this day.[30] Taiwan stations several tens of thousands of troops on Jinmen and 10,000 on Mazu. The latter number in particular is comparable to what China might be able to put ashore on such an island within hours. Moreover, Taiwan would have to traverse a greater distance to reinforce its garrisons on these islands than China would have to cover in building up any beachhead. Given geography, Taiwan also might concede the advantage in the air to China in such a scenario; in such a location, PRC fighters could benefit from shore-based air controllers, and would waste little fuel and time flying to the combat theater from their bases on the mainland.

But as for defending the main island against invasion, Taiwan is in a fairly good military position. It has large ground forces, good internal lines of communication, advanced munitions to use against an enemy that must expose itself to attack, and an enemy with limited technological excellence and operational proficiency. Were China to attempt an all-out invasion, it could suffer not just defeat, but also one of the most staggering losses of modern military history. It would not be militarily necessary for U.S. combat forces to come to Taiwan's help in such a war. Whether it was deemed politically desirable or not would largely be a function of how the war began, and of whether Washington considered it essential under the circumstances to demonstrate unimpeachable support for Taiwan. Regardless, any demands on U.S. combat forces would be modest.

# Notes

## 1. Thinking the Unthinkable

1. Joseph Cirincione, "Did China Threaten to Bomb Los Angeles?" *Proliferation Brief*, vol. 4, no. 4, March 2000, Carnegie Endowment for International Peace, http://www.carnegieendowment.org/publications/index.cfm?fa=view&id=651 [accessed March 19, 2006]; the references to Somalia, Haiti, and Bosnia are from an account in the *Washington Post*, June 21, 1998. Robert L. Suettinger suggests it was General Xiong Guang-kai, then a deputy chief of staff of China's People's Liberation Army, who was responsible for intelligence and chatting up foreign visitors; see his *Beyond Tiananmen: The Politics of U.S.–China Relations 1989–2000* (Washington, D.C.: Brookings, 2003), p. 248.

2. Cirincione, "Did China Threaten to Bomb Los Angeles?"

3. For an American view that Taiwan has a peripheral relevance to U.S. interest, see Ted Galen Carpenter, *America's Coming War with China: A Collision Course over Taiwan* (New York: Palgrave MacMillan, 2006).

4. Suettinger, *Beyond Tiananmen*, p. 248.

5. Ibid.

6. See Suettinger, *Beyond Tiananmen*, p. 255.

## 2. An Emerging Rival?

1. *Newsweek*, May 9, 2005; *Time*, June 27, 2005; *Economist*, July 30–August 5, 2005; *Atlantic Monthly*, June 2005.

2. When Napoleon's statement is quoted, there is sometimes also a reference to the phrase "sleeping dragon." We are grateful to Grace Chung for doing the Lexis/Nexis search.

3. Kurt M. Campbell, "China Watchers Fighting a Turf War of Their Own," *New York Times*, May 20, 2000, p. B-13.

4. "The National Security Strategy of the United States of America," the White House, Washington, D.C., September 17, 2002, http://www.whitehouse.gov/nsc/nss9.html (accessed November 5, 2005); "Quadrennial

Defense Review Report," Office of the Secretary of Defense, U.S. Department of Defense, February 6, 2006, http://www.comw.org/qdr/qdr2006.pdf (accessed April 8, 2006).

5. "4.3 Structure of Manufacturing," in *World Bank, 2005 World Development Indicators* (Washington, D.C.: World Bank, 2005), pp. 206– 209.

6. "That Blur? It's China, Moving up in the Pack," *New York Times*, December 21, 2005, pp. C1–C2.

7. "Young Seen as Leading Chinese Consumer Drive," *Financial Times*, October 13, 2005.

8. "Top Advisory Panel Warns of an Erosion of the U.S. Competitive Edge in Science," *New York Times*, October 13, 2005, p. A22.

9. Fareed Zakaria, "Does the Future Belong to China?" *Newsweek*, May 9, 2005, available at www.msnbc.msn.com/id/7693580/site/newsweek.

10. http://www.cia.gov/cia/publications/factbook/docs/rankorderguide.html (accessed November 18, 2006).

11. David Shambaugh, *Modernizing China's Military: Progress, Problems, and Prospects* (Berkeley: University of California Press, 2003), pp. 222–224; Stockholm International Peace Research Institute, "Transfers of Major Conventional Weapons to China, 1994–2003" (http://web.sipri.org/contents/armstrad/trend_ind_CHI_94-03.pdf [accessed July 27, 2004]).

12. U.S. Department of Defense, Annual Report on the Military Power of the People's Republic of China: Report to Congress Pursuant to the FY 2000 National Defense Authorization Act, July 19, 2005 (http://www.defenselink.mil/news/Jul2005/d20050719china.pdf [accessed July 19, 2005]), quoted passage from Executive Summary.

13. Department of Defense, Annual Report on the Military Power of the People's Republic of China: Report to Congress Pursuant to the FY 2000 National Defense Authorization Act, July 19, 2005 (http://www.defenselink.mil/news/Jul2005/d20050719china.pdf [accessed July 19, 2005]), pp. 7, 12–13; cited pages on pp. 7 and 13.

14. Robert D. Kaplan, "How We Would Fight China," *Atlantic Monthly*, June 2005. Kaplan's analysis is outside the mainstream in that it concludes that conflict is inevitable, not just possible. It is also one-sided in that he examines only the military dimension without assessing the two countries' profound economic interdependence.

15. For a gentle warning of America's waning influence vis-à-vis China in Southeast Asia, see "China and ASEAN: A Growing Relationship," speech by Ambassador Chan Heng Chee, Singapore's ambassador to the United States, at the Asia Society Texas Annual Ambassadors' Forum & Corporate Conference, Houston, February 3, 2006,

http://app.mfa.gov.sg/pr/read _content.asp?View,4416 (accessed April 8, 2006).

16. Joseph S. Nye Jr., *Understanding International Conflicts: An Introduction to Theory and History*, 3rd ed. (New York: Longman, 2000), p. 17.


3. Competition versus Opposition

1. Geoffrey Blainey, *The Causes of War* (New York: Free Press, 1973), pp. 115–119.

2. Keith Crane, Roger Cliff, Evan Medeiros, James Mulvenon, and William Overholt, *Modernizing China's Military: Opportunities and Constraints* (Santa Monica, Calif.: Rand, 2005), pp. xvi–xxvii, 46.

3. Michael D. Swaine and Ashley J. Tellis, *Interpreting China's Grand Strategy: Past, Present, and Future* (Santa Monica, Calif.: Rand, 2000), pp. 231–241.

4. Alastair I. Johnston, *Cultural Realism: Strategic Culture and Grand Strategy in Chinese History* (Princeton, N.J.: Princeton University Press, 1955); Swaine and Tellis, *Interpreting China's Grand Strategy*, pp. 231–241.

5. China may have certain military advantages for any war on its territory, and the United States for any war at sea or over islands—but neither country is likely to perceive itself as having a decisive systematic advantage for warfare in general. For related arguments see Barry R. Posen, "Command of the Commons: The Military Foundation of U.S. Hegemony," *International Security* 28, no. 1 (Summer 2003): 5–46; and Robert S. Ross, "The Geography of the Peace: East Asia in the Twenty-first Century," *International Security* 23, no. 4 (Spring 1999): 81–118.

6. Henry A. Kissinger, "China: Containment Won't Work," *Washington Post*, June 13, 2005, p. A19.

7. Nicholas R. Lardy, *Integrating China into the Global Economy* (Washington, D.C.: Brookings, 2002), pp. 1–28; and Alastair Iain Johnston, "Is China a Status Quo Power?," *International Security* 27, no. 4 (Spring 2003): 5–56.

8. See Philip Bobbitt, *The Shield of Achilles* (London: Penguin Books, 2002), pp. 798–823.

9. Monty G. Marshall and Ted Robert Gurr, "Peace and Conflict 2005" (College Park, Md.: Center for International Development and Conflict Management, May 2005), available at www.cidcm.umd.edu, pp. 11–13.

10. For a more general articulation of this broad argument see G. John Ikenberry, "Institutions, Strategic Restraint, and the Persistence of

American Postwar Order," *International Security* 23, no. 3 (Winter 1998/99): 43–78.

11. Richard N. Haass, *The Opportunity: America's Moment to Alter History's Course* (New York: Public Affairs, 2005), p. 20.

12. David Zweig and Bi Jianhai, "China's Global Hunt for Energy," *Foreign Affairs* 84, no. 5 (September/October 2005): 37.

13. International Institute for Strategic Studies, *The Military Balance 2005/2006* (Oxfordshire, U.K.: Routledge, 2005).

14. Princeton Lyman, "China's Rising Role in Africa," Presentation to the U.S.-China Commission, July 21, 2005; www.cfr.org/publications/8436/chinas_rising_role_in_africa.html [accessed September 17, 2006].

15. Zheng Bijian, "China's 'Peaceful Rise' to Great-Power Status," *Foreign Affairs* 84, no. 5 (September/October 2005): 18–19.

16. Richard C. Bush, *Untying the Knot* (Washington, D.C.: Brookings, 2005), pp. 29–30.

17. See Kurt M. Campbell, "Foreign Policy and National Security Just Became Twice as Hard," testimony before the House Committee on Armed Services, September 27, 2005.

18. Katinka Barysch, *Embracing the Dragon: The EU's Partnership with China* (London: Centre for European Reform, 2005), pp. 21–26.

19. Zhao Mei, "Chinese Views of America: A Survey," in Carola McGiffert, *Chinese Images of the United States* (Washington, D.C.: Center for Strategic and International Studies, 2005), p. 62.

20. Wang Jisi, "China's Search for Stability with America," *Foreign Affairs* 84, no. 5 (September/October 2005): 39–48.

21. Robert L. Suettinger, *Beyond Tiananmen: The Politics of U.S.-China Relations* 1989–2000 (Washington, D.C.: Brookings, 2003), p. 7.

22. Richard H. Solomon, *Chinese Negotiating Behavior* (Washington, D.C.: U.S. Institute of Peace, 1999), p. 31.

23. Kishore Mahbubani, "Understanding China," *Foreign Affairs* 84, no. 5 (September/October 2005): 53.

24. Sheldon W. Simon, "Southeast Asia's Defense Needs: Change or Continuity?" in Ashley J. Tellis and Michael Wills, eds., *Strategic Asia 2005–06: Military Modernization in an Era of Uncertainty* (Seattle: National Bureau of Asian Research, 2005), p. 274.

25. Agence France Presse, "Philippines Cannot Rely on U.S. Defence: Military Chief," December 4, 1999, available at www.nexis.com/research/search/documentDisplay?_m=ce0567bae1e3858b835450e. . .

26. On the seabed petroleum issue see Selig S. Harrison, "Seabed Petroleum in Northeast Asia: Conflict or Cooperation?" in Selig S. Harri-

son, ed., *Seabed Petroleum in Northeast Asia: Conflict or Cooperation?* (Washington, D.C.: Woodrow Wilson Center for Scholars, 2005), p. 7.

27. For a good discussion see Zbigniew Brzezinski, *The Choice: Global Domination or Global Leadership* (New York: Basic Books, 2004), pp. 107–122.

28. Michael J. Green, *Japan's Reluctant Realism* (New York: Palgrave, 2001).

29. Mike Mochizuki and Michael O'Hanlon, "Calming the Japan-China Rift," *Washington Times*, April 21, 2005.

30. See R. Evan Ellis, *U.S. National Security Implications of Chinese Involvement in Latin America* (Carlisle, Pa.: Army War College, Strategic Studies Institute, 2005).

31. Jay Solomon, "FBI Sees Big Threat from Chinese Spies: Businesses Wonder," *Wall Street Journal*, August 10, 2005, p. 1.

32. Bill Gertz, "Chinese Technology Theft on the Rise, U.S. Says," *Washington Times*, June 27, 2005, p. 16.

33. U.S. House of Representatives, Select Committee, U.S. National Security and Military/Commercial Concerns with the People's Republic of China (Washington, D.C.: U.S. Congress, 1999), pp. ii–xxxvii.

34. Ted C. Fishman, *China, Inc.: How the Rise of the Next Superpower Challenges America and the World* (New York: Scribner, 2005), p. 293.

35. See Nicholas R. Lardy, "United States–China Ties: Reassessing the Economic Relationship," testimony before the House Committee on International Relations, October 21, 2003, available at www.iie.com/publications/papers/lardy1003.htm.

36. Lael Brainard and Michael O'Hanlon, "A Test of American Independence," *Financial Times*, July 26, 2005.

37. Ibid.

38. C. Fred Bergsten, Bates Gill, Nicholas R. Lardy, and Derek Mitchell, *China: The Balance Sheet, What the World Needs to Know Now about the Emerging Superpower* (New York: Public Affairs, 2006), pp. 4, 23–39.

39. For a version of Zoellick's appeal see Deputy Secretary of State, Robert B. Zoellick, "Whither China: From Membership to Responsibility?," remarks to National Committee on U.S.–China Relations, New York City, September 21, 2005, http://www.state.gov/s/d/rem/53682.htm (accessed October 31, 2005).

40. John Hill, "U.S. Quadrennial Defense Review Sparks Anger in China," *Jane's Intelligence Review* (April 2006): 46–47.

41. On the American side see Zoellick, "Whither China"; and on the Chinese side, *China's Peaceful Rise: Speeches of Zheng Bijian, 1997–2005* (Washington, D.C.: Brookings, 2005).

42. In this regard we share the view of our late, former Brookings colleague A. Doak Barnett.

43. In his well-known book, Thomas Barnett lucidly discusses the internal Pentagon dynamics that have made some designate China as the next great threat, and argues against the likelihood of general war between the United States and the PRC, as we do. However, in our judgment there are real reasons to consider war over Taiwan entirely plausible. For Barnett's view see Thomas P. M. Barnett, *The Pentagon's New Map: War and Peace in the Twenty-first Century* (New York: G. P. Putnam's Sons, 2004), pp. 96–106.

44. Not only the PRC government, but also the Chinese population, are passionate about the Taiwan question. See, for example, Jia Qingguo, "Partners or Competitors: A Choice to Be Made," in Robert M. Hathaway and Wilson Lee, eds., *George W. Bush and East Asia: A First-Term Assessment* (Washington, D.C.: Woodrow Wilson International Center for Scholars, 2005), pp. 117–129; and Zhao Mei, "Chinese Views of America: A Survey," in McGiffert, *Chinese Images of the United States*, p. 71.

## 4. The Lost Island

1. On the early history of Taiwan see John Robert Shepherd's splendid *Statecraft and Political Economy on the Taiwan Frontier, 1600–1800* (Stanford, Calif.: Stanford University Press, 1996); and the early chapters of Murray A. Rubinstein, ed., *Taiwan: A New History* (Armonk, N.Y.: M. E. Sharpe, 1999).

2. For an account of Taiwan's Sinicization through the history of one family see Johanna Menzel Meskill, *A Chinese Pioneer Family: The Lins of Wu-feng, Taiwan, 1729–1895* (Princeton, N.J.: Princeton University Press, 1979).

3. On the sociology and politics of religion see David K. Jordan, *Gods, Ghosts, & Ancestors: Folk Religion in a Taiwanese Village* (Berkeley: University of California Press, 1972); and Arthur P. Wolf, ed., *Religion and Ritual in Chinese Society* (Stanford, Calif.: Stanford University Press, 1974).

4. For the best single volume on U.S.-Taiwan relations after 1945 see Nancy Bernkopf Tucker, *Taiwan, Hong Kong, and the United States, 1945–1992: Uncertain Friendships* (New York: Twayne, 1994). For some key issues in that history see Richard C. Bush, *At Cross Purposes: U.S.-Taiwan Relations since 1942* (Armonk, N.Y.: M. E. Sharpe, 2004).

5. On the U.S.–ROC alliance see John W. Garver, *The Sino-American Alliance: Nationalist China and American Cold War Strategy in Asia*

(Armonk, N.Y.: M. E. Sharpe, 1997); and Robert Accinelli, *Crisis and Commitment: United States Policy toward Taiwan, 1950–1955* (Chapel Hill: University of North Carolina Press, 1996). On Mao see Shu Guang Zhang, *Deterrence and Strategic Culture: Chinese-American Confrontations, 1949–1958* (Ithaca, N.Y.: Cornell University Press, 1992); and Chen Jian, *Mao's China and the Cold War* (Chapel Hill: University of North Carolina Press, 2001).

6. The best one-volume treatment is Denny Roy, *Taiwan: A Political History* (Ithaca, N.Y.: Cornell University Press, 2003).

7. On this theme see Alan M.Wachman, *Taiwan: National Identity and Democratization* (Armonk, N.Y.: M. E. Sharpe, 1994).

8. The Election Study Center of Taiwan's National Chengchi University conducts polls on changes in Taiwan residents' sense of identity. See its Web site: www2.nccu.tw/~s00/eng/data/Political%20Attitude02.htm.

9. For Chiang's and Deng's indirect interaction see Jay Taylor, *The Generalissimo's Son: Chiang Ching-kuo and the Revolutions in China and Taiwan* (Cambridge, Mass.: Harvard University Press, 2000).

10. For a detailed look at the shoe industry's migration see You Tien Hsing, *Making Capitalism in China: The Taiwan Connection* (New York: Oxford University Press, 1998).

11. "Taiwan's Trade Surplus with China Tops U.S. $31.8 Billion," Central News Agency, February 24, 2006, Foreign Broadcast Information Service, CPP20060224968056 (accessed February 25, 2006); Bruce Einhorn, "Why Taiwan Matters," *Business Week*, May 16, 2005, p. 76; "Taiwan's Role in Peace and Stability in East Asia: A Discussion with Dr. Ma Ying-jeou," Brookings Institution, March 23, 2006, transcript produced from a recording, p. 16, http://www.brookings.edu/comm/events/20060323.pdf (cited April 8, 2006).

12. "Taiwan Chip Output to Start in 10 Days—Production Schedule Relies on Restoring Power Knocked Out by Quake," *Wall Street Journal*, September 24, 1999, p. A-12.

13. Einhorn, "Why Taiwan Matters."

14. For an account of the secret contacts see Richard C. Bush, *Untying the Knot: Making Peace in the Taiwan Strait* (Washington, D.C.: Brookings, 2005), pp. 288–290. For a summary of the growing social and economic integration see ibid., pp. 28–35.

15. For the best account of the 1995–1996 crisis see Robert L. Suettinger, *Beyond Tiananmen: The Politics of U.S.–China Relations 1989–2000* (Washington, D.C.: Brookings, 2003), pp. 200–263.

16. These are discussed in depth in Bush, *Untying the Knot*, chap. 3.

17. For an assessment of this episode see ibid., pp. 55–57, 218–221.

## 5. The Taiwan Tinderbox

1. For a broader discussion of U.S. policy see Richard C. Bush, *Untying the Knot: Making Peace in the Taiwan Strait* (Washington, D.C.: Brookings, 2005), chap. 9.

2. The "three communiqués" between the United States and the People's Republic of China were the Shanghai Communiqué of 1972, which set the guidelines for the two countries' initial rapprochement; the December 1978 joint communiqué on the normalization of relations, by which the United States recognized the PRC as the government of China and announced the establishment of diplomatic relations; and the August 1982 communiqué on arms sales to Taiwan, in which Washington pledged to exercise restraint in its arms sales policy in light of Beijing's peaceful-unification policy. The Taiwan Relations Act was passed by Congress in March 1979 and signed by President Carter in April 1979. It established the legal framework for continuing relations with Taiwan on an unofficial basis, expressed concern about Taiwan's security, and authorized continued arms sales for Taiwan. The "six assurances" were pledges that President Reagan made to Taiwan at the time of the August 1982 arms sales communiqué to reassure President Chiang Ching-kuo that the United States had not sold out the island's political or security interests. For more information, see "The 'Sacred Texts' of United States-China-Taiwan Relations," in Richard C. Bush, *At Cross Purposes: U.S.-Taiwan Relations since 1942* (Armonk, N.Y.: M.E. Sharpe, 2004), pp. 124–178.

3. U.S. Department of Defense, Annual Report on the Military Power of the People's Republic of China: Report to Congress Pursuant to the FY 2000 National Defense Authorization Act, May 28, 2004, p. 7 (hereinafter cited as 2004 Pentagon Report), http://www.defenselink.mil/pubs/d20040528PRC.pdf, pp. 7, 11 (accessed June, 1 2004).

4. Emerson M. S. Niou, "Understanding Taiwan Independence and Its Policy Implications," *Asian Survey* 64, no. 4 (July–August 2004): 558.

5. The public American warnings were conveyed in "Overview of U.S. Policy toward Taiwan," testimony by James A. Kelly at the hearing "The Taiwan Relations Act: The Next Twenty-five Years," House International Relations Committee, April 21, 2004 (www.state.gov/p/eap/rls/rm/2004/31649pf.htm).

6. A few Chinese scholars have understood this, but that thinking has not yet penetrated government policy.

7. For Ma's views see "Taiwan's Role in Peace and Stability in East Asia: A Discussion with Dr. Ma Ying-jeou" (Washington, D.C.: Brookings, March 23, 2006), transcript produced from a recording, p. 16, http://www.brookings.edu/comm/events/20060323.pdf (cited April 8, 2006).

8. Any constitutional amendment that passed the legislature also would have to face a popular referendum and get a majority of eligible (not of participating) voters. Practically speaking, that works out to 60 to 65 percent of participating voters, again a supermajority.

## 6. Adding Fuel to the Fire

1. Avery Goldstein, *Rising to the Challenge: China's Grand Strategy and International Security* (Stanford, Calif.: Stanford University Press, 2005), pp. 178–193.

2. U.S. Department of Defense, "Annual Report to Congress: The Military Power of the People's Republic of China, 2006" (Washington, D.C., 2006), p. 20.

3. Information Office of the State Council of the People's Republic of China, *China's National Defense in 2004* (Beijing, 2004), chap. 4 (english.people.com.cn/whitepaper/defense2004.htm); and U.S. Department of Defense, "Annual Report to Congress: The Military Power of the People's Republic of China, 2005" (Washington, D.C., 2005), p. 21, available at www.dod.mil/news/Jul2005/d20050719china.pdf.

4. Then secretary of defense Donald H. Rumsfeld, Remarks before the International Institute for Strategic Studies symposium, Singapore, June 4, 2005, available at www.defenselink.mil/speeches/2005/sp20050604-secdef1561.html.

5. See, for example, Rear Admiral (Ret.) Eric A. McVadon, "Recent Trends in China's Military Modernization," before the U.S.-China Economic and Security Review Commission (Washington, D.C., September 15, 2005), p. 1.

6. Bates Gill and Michael O'Hanlon, "China's Military, Take 3," *National Interest* 58 (Winter 1999/2000): 118.

7. U.S. Department of Defense, "Annual Report to Congress: Military Power of the People's Republic of China, 2006," p. 21.

8. See ibid., p. 50.

9. Ibid., p. 46.

10. Republic of China, Ministry of National Defense, "National Defense Report, 2004" (Taipei, 2004), pp. 29, 52.

11. International Institute for Strategic Studies, *The Military Balance 2005/2006* (Colchester, U.K.: Routledge, 2005), pp. 270–276; Michael E. O'Hanlon, *Defense Policy Choices for the Bush Administration*, 2nd ed. (Washington, D.C.: Brookings, 2002), pp. 154–203; Robert Hewson, "China Boosts Its Air Assets with Ilyushin Aircraft," *Jane's Defence Weekly*, September 21, 2005, p. 16; International Institute for Strategic Studies, *The Military Balance 2000/2001* (London: Oxford University Press, 1999),

pp. 194–197; and U.S. Department of Defense, "Annual Report to Congress: The Military Power of the People's Republic of China, 2006," p. 4.

12. U.S. Department of Defense, "Annual Report to Congress: The Military Power of the People's Republic of China, 2005," p. 17.

13. David Shambaugh, *Modernizing China's Military: Progress, Problems, and Prospects* (Berkeley: University of California Press, 2002), pp. 105–107.

14. For example, on its airpower doctrine, see Kenneth W. Allen and Jeffrey M. Allen, "Controlling the Airspace over the Taiwan Strait: Basic Issues and Concepts," in Steve Tsang, ed., *If China Attacks Taiwan: Military Strategy, Politics, and Economics* (Colchester, U.K.: Routledge, 2005), pp. 100–105.

15. U.S. Department of Defense, "Annual Report to Congress: The Military Power of the People's Republic of China, 2005," p. 3; and U.S. Department of Defense, "Annual Report to Congress: Military Power of the People's Republic of China, 2006," p. 3.

16. Robyn Lim, "China's Muddled Maritime Strategy," *Asian Wall Street Journal*, August 23, 2005.

17. U.S. Department of Defense, "Annual Report to Congress: The Military Power of the People's Republic of China, 2006," pp. 7, 13, 15. Ellis Joffe, "China's Military Buildup: Beyond Taiwan?" in Andrew Scobell and Larry M. Wortzel, eds., *Shaping China's Security Environment: The Role of the People's Liberation Army* (Carlisle, Pa.: Strategic Studies Institute, 2006), pp. 42–45.

18. See U.S. Department of Defense, "FY04 Report to Congress on PRC Military Power: Annual Report on the Military Power of the People's Republic of China" (Washington, D.C., 2004), pp. 17, 21–26, and 37–41.

19. Information Office of the State Council of the People's Republic of China, *China's National Defense in 2004* (Beijing, 2004), chap. 3 (english.people.com.cn/whitepaper/defense2004.htm).

20. U.S. Department of Defense, "Annual Report to Congress: The Military Power of the People's Republic of China, 2005," p. 16.

21. Keith Crane, Roger Cliff, Evan Medeiros, James Mulvenon, and William Overholt, *Modernizing China's Military: Opportunities and Constraints* (Santa Monica, Calif.: Rand, 2005), pp. 154–190; Douglas Barrie, "Cruising Along: Beijing's Ambitious Guided-Weapons Funding Continues to Pay Dividends for Armed Forces," *Aviation Week and Space Technology*, July 28, 2005, p. 31; and "Chinese Puzzle," *Jane's Defence Weekly*, January 21, 2004, pp. 24–29.

22. U.S. Department of Defense, "Annual Report to Congress: The Military Power of the People's Republic of China, 2006," p. 5.

23. Christopher F. Foss, "China Modifies TY-90 Missile for Surface Launch," *Jane's Defence Weekly*, June 2, 2004, p. 15; Ronald O'Rourke, *China Naval Modernization: Implications for U.S. Navy Capabilities* (Washington, D.C.: Congressional Research Service, 2005), p. 5; U.S. Department of Defense, "FY04 Report to Congress on PRC Military Power: Annual Report on the Military Power of the People's Republic of China" (Washington, D.C., 2004), pp. 5, 14, 18–19, 28–33, and 42–43; Republic of China, Ministry of National Defense, "National Defense Report, 2004," pp. 49–50; and "Watching Warily," *Aviation Week and Space Technology*, July 25, 2005, p. 30.

24. Republic of China, Ministry of National Defense, "National Defense Report, 2004," p. 49.

25. See U.S. Department of Defense, "FY04 Report to Congress on PRC Military Power: Annual Report on the Military Power of the People's Republic of China," pp. 5, 14, 18–19, 28–33, and 42–43; Republic of China, Ministry of National Defense, "National Defense Report, 2004," pp. 49–50; and U.S. Department of Defense, "Annual Report to Congress: The Military Power of the People's Republic of China, 2005," pp. 35–36.

26. U.S. Department of Defense, "Annual Report to Congress: The Military Power of the People's Republic of China, 2006," p. 3.

27. David Shambaugh, "China's Military Modernization: Making Steady and Surprising Progress," in Tellis and Wills, eds., *Strategic Asia 2005–06: Military Modernization in an Era of Uncertainty* (Seattle: National Bureau of Asian Research, 2005), p. 97.

28. Wendell Minnick, "Taiwan Receives AIM-120C Missiles," *Jane's Defence Weekly*, December 3, 2003, p. 16.

29. Wendell Minnick, "Taiwan Boosts Submarine Force with Harpoons," *Jane's Defence Weekly*, September 28, 2005, p. 18; and Wendell Minnick, "Identity Crisis," *Jane's Defence Weekly*, June 30, 2004, pp. 25–29.

30. Glenn Kessler, "Ex-President Says Taiwan Needs Missiles," *Washington Post*, October 18, 2005.

31. See U.S. Department of Defense, "FY04 Report to Congress on PRC Military Power: Annual Report on the Military Power of the People's Republic of China," p. 47.

32. Richard Halloran, "U.S. Pressures Taiwan to Focus on Defense Policy," *Washington Times*, August 23, 2005, p. 1.

33. Michael D. Swaine, "Taiwan's Defense Reforms and Military Modernization Program: Objectives, Achievements, and Obstacles," in Nancy Bernkopf Tucker, ed., *Dangerous Strait: The U.S.–Taiwan–China Crisis* (New York: Columbia University Press, 2005), pp. 131–161.

34. Jonathan Karp, "Taiwan to Get Better U.S. Military Technology," *Wall Street Journal*, June 24, 2005, p. 11.

35. For an analysis of the legal effect (or lack thereof) of the Taiwan Relations Act, see Richard C. Bush, "The Sacred Texts of United States–China–Taiwan Relations," in *At Cross Purposes: U.S.–Taiwan Relations since 1942* (Armonk, N.Y.: M. E. Sharpe, 2004), chap. 5.

36. National Institute for Defense Studies, *East Asian Strategic Review 2005* (Tokyo: National Institute for Defense Studies, 2005), p. 115.

37. These reasons do not include the canard that the United States wants to keep Taiwan's wealth and technology out of PRC hands, or that it wishes another "unsinkable aircraft carrier" with which to contain a rising China in the future. These highly theoretical arguments are belied by the fact that U.S. policy has never opposed Chinese reunification provided that it be peaceful and on terms acceptable to both sides. Moreover, they overstate the long-term strategic significance of Taiwan, which, while an important U.S. ally and friend, and a strong economic partner, at the end of the day is an island with a population one-sixtieth that of mainland China.

38. See James Mann, *Rise of the Vulcans* (New York: Penguin Books, 2004), pp. 284–286; Ivo H. Daalder and James M. Lindsay, *America Unbound: The Bush Revolution in Foreign Policy* (Washington, D.C.: Brookings, 2003), pp. 69–70.

39. For a similar analysis see Mitchell B. Reiss, "Prospects for Nuclear Proliferation in Asia," in Tellis and Wills, eds., *Strategic Asia 2005-06*, pp. 340–341; and Richard N. Haass, *The Opportunity: America's Moment to Alter History's Course* (New York: Public Affairs, 2005), p. 151.

40. See for example, Geoffrey Blainey, *The Causes of War* (New York: Free Press, 1973), pp. 35–56, 108–126; and Victor D. Cha, "Hawk Engagement and Preventive Defense on the Korean Peninsula," *International Security* 27, no. 1 (Summer 2002): 40–78.

41. Sun Tzu, *The Art of War*, translated and with an introduction by Samuel B. Griffith (London: Oxford University Press, 1963), p. 77. Sun Tzu is the previous romanization of the name. Sun Zi is now more common.

42. See Barry M. Blechman and Stephen S. Kaplan, *Force without War: U.S. Armed Forces as a Political Instrument* (Washington, D.C.: Brookings, 1978), pp. 23–57.

43. Ashton B. Carter and William J. Perry, *Preventive Defense: A New Security Strategy for America* (Washington, D.C.: Brookings, 1999), pp. 97–99; and Robert L. Suettinger, *Beyond Tiananmen: The Politics of U.S.–China Relations, 1989–2000* (Washington, D.C.: Brookings, 2003), p. 255.

44. Suettinger, *Beyond Tiananmen*, p. 260.

45. Shambaugh, *Modernizing China's Military*, pp. 102–103.

46. On this see Sean M. Lynn-Jones, "A Quiet Success for Arms Control: Preventing Incidents at Sea," *International Security* 9, no. 4 (Spring 1985), reprinted in Steven E. Miller and Stephen Van Evera, eds., *Naval Strategy and National Security* (Princeton, N.J.: Princeton University Press, 1988), pp. 359–389; Ashton B. Carter and William J. Perry, *Preventive Defense: A New Security Strategy for America* (Washington, D.C.: Brookings, 1999), p. 109; and Richard C. Bush, *Untying the Knot: Making Peace in the Taiwan Strait* (Washington, D.C.: Brookings, 2005), pp. 277–278.

47. Carter and Perry, *Preventive Defense*, pp. 97–99.

48. See map following p. 139 in Akikazu Hashimoto, Mike Mochizuki, and Kurayoshi Takara, eds., *The Okinawa Question and the U.S.–Japan Alliance* (Washington, D.C.: George Washington University Press, 2005).

49. International Institute for Strategic Studies, *The Military Balance 2004–2005* (London: Oxford University Press, 2004), pp. 31–32; and U.S. Department of Defense, Washington Headquarters Services, Directorate for Information Operations and Reports, "Active Duty Military Personnel Strengths by Regional Area and by Country" (Washington, D.C., March 31, 2005) (http://web1.whs.osd.mil), accessed July 28, 2005.

50. U.S. Department of Defense, "Annual Report to Congress: The Military Power of the People's Republic of China, 2005," p. 44.

51. International Institute for Strategic Studies, *The Military Balance 2004–2005*, p. 171; and Shambaugh, *Modernizing China's Military*, p. 103.

52. International Institute for Strategic Studies, *The Military Balance 2004–2005*, pp. 170–173.

53. For a good history see John Keegan, *The First World War* (New York: Alfred A. Knopf, 1999); also see Steven E. Miller, Sean M. Lynn-Jones, and Stephen Van Evera, *Military Strategy and the Origins of the First World War* (Princeton, N.J.: Princeton University Press, 1991).

54. Keegan, *The First World War*, p. 73.

55. Barbara Tuchman, *The Guns of August* (New York: Bantam Books, 1980), p. 135.

56. Blainey, *The Causes of War*, pp. 144–145.

57. This is a tricky statement. As a legal formulation, it means that Taiwan is a sovereign entity, not subordinate to any other state (i.e., China). On that, virtually everyone in Taiwan agrees. But Taiwanese politicians like the double meaning of the word "independent," because they can

appeal to people who would like a Republic of Taiwan and say to others that they are not saying anything new.

58. Michael B. Oren, *Six Days of War: June 1967 and the Making of the Modern Middle East* (Oxford, U.K.: Oxford University Press, 2002), pp. 262–271.

59. Sean M. Lynn-Jones, "A Quiet Success for Arms Control: Preventing Incidents at Sea," *International Security* 9, no. 4 (Spring 1985), reprinted in Steven E. Miller and Stephen Van Evera, eds., *Naval Strategy and National Security* (Princeton, N.J.: Princeton University Press, 1988), pp. 362, 382.

60. For a concise review of the history see Raymond L. Garthoff, "The Cuban Missile Crisis: An Overview," in James A. Nathan, ed., *The Cuban Missile Crisis Revisited* (New York: St. Martin's Press, 1992), pp. 41–53; and Raymond L. Garthoff, *Reflections on the Cuban Missile Crisis* (Washington, D.C.: Brookings, 1987), pp. 20–22.

61. Ronald E. Powaski, *March to Armageddon* (Oxford, U.K.: Oxford University Press, 1987), pp. 103–106.

62. Garthoff, "The Cuban Missile Crisis," in Nathan, *The Cuban Missile Crisis Revisited*, p. 46.

63. McGeorge Bundy, *Danger and Survival* (New York: Vintage Books, 1988), pp. 453–458.

## 7. China Might Think It Would Win

1. On the estimate that the United States has two-thirds of the world's projectable military power see Michael E. O'Hanlon, *Expanding Global Military Capacity for Humanitarian Intervention* (Washington, D.C.: Brookings, 2003), pp. 51–83.

2. For a good general argument along these lines see Thomas J. Christensen, "Posing Problems without Catching Up: China's Rise and Challenges for U.S. Security Policy," *International Security* 25, no. 4 (Spring 2001), pp. 5–40.

3. U.S. Department of Defense, "Annual Report to Congress: The Military Power of the People's Republic of China, 2006" (Washington, D.C., 2006), p. 29.

4. Republic of China, Ministry of National Defense, National Defense Report, 2004 (Taipei: Ministry of National Defense, 2004), p. 49.

5. John Hill, "Missile Race Heightens Tension across Taiwan Strait," *Jane's Intelligence Review* (January 2005), pp. 44–45.

6. Anthony H. Cordesman and Abraham R. Wagner, *The Lessons of Modern War*, vol. 2: *The Iran-Iraq War* (Boulder, Colo.: Westview Press, 1990), pp. 205–206; and Daniel L. Byman and Matthew C. Waxman,

"Kosovo and the Great Air Power Debate," *International Security* 24, no. 4 (Spring 2000), pp. 37–38.

7. James C. Mulvenon, Murray Scot Tanner, Michael S. Chase, David Frelinger, David C. Gompert, Martin C. Libicki, and Kevin L. Pollpeter, *Chinese Responses to U.S. Military Transformation and Implications for the Department of Defense* (Santa Monica, Calif.: Rand Corporation, 2006), pp. 116–120.

8. Robert C. Suettinger, *Beyond Tiananmen: The Politics of U.S.– China Relations 1989–2000* (Washington, D.C.: Brookings, 2003), p. 226.

9. John Hill, "Missile Race Heightens Tension Across Taiwan Strait," *Jane's Intelligence Review* (January 2005), pp. 44–45.

10. William C. Triplett II, "Potential Applications of PLA Information Warfare Capabilities to Critical Infrastructure," in Colonel Susan M. Puska, ed., *People's Liberation Army after Next* (Carlisle, Pa.: U.S. Army War College, Strategic Studies Institute, 2000), pp. 94–95.

11. James C. Mulvenon et al., *Chinese Responses to U.S. Military Transformation,* pp. 83–94.

12. Central Intelligence Agency, *The World Factbook 2005* (Washington, D.C., 2005) (available at www.cia.gov/cia/publications/factbook/geos/tw.html).

13. For a concurring view see Bernard D. Cole, "Command of the Sea?: Can the PLA Secure the Control of the Sea and Cut Off Taiwan from the Outside World?," paper presented at Conference on the Taiwan Strait at St. Antony's College, Oxford, England, February 27–28, 2004.

14. Bruce G. Blair, *Strategic Command and Control: Redefining the Nuclear Threat* (Washington, D.C.: Brookings, 1985), pp. 90–92, 132–137; Denny Roy, "Tensions in the Taiwan Strait," *Survival* 42, no. 1 (Spring 2000), p. 85; and Michael E. O'Hanlon, *Technological Change and the Future of Warfare* (Washington, D.C.: Brookings, 2000), pp. 176–181.

15. Shambaugh, "Taiwan's Eroding Military Advantage," pp. 130–31.

16. See Government Information Office, *Taiwan Yearbook 2004* (Taipei, 2004); and General Accounting Office, Container Security: Expansion of Key Customs Programs Will Require Greater Attention to Critical Success Factors, GAO-03-770 (Washington, D.C., July 2003), p. 5.

17. Paul H. B. Godwin, "The Use of Military Force against Taiwan: Potential PRC Scenarios," in Parris H. Chang and Martin L. Lasater, eds., *China Crosses the Taiwan Strait: The International Response* (Lanham, Md.: University Press of America, 1993), pp. 21–22.

18. Republic of China, *Republic of China Yearbook* 1999 (Taipei, 1999) (available at www.gio.gov.tw/info/yb97/html/content.htm).

19. Michael E. O'Hanlon, *Defense Policy Choices for the Bush Administration* (Washington, D.C.: Brookings, 2002), p. 189.

20. Michael R. Gordon and General Bernard E. Trainor, *The Generals' War: The Inside Story of the Conflict in the Gulf* (Boston: Little, Brown, 1995), pp. 343–345.

21. See, for example, Andrew F. Krepinevich Jr., *The Conflict Environment in 2016: A Scenario-Based Approach* (Washington, D.C.: Center for Strategic and Budgetary Assessments, 1996), p. 7.

22. For a very good general discussion of modern mine and countermine technologies see Owen Cote, *The Future of Naval Aviation* (Cambridge, Mass.: MIT Security Studies Program, 2006), pp. 37-38 (available at http://web.mit.edu/ssp/).

23. See Congressional Budget Office, *U.S. Naval Forces: The Sea Control Mission* (Washington, D.C.: Congressional Budget Office, 1978).

24. See Lyle Goldstein and William Murray, as well as Michael E. O'Hanlon, "Damn the Torpedoes: Debating Possible U.S. Navy Losses in a Taiwan Scenario," *International Security* 29, no. 2 (Fall 2004): 202–206.

25. See, for example, Rear Admiral (Ret.) Eric A. McVadon, "Recent Trends in China's Military Modernization," before the U.S.-China Economic and Security Review Commission, Washington, D.C., September 15, 2005, p. 4.

26. Michael E. O'Hanlon, *Neither Star Wars Nor Sanctuary: Constraining the Military Uses of Space* (Washington, D.C.: Brookings, 2004), pp. 91–104.

## 8. Spiraling Out of Control

1. Joshua M. Epstein, "Dynamic Analysis and the Conventional Balance in Europe," *International Security* 12, no. 4 (Spring 1988).

2. Richard K. Betts, *Surprise Attack* (Washington, D.C.: Brookings, 1982), p. 5.

3. Lon Nordeen Jr., *Air Warfare in the Missile Age* (Washington, D.C.: Smithsonian Institution Press, 1985), pp. 201–203.

4. James F. Dunnigan, *How to Make War*, 3rd ed. (New York: William Morrow, 1993), p. 347.

5. For analyses that remain mostly correct today see Owen Cote, *The Future of Naval Aviation* (Cambridge, Mass.: MIT Security Studies Program, 2006), pp. 34–37 (available at http://web.mit.edu/ssp/); Owen Cote and Harvey Sapolsky, *Antisubmarine Warfare after the Cold War* (Cambridge, Mass.: MIT Security Studies Program, 1997), p. 13; and Tom Stefanick, *Strategic Antisubmarine Warfare and Naval Strategy* (Lexington, Mass.: Lexington Books, 1987), pp. 35–49.

6. Michael Swaine, introduction in Michael Swaine, ed., *Managing Sino American Crises: Case Studies and Analysis* (Washington, D.C.. Carnegie Endowment, 2006).

7. Michael E. O'Hanlon, *Defense Strategy for the Post-Saddam Era* (Washington, D.C.: Brookings, 2005), pp. 27–38.

8. Stephen Biddle, *Military Power: Explaining Victory and Defeat in Modern Battle* (Princeton, N.J.: Princeton University Press, 2004), pp. 29–77; William Owens, *Lifting the Fog of War* (New York: Farrar, Straus, & Giroux, 2000); and Michael E. O'Hanlon, *Technological Change and the Future of Warfare* (Washington, D.C.: Brookings, 2000), pp. 106–167.

9. Andrew F. Krepinevich Jr., *The Conflict Environment of 2016: A Scenario-Based Approach* (Washington, D.C.: Center for Strategic and Budgetary Assessments, 1996).

10. Desmond Ball, "China Pursues Space-Based Intelligence-Gathering Capabilities," *Jane's Intelligence Review* (December 2003), pp. 36–39; see also, Rear Admiral Eric A. McVadon, "China's Maturing Navy," *Naval War College Review*, vol. 59, no. 2 (Spring 2006), pp. 98–99.

11. Michael E. O'Hanlon, *Neither Star Wars Nor Sanctuary: Constraining the Military Uses of Space* (Washington, D.C.: Brookings, 2004), pp. 91–104; Bill Gertz, "Chinese Missile Has Twice the Range U.S. Anticipated," *Washington Times*, November 20, 2002, p. 3; Barry Watts, *The Military Uses of Space: A Diagnostic Assessment* (Washington, D.C.: Center for Strategic and Budgetary Assessments, 2001); Bob Preston, Dana J. Johnson, Sean J. A. Edwards, Michael Miller, and Calvin Shipbaugh, *Space Weapons, Earth Wars* (Santa Monica, Calif.: Rand, 2002); and Benjamin Lambeth, *Mastering the Ultimate High Ground: Next Steps in the Military Uses of Space* (Santa Monica, Calif.: Rand, 2003).

12. Then secretary of defense Donald H. Rumsfeld, "Quadrennial Defense Review Report" "(Washington, D.C.: U.S. Department of Defense, February 2006), p. 29.

13. William M. Arkin, "America's New China War Plan," Washingtonpost .com, May 24, 2006, available at blog.washingtonpost.com/earlywarning/ 2006/05/Americas_new_china_war_plan.html.

14. For a similar analysis of China's possible strategic calculus see Michael D. Swaine, "Chinese Crisis Management: Framework for Analysis, Tentative Observations, and Questions for the Future," in Andrew Scobell and Larry M. Wortzel, eds., *Chinese National Security Decision-making under Stress* (Carlisle, Pa.: Army War College, Strategic Studies Institute, 2005), pp. 32–33.

15. Michael J. Green, *Japan's Reluctant Realism* (New York: Palgrave, 2001), pp. 108–109; Kishore Mahbubani, "Understanding China," *Foreign*

*Affairs* 84, no. 5 (September/October 2005): 57; and David Pilling, "Issue of Taiwan Raises Stakes between Tokyo and Beijing," *Financial Times*, February 25, 2005, p. 10.

16. International Institute for Strategic Studies, *The Military Balance 2004–2005* (Oxford, U.K.: Oxford University Press, 2004), pp. 176–177; Christopher W. Hughes, "Japanese Military Modernization: In Search of a 'Normal' Security Role," in Ashley J. Tellis and Michael Wills, eds., *Strategic Asia 2005–06: Military Modernization in an Era of Uncertainty* (Seattle: National Bureau of Asian Research, 2005), pp. 129–130.

17. Jong-Heon Lee, "South Korea Fears Regional Military Conflicts," United Press International Wire Service, March 8, 2005; and British Broadcasting Corporation, "South Korean President Rejects Regional Expansion of U.S. Military Role," March 8, 2005 (available at www .bbc.co.uk).

18. Jonathan D. Pollack, "The Strategic Futures and Military Capabilities of the Two Koreas," in Tellis and Wills, eds., *Strategic Asia 2005–06*, pp. 153–154.

19. See, for example, Richard W. Baker and Charles E. Morrison, eds., *Asia Pacific Security Outlook 2005* (Tokyo: Japan Center for International Exchange, 2005), p. 146; and Dana R. Dillon and John J. Tkacik Jr., "China and ASEAN: Endangered American Primacy in Southeast Asia," backgrounder no. 1886, October 19, 2005, p. 5 (available at www.heritage.org).

20. Paul Dibb, "U.S.–Australia Alliance Relations: An Australian View," *Strategic Forum* 216 (August 2005): 5.

21. David Zweig and Bi Jianhai, "China's Global Hunt for Energy," *Foreign Affairs* 84, no. 5 (September/October 2005): 30.

22. Hugh White, "Australian Strategic Policy," in Tellis and Wills, eds., *Strategic Asia 2005–06*, pp. 325–326.

23. International Institute for Strategic Studies, *The Military Balance 2004–2005*, pp. 167–168, 187–192.

24. Sheldon W. Simon, "Southeast Asia's Defense Needs: Change or Continuity?" in Tellis and Wills, eds., *Strategic Asia 2005–06*, pp. 279, 285.

25. Stephen P. Cohen, *India: Emerging Power* (Washington, D.C.: Brookings, 2001), pp. 256–264.

26. The Treaty of Friendship, Cooperation, and Mutual Assistance between the People's Republic of China and the Democratic People's Republic of Korea (available at www.ioc.u-tokyo.ac.jp/~worldjpn/documents/texts/docs/19610711.T1E.html) was signed in 1961. Moreover, literally speaking it only obliges its two signatories to help each other when one is "subjected to armed attack"; the obligations in the event one of them does

the attacking are much less clear. See also Bates Gill, Testimony before the Senate Foreign Relations Committee on Regional Implications of the Changing Nuclear Equation on the Korean Peninsula, March 12, 2003, available at www.csis.org/hill/030312gill.pdf.

27. BBC, "Shanghai Plan to Fight Extremism," June 15, 2001, available at news.bbc.co.uk/1/hi/world/asia-pacific/1389493.stm; and Ministry of Foreign Affairs of the People's Republic of China, "Shanghai Cooperation Organization," July 1, 2004, available at www.fmprc.gov.cn/eng/topics/sco/t57970.htm.

28. Raza Naqvi, "Shanghai Bloc Expands Reach," *Washington Times*, August 20, 2005.

29. Associated Press, "U.S. Is Watching Russia-China Drill," *International Herald Tribune*, August 19, 2005.

30. Shu Guang Zhang, "Between 'Paper' and 'Real Tigers': Mao's View of Nuclear Weapons," in John Lewis Gaddis, Philip H. Gordon, Ernest R. May, and Jonathan Rosenberg, *Cold War Statesmen Confront the Bomb* (Oxford, U.K.: Oxford University Press, 1999), pp. 213–215.

31. Robert S. Ross, "Navigating the Taiwan Strait: Deterrence, Escalation Dominance, and U.S.–China Relations," *International Security* 27, no. 2 (Fall 2002), pp. 56–61.

32. China's strategic thinkers are, for example, beginning to give more attention to the theory of escalation control and war termination, but these concepts remain relatively new for them—and in any case, there is always a major potential gap between theory and practice in this domain. See Lonnie D. Henley, "War Control: Chinese Concepts of Escalation Management," in Andrew Scobell and Larry M. Wortzel, eds., *Shaping China's Security Environment: The Role of the People's Liberation Army* (Carlisle, Pa.: Strategic Studies Institute, 2006), pp. 81–103. John Wilson Lewis and Xue Litai, *Imagined Enemies: Chian Prepares for Uncertain War* (Stanford, Calif.: Stanford University Press, 2006), p. 273.

33. Scholar David Schwartz wrote "NATO's Nuclear Addiction." See David N. Schwartz, *NATO's Nuclear Dilemmas* (Washington, D.C.: Brookings, 1983), pp. 13–34.

34. Robert Jervis, *The Illogic of American Nuclear Strategy* (Ithaca, N.Y.: Cornell University Press, 1984), pp. 167–168.

35. The clearest threat concerning Taiwan came in the 1954–55 offshore islands crisis; see Robert Accinelli, *Crisis and Commitment: United States Policy toward Taiwan, 1950–1955* (Chapel Hill: University of North Carolina Press, 1996), pp. 214–215. Also see Richard K. Betts, *Nuclear Blackmail and Nuclear Balance* (Washington, D.C.: Brookings, 1987), p. 59; Shu Guang Zhang, "Between 'Paper' and 'Real Tigers,'" pp. 198–202;

and Robert Accinelli, "'A Thorn in the Side of Peace': The Eisenhower Administration and the 1958 Offshore Islands Crisis," in Robert S. Ross and Jiang Changbin, eds., *Reexamining the Cold War: U.S.–China Diplomacy, 1954–1973* (Cambridge, Mass.: Harvard University Asia Center, 2001), pp. 106–140.

36. Bradley Roberts, "China," in James J. Wirtz and Jeffrey A. Larsen, eds., *Rockets' Red Glare Missile Defenses and the Future of World Politics* (Boulder, Colo.: Westview, 2001), pp. 204–206.

37. Betts, *Nuclear Blackmail and Nuclear Balance*, p. 229.

38. McGeorge Bundy, *Danger and Survival: Choices about the Bomb in the First Fifty Years* (New York: Vintage Books, 1988), pp. 273–287.

39. Betts, *Nuclear Blackmail and Nuclear Balance*, pp. 123–131.

40. See Herman Kahn, *On Escalation: Metaphors and Scenarios* (New York, 1965); Thomas Schelling, *Arms and Influence* (New Haven, Conn.: Yale University Press, 1996), p. 93; and Lawrence Freedman, "The First Two Generations of Nuclear Strategists," in Peter Paret, ed., *Makers of Modern Strategy from Machiavelli to the Nuclear Age* (Princeton, N.J.: Princeton University Press, 1986), pp. 762–766.

41. Scott D. Sagan, *The Limits of Safety: Organizations, Accidents, and Nuclear Weapons* (Princeton, N.J.: Princeton University Press, 1993); and George Quester, "If the Nuclear Taboo Gets Broken," *Naval War College Review* 58, no. 2 (Spring 2005), p. 76.

42. A fascinating book about this danger during the Cold War is Bruce G. Blair, *Strategic Command and Control: Redefining the Nuclear Threat* (Washington, D.C.: Brookings, 1985), esp. pp. 182–211.

43. Bradley Roberts, "China," in James J. Wirtz and Jeffrey A. Larsen, eds., *Rockets' Red Glare*, pp. 186–187.

44. Richard McGregor and Demetri Sevastopulo, "Beijing Plays Down General's Threats," *London Financial Times*, July 18, 2005; Joe McDonald, "Chinese General Threatens U.S. over Taiwan," *Washington Post*, July 15, 2005; Andrew Yeh, "China Acts to Ease Fears over N-Arms Policy," *London Financial Times*, July 25, 2005; and "China Punishes General for Talk of Strike at U.S.," *International Herald Tribune*, December 22, 2005.

45. Robert Suettinger, *Beyond Tiananmen: The Politics of U.S.-China Relations, 1989–2000* (Washington, D.C.: Brookings, 2003), p. 248.

46. See, for example, Pan Zhenqiang, "China's Insistence on No-First-Use," *China Security* 1 (Autumn 2005): 5; and Shen Dingli, "Nuclear Deterrence in the 21st Century," *China Security* 1 (Autumn 2005): 13.

47. For the classic argument on this dynamic, in regard to U.S.–Soviet competition in particular, see Barry R. Posen, *Inadvertent Escalation:*

*Conventional War and Nuclear Risks* (Ithaca, N.Y.: Cornell University Press, 1991), pp. 1–16, 135–158.

48. See Bruce G. Blair, *The Logic of Accidental Nuclear War* (Washington, D.C.: Brookings, 1993), pp. 23–26; and Bruge G. Blair, *Strategic Command and Control: Redefining the Nuclear Threat* (Washington, D.C.: Brookings, 1985), pp. 282–287.

49. Steve Fetter, "Nuclear Strategy and Targeting Doctrine," in Harold A. Feiveson, ed., *The Nuclear Turning Point* (Washington, D.C.: Brookings, 1999), pp. 47–59; Desmond Ball and Jeffrey Richelson, eds., *Strategic Nuclear Targeting* (Ithaca, N.Y.: Cornell University Press, 1986); and David Mosher and Michael E. O'Hanlon, *The START Treaty and Beyond* (Washington, D.C.: Congressional Budget Office, 1991), pp. 21–25.

50. See, for example, Lawrence Freedman, *The Evolution of Nuclear Strategy* (New York: St. Martin's Press, 1983), pp. 76–90.

## 9. From Standoff to Stand-down

1. As a corollary, the United States should support, and encourage China to support, Taiwan's greater participation in international organizations (as an observer, perhaps). Beijing will be more likely to win over the Taiwan public if it allows participation. Taipei can make a contribution to the substantive work of those organizations—and that should be its motivation, not scoring symbolic sovereignty points.

2. C. Fred Bergsten, Bates Gill, Nicholas R. Lardy, and Derek Mitchell, *China: The Balance Sheet: What the World Needs to Know Now about the Emerging Superpower* (New York: Public Affairs, 2006), pp. 104–105.

3. Lael Brainard and Michael E. O'Hanlon, "A Test of American Independence," *Financial Times*, July 26, 2005.

4. Tim Judah, *Kosovo: War and Revenge* (New Haven, Conn.: Yale University Press, 2000), pp. 272–279; and Ivo H. Daalder and Michael E. O'Hanlon, *Winning Ugly: NATO's War to Save Kosovo* (Washington, D.C.: Brookings, 2000), pp. 165–175.

5. Michael E. O'Hanlon could imagine that Washington might confidentially also apply a fair amount of pressure on Taipei to clarify publicly that such a new constitution was not intended to pursue an independence agenda. The United States might further indicate that its willingness to come quickly to Taiwan's military aid against limited Chinese attacks could be influenced by Taiwan's response. The United States might well do so even as it remained committed to ensuring that, in the final analysis, Taiwan would not be conquered by China. Richard C. Bush believes that

Taipei would readily give such an assurance but that it would have no impact on the intentions of a mistrustful Beijing. Washington would work very hard at this stage of the crisis to urge Taipei to coordinate closely with the United States both militarily and politically, to exercise restraint, and generally to not make the situation worse.

6. See Raymond L. Garthoff, *A Journey through the Cold War* (Washington, D.C.: Brookings, 2001), pp. 168–187.

7. For relevant history and a number of relevant observations about policy tools and instruments see Ashton B. Carter and William J. Perry, *Preventive Defense: A New Security Strategy for America* (Washington, D.C.: Brookings, 1999), pp. 92–122.

8. James A. Baker, III, *The Politics of Diplomacy* (New York: G. P. Putnam's Sons, 1995), pp. 569–578.

## Appendix: Why China Could Not Seize Taiwan

1. For an earlier version of a similar agreement see Michael O'Hanlon, "Why China Cannot Conquer Taiwan," *International Security* 25, no. 2 (Fall 2000): 51–86.

2. See U.S. Department of Defense, *FY04 Report to Congress on PRC Military Power: Annual Report on the Military Power of the People's Republic of China* (2004), p. 50.

3. U.S. Department of Defense, *Annual Report to Congress: The Military Power of the People's Republic of China, 2005* (2005), p. 42.

4. See U.S. Marine Corps, "Operational Maneuver from the Sea," *Marine Corps Gazette* (June 2006).

5. See U.S. Department of Defense, *FY04 Report to Congress on PRC Military Power: Annual Report on the Military Power of the People's Republic of China* (2004), p. 37.

6. See, for example, Rear Admiral (Ret.) Eric A. McVadon, "Recent Trends in China's Military Modernization," before the U.S.–China Economic Security Review Commission, Washington, D.C., September 15, 2005, p. 3.

7. Ministry of National Defense, Republic of China (Taiwan), *2004 National Defense Report* (Taipei, Taiwan: Ministry of National Defense, 2004), p. 29.

8. Epstein, *Measuring Military Power*, pp. 208–209, 223.

9. Personal communication from Shuhfan Ding, Institute of International Relations, National Chengchi University, Taipei, Taiwan, April 14, 2000; see also David Shambaugh, "China's Military Views the World," *International Security* 24, no. 3 (Winter 1999/2000): 61.

10. The U.S. experience against Iraq in Desert Storm in 1991 provides a good window into how hard it is to shut down an enemy's air force.

Coalition aircraft averaged dozens of strike sorties a day against Iraqi air-fields during the war's first week, yet did not stop the Iraqi air force from flying about forty sorties a day. That was a time when coalition aircraft completely ruled the skies, moreover. In the airfield attacks, British planes were dropping advanced runway-penetrating weapons, precisely and from low altitude. They carried some thirty bomblets apiece, each bomblet con-sisting of two charges: a primary explosive to create a small hole in the runway, and a second explosive to detonate below its surface, causing a crater of 10 to 20 meters' width (depending largely on soil conditions). A standard attack would have used eight aircraft, each dropping two weapons, to shut down a standard NATO-length runway of 9,000 feet by 150 feet—a difficult mission, given the need to drop the weapons at pre-cise and quite low altitudes. See Thomas A. Keaney and Eliot A. Cohen, *Gulf War Air Power Survey Summary Report* (Washington, D.C.: U.S. Government Printing Office, 1993), pp. 56–65; U.S. General Accounting Office, *Operation Desert Storm: Evaluation of the Air Campaign* GAO/NSIAD-97-134 (June 1997), pp. 209–212; Christopher S. Parker, "New Weapons for Old Problems," *International Security* 23 no. 4 (Spring 1999): 147; Duncan Lennox, ed., *Jane's Air-Launched Weapons* (Surrey, U.K.: Jane's Information Group, 1999), issue 33 (August 1999); Christo-pher M. Centner, "Ignorance Is Risk: The Big Lesson from Desert Storm Air Base Attacks," *Airpower Journal* VI, no. 4 (Winter 1992): 25–35 (avail-able at www.airpower.maxwell.af.mil/airchronicles/apj/center.html); and personal communication from Dave C. Fidler, Wing Commander Air 1, U.K. embassy, Washington, D.C., April 14, 2000.

11. Kenneth W. Allen and Jeffrey M. Allen, "Controlling the Airspace over the Taiwan Strait: Basic Issues and Concepts," in Steve Tsang, ed., *If China Attacks Taiwan: Military Strategy, Politics, and Economics* (Col-chester, U.K.: Routledge, December 2005), pp. 94–121.

12. Typically about two to six Harpoon-size missiles would be needed to destroy a large surface vessel. See *Jane's Naval Review 1987* (London: Jane's Publishing, 1987), p. 124. In flying some three hundred sorties against British forces in the 1982 Falklands War, and attacking U.K. ships on the open oceans where they are harder to spot than when approaching shore, Argentina sank four British ships with bombs and hit another six with bombs that did not detonate because they had been improperly fused. Argentina sank a total of six ships, including those hit by Exocets and other weapons. See Lon O. Nordeen, *Air Warfare in the Missile Age*, 2nd ed. (Washington, D.C.: Smithsonian Institution Press, 2002), pp. 201–203.

13. Most likely, aircraft attrition rates per sortie would be no more than 5 percent, actually quite high by historical standards. Higher rates are possible; for example, Argentina may have suffered attrition rates per

sortie as high as 20 to 30 percent or so in the Falklands War. But the only aircraft likely to do this poorly in a China-Taiwan confrontation would be China's older planes, particularly if flying low-altitude missions near or over Taiwan (where the latter's air defenses would be most effective). See Nordeen, *Air Warfare in the Missile Age*, pp. 201–203; O'Balance, "The Falklands, 1982," in Bartlett, ed., *Assault from the Sea*, pp. 435–436; Epstein, *Measuring Military Power*, pp. 151–152; and Posen, "Measuring the European Conventional Balance," p. 104.

14. See Department of Defense, *FY04 Report to Congress on PRC Military Power: Annual Report on the Military Power of the People's Republic of China* (2004), p. 40; and International Institute for Strategic Studies, *The Military Balance 2005/2006* (Colchester, U.K.: Routledge, 2005), pp. 270–276.

15. See James F. Dunnigan, *How to Make War: A Comprehensive Guide to Modern Warfare for the Post–Cold War Era*, 3rd ed. (New York: William Morrow, 1993), pp. 284–292.

16. Keegan, *The Second World War*, pp. 376–385.

17. Wendell Minnick, "Washington Establishes Military Hotline with Taipei," *Jane's Defence Weekly* (October 29, 2003), p. 14.

18. Swaine, *Taiwan's National Security, Defense Policy, and Weapons Procurement Processes*, p. 60.

19. International Institute for Strategic Studies, *The Military Balance 1981/1982* (London: International Institute for Strategic Studies, 1982), pp. 92–93.

20. Nordeen, *Air Warfare in the Missile Age*, pp. 201–203.

21. Office of Technology Assessment, *Proliferation of Weapons of Mass Destruction* (Washington, D.C.: Office of Technology Assessment, 1993), pp. 45–67.

22. Trevor N. Dupuy, *Attrition: Forecasting Battle Casualties and Equipment Losses in Modern War* (Fairfax, Va.: HERO Books, 1990), p. 58; and Anthony H. Cordesman and Abraham R. Wagner, *Lessons of Modern War*, vol. 2: *The Iran-Iraq War* (Boulder, Colo.: Westview Press, 199), p. 518.

23. See Utgoff, *The Challenge of Chemical Weapons*, pp. 148–188; and Dupuy, *Attrition*, p. 58.

24. Robert G. Nagler, *Ballistic Missile Proliferation: An Emerging Threat* (Arlington, Va.: System Planning Corporation, 1992), p. 10.

25. See Dunnigan, *How to Make War*, pp. 284–292. The typical lateral inaccuracy of gunfire or artillery fire is proportional to the distance over which the round must travel, meaning that a shot to five hundred

meters would be expected to have one-tenth the miss distance of a shot to five kilometers.

26. For a concurring view see McVadon, "PRC Exercises, Doctrine, and Tactics toward Taiwan," pp. 254–255.

27. Robert Hewson, "China Boosts Its Air Assets with Ilyushin Aircraft," *Jane's Defence Weekly* (September 21, 2005), p. 16.

28. For historical perspective see James A. Huston, "The Air Invasion of Holland," *Military Review,* (September 1952), pp. 13–27; and Gerard M. Devlin, *Paratrooper: The Saga of U.S. Army and Marine Parachute and Glider Combat Troops during World War II* (New York: St. Martin's Press, 1979).

29. Schmidt, *Moving U.S. Forces*, pp. 48, 54, 80–81.

30. For a similar view see Michael D. Swaine and Roy D. Kamphausen, "Military Modernization in Taiwan," in Ashley J. Tellis and Michael Wills, *Strategic Asia 2005–2006: Military Modernization in an Era of Uncertainty* (Seattle: National Bureau of Asian Research, 2005), p. 417.

# Index

Page numbers followed by *t* indicate tables.

Aegis radar systems, 146
aerial refueling, 26
Afghanistan, 106, 155, 168
Ahtisaari, Martti, 176
AIM-120C air-to-air missile, 106
aircraft carriers, 104, 126, 140, 142,
    143–144, 146, 157, 183
air defense systems, 105
air forces, 110, 116–117, 133, 140
    preemptive strike and, 134
    war triggers and, 120
air superiority, 130
American Civil War, 68, 94
amphibious assault, 125–126, 138
    exercises, 5, 104
    keys to successful, 129–130
antipoverty campaign, 13, 21, 23, 41
antisecession law (China, 2005), 78,
    83, 84, 88, 96, 109, 162
antisubmarine warfare (ASW),
    139–140, 141, 150, 151
Arab-Israeli wars, 120, 143, 155
Arkin, William, 147
Asian financial crisis, 30
Asia-Pacific Economic Cooperation
    summit, 48
Asia-Pacific region, 11, 27
    U.S. bases in, 126, 140, 141,
        149–151, 157
    U.S. force modernization in, 109
    U.S. forces in, 27, 114, 115*t*, 147,
        177
    U.S. hegemony in, 18, 19
    *See also* war potential

"assassin's mace" weapons, 105
Association of Southeast Asian
    Nations, 29, 45, 152
*Atlantic Monthly* (magazine), 17, 27
atmospheric nuclear detonation, 127,
    135, 183
Australia, 30, 41, 42, 45, 54, 151, 172,
    176

Baker, James, 181
balance of interests, 109, 147
*Balkan Ghosts* (Kaplan), 27
Balkan wars, 8–9, 106, 145, 176
ballistic missiles, 3, 5–6, 131, 179
    medium-range, 82, 121, 122
    mobile short-range, 106
    *See also* ICBMs
Bay of Pigs, 129
Belgrade Chinese embassy accidental
    bombing, 8–9, 44
Betts, Richard, 154
Bi Jianhai, 39
blockade of Taiwan scenario, 130,
    132–134, 136–142, 147, 175–180
    as most promising option, 158–159
    Taiwan potential response to,
        179–180
    three major factors in, 135
    U.S. potential breaking of,
        139–142, 149, 159, 180–181
"Blue" faction, 89, 91–92, 170
Brazil, 56
Britain, 101, 129, 137, 149, 151
    Falklands War, 129, 142, 144

Bundy, McGeorge, 122
Bush, George W., 18, 27, 29
    Asian security strategy and, 18
    Australian reception to, 30
    Chinese policies and, 35, 147, 169
    democratization policy of, 43
    Taiwan policy and, 14, 74, 78, 79,
        80–81, 86, 87, 108, 110–111, 169

Campbell, Kurt, 18
capitalism, 41, 42, 43, 61, 70
casualty aversion, 1, 110, 144, 147
central Asia, 28, 152
Chávez, Hugo, 39
Chen Shui-bian, 7, 62, 63, 73–74, 75,
        78–80, 85–87, 91–93, 96
    internal constraints on, 162
    political opponents of, 89
Chiang Ching-kuo, 64–65, 68, 69, 77
Chiang Kai-shek, 60–62, 64, 65, 67, 75
Chi Haotian, 114
China, 12–33, 65, 81, 151
    cultural heritage of, 31–32
    economic growth of. See under
        economy; manufacturing; trade
    effects of rise of, 39
    great power potential of, 13, 14, 15,
        17–33, 36, 54
    human rights and, 23, 40, 49, 95
    image concerns of, 91
    Japanese conflict with, 11, 44–46,
        59, 74–75, 150, 161
    media focus on, 17
    national interest outlook of, 42
    nationalism and, 21, 30, 44, 46, 80
    peaceful rise policy of, 41–42
    problems and challenges of, 41, 53
    prosperity-for-legitimacy bargain of,
        20
    public opinion in, 44, 55, 80, 90,
        183
    UN Security Council and, 39, 56,
        71
    See also Chinese Communist Party;
        Taiwan; war potential
China, Inc. (Fishman), 49

Chinese civil war, 68, 70, 75
Chinese Communist Party, 29, 80
    anti-Maoist reform in, 12–13, 20,
        40, 41, 42, 65
    corruption and, 41, 48
    economic growth and, 19–20, 65
    fears of U.S. undermining of, 43
    future leaders of, 93, 94–95, 97
    international status quo and, 37
    leadership skills of, 21, 43
    "one country, two systems" model
        and, 8, 70, 71, 89
    pragmatism of, 40–44, 46, 65
    Taiwan and, 13–14, 60–61, 65, 67,
        68, 74–75, 94, 183
Christopher, Warren, 4
Clausewitz, Karl von, 82
Clinton, Bill, 18, 177
    China policy of, 5, 8–9, 14, 35
    Taiwan policy of, 3–7, 72, 79
Cohen, William, 114
Cold War, 18, 145, 150, 154–155,
        168
    antisubmarine warfare and, 141
    deterrence and, 153
    end of, 19, 37, 185
    Taiwan's position in, 60–61, 65
    See also Cuban Missile Crisis
cold war (potential Chinese-U.S.), 11,
        27, 110
colonialism, 29, 32, 37, 38, 45–46, 57,
        58, 62
Committee on Foreign Investments
    in the United States, 51, 173
communism. See Chinese Communist
    Party; ideology
computers
    Chinese assembly of, 9, 20, 21, 66,
        172
    cyberattacks and, 134
    dual-use, 52
    RMA hypothesis and, 145, 146
Congress, U.S., 6, 49
    Taiwan supporters in, 4, 68, 72, 80,
        95–96, 108, 162, 167
CONPLAN (conceptual plan), 147

consumer goods, 13, 20, 22, 50,
172–173
containment policy, 55, 61
Cornell University, 2, 4, 18, 72, 79
corporations, U.S., 17–18
corruption, 41, 48
counterinsurgency, 145
counterintelligence tools, 52, 53
counterterrorism, 29
Cox Commission, 49
cruise missiles, 81, 109, 119, 132, 137,
144, 184
hypersonic antiship, 146
Cuban Missile Crisis, 12, 101,
121–123, 147, 158, 168, 177,
182, 185
currency, 23, 30, 47, 49, 66, 105, 131
cyberattacks, 134

Dalai Lama, 43
debt, U.S., 13, 23, 47, 173
defense budget
Chinese allocation of, 105
Chinese size of, 25–26, 36, 81
China vs. Taiwan, 101–102, 107
U.S. size of, 125
Defense Department (U.S.), 18–19,
26–27, 54, 82, 88, 101, 109, 147
Defense Intelligence Agency (U.S.),
130
Dell computers, 9, 66
Democratic Party (U.S.), 95, 96, 163
democratic peace theory, 40
Democratic Progressive Party
(Taiwan), 7, 69, 71, 73–74, 79,
86
independence goal and, 74, 90, 97
potential comeback of, 93–97
democratization, 3, 6, 7, 14, 43, 61,
67–68, 72, 84, 110, 118, 123
Deng Xiaoping, 19–20, 65, 68
destroyers, 81, 153
deterrence, 78, 82–88, 100, 123, 153,
154. See also dual deterrence
policy
diesel submarines, 105

diplomacy
China and, 3, 27–30, 39, 41, 47, 71,
151
Chinese-Taiwan war potential and,
166, 176–178, 183, 186
dollars, 23
Downer, Alexander, 151
dual deterrence policy, 78, 90, 96,
108–109, 163–164
Dubai Ports World, 251

earthquake, Taiwan (1999), 66
East Sea Fleet (China), 116
economic warfare, 171–173, 174
Economist (magazine), 17
economy
China-Taiwan interactions and, 9,
20, 41, 66–67, 69, 79
China's growth of, 13, 17–18,
19–24, 30–32, 36, 41, 44, 65, 81
China's problems/challenges of, 41,
53
Chinese-U.S. interactions and, 9,
22, 38–39, 47–51, 99, 161,
171–173
as cyberwar target, 134
GDPs and, 20–21, 23, 36, 135
Japan's size of, 39
knowledge-based, 56
Taiwan's wealth and, 14, 62, 65–66
war potential and, 12, 47–50, 56,
138, 149, 171–172
See also globalization;
manufacturing; trade
education system, 56, 63
embargo, 171–173, 174
EMP burst, 135, 183, 184
energy sources, 28, 30, 38, 39
Chinese investments and, 48–49, 161
See also oil
environmental policies, 10, 20, 39
EP-3 incident (2001), 9, 44, 114
espionage, 114, 123
industrial, 49, 52
European Union, 70, 176
Exocet missile, 144

fair trade, 48
Falklands War, 129, 142, 144
Fishman, Ted, 49
fixed underwater arrays (SOSUS), 144
floating minisensors, 146
foreign investments
    by China, 13, 47–51, 173
    by Taiwan in China, 41, 66
    by United States, 66
France, 59, 101
Freeman, Charles ("Chas"), 1, 2, 5,
    11, 156
free trade, 19, 20, 29, 48
Fujian province, 59
Futenma base, 116

Germany, 21, 36, 38, 39, 47
Gibson, Charlie, 108
globalization, 18–20, 37, 39, 44, 50,
    66–67, 161
GPS range finders, 142
Green, Michael, 46
"Green" faction, 89, 90, 91, 118
gross domestic product, 20–21, 23,
    36, 135
Guam, 54, 114, 116, 141, 157

Haass, Richard, 38
Han Dynasty, 31
Hobbes, Thomas, 36
Hong Kong, 3, 8, 70
"How We Would Fight China"
    (Kaplan), 27
Hsinchu Science Park, 9
Hu Jintao, 30, 48–49, 50, 57, 94–95
human rights, 2, 43, 68
    Chinese abuses of, 23, 40, 49, 95
Hussein, Saddam, 149

ICBMs, 1, 26, 102, 142, 156, 184
ideology
    China-Taiwan relations and, 13–14,
        57, 60–61, 65, 67–71, 74–75
    China-Taiwan unification model
        and, 8, 70, 71, 89
    China's pragmatism vs., 42–44

Chinese technocrats and, 21, 43
    end of Maoist, 20, 40, 41, 42, 65
    U.S.-Chinese relations and, 10,
        12–13, 43, 56
income gap, 41, 53
India, 28–29, 54, 55, 152, 168, 176
Indonesia, 42
industrial espionage, 49, 52
intellectual property, 2, 43, 48, 49
interest rates, 23, 47
International Institute for Strategic
    Studies symposium, 101
International Monetary Fund, 19
international system, 8, 9, 55–56, 123
    Chinese improved integration into,
        27–29, 38, 39, 41–44, 56
    Chinese potential war on Taiwan
        and, 129, 136, 175–176
    rising-power–established-power
        dynamic and, 13, 30–31, 32, 36,
        38, 39, 56
    Taiwan's place in, 7, 61, 70, 71, 86
    two-China issue and, 3, 4, 60–61,
        68, 71, 75, 78
    U.S. decline in, 27–29, 56
    See also diplomacy; war potential
Internet, 20, 80
Iran, 9, 28, 38, 40, 95, 120, 155
Iraq, 24, 38, 144, 149
Iraq-Iran War, 131
Iraq War, 46, 74, 95, 106, 110, 116,
    131, 145, 151
Islam, 29, 151
Israel, 81, 120, 143, 155

Jaffe, Amy, 39
Japan, 18, 55, 65, 95, 120, 173, 176
    China and, 11, 20, 29–30, 44–46,
        59, 74–75, 150, 161
    defense budget of, 101
    economy of, 21, 39
    limited security role of, 46
    rise of, 29, 32, 36, 39, 45–46, 50,
        57, 59, 62, 69, 74–75
    Taiwan and, 57, 59, 62, 64, 169,
        171

U.S. alliance with, 14, 30, 44, 46,
     54, 114, 116, 126, 149, 179
Jervis, Robert, 154
Jiang Zemin, 5
Jinmen, shelling of, 61, 65, 113

Kadena base, 116, 184
Kahn, Herman, 155
Kaohsiung Harbor, 136
Kaplan, Robert, 27
Kargil region, 168
Kazakhstan, 152
Kennedy, John F., 77, 122, 147, 177
Khrushchev, Nikita, 122
Kilo (diesel submarine), 105
Kissinger, Henry, 36–37, 40
*Kitty Hawk* (aircraft carrier), 120
KMT. *See* Nationalist Party
Korean War, 154, 168
Kosovo War, 8–9, 145, 176
Krepinevich, Andrew, 145
Kuomintang. *See* Nationalist Party
Kyrgyzstan, 152

labor
   Chinese low-waged, 20, 50, 66, 173
   Taiwan, 65–66
Lardy, Nicholas, 50
Latin America, 30, 48–49, 51
Law of the Sea, 45
Lebanon, 110, 147
Lee Teng-hui, 3, 7, 69–73, 75
   background of, 62, 63
   U.S. visit of, 2–6, 18, 72, 79, 80,
     174
*Liberty*, USS, 120
Lincoln, Abraham, 68, 94
Liu Huaqui, 5–6
Los Angeles, 1, 5, 11, 156

Macau, 70
macroeconomic imbalances, 47–48
Mahbubani, Kishore, 43
Malaysia, 45
Manchu government, 59
Mandarin Chinese, 60, 62

manufacturing, 29, 66, 79
   Chinese assembly and, 9, 20, 21,
     50, 66, 172
   Chinese growth share of, 20, 39,
     65, 172
   U.S. as Chinese market for, 21–22
manufacturing value added (MVA),
   20
Mao Zedong, 17, 20, 40, 41, 60, 61,
   65, 67, 153
Marxism, 21, 67
Matsu (Mazu), shelling of, 65, 113
Ma Ying-jeou, 91, 92–93
medium-range missiles, 82, 121, 122
middle class, Chinese, 13, 21, 23
Military Maritime Accord (1998), 114
military power
   basic data, 103*t*
   Chinese buildup of, 18, 24–27, 30,
     31, 36, 54, 80–82, 88, 90, 94,
     100–107, 109, 116–117, 130, 147
   Chinese technological espionage
     and, 49
   Chinese-U.S. 1995–1996 standoff
     and, 2, 3, 5–6, 14, 18
   Chinese-U.S. mutual ambivalence
     and, 53–55
   Chinese weaknesses in, 103–104
   exercises/maneuvers and, 114–115
   fixed land bases and, 145–146
   massive mobilization and, 117–118
   Taiwan and, 71, 78, 100, 101–102,
     103*t*, 106–107, 118
   U.S. Asian-Pacific Theater forces
     and, 115*t*
   U.S. dominance in, 19, 24, 52, 56,
     103*t*, 125
   U.S. strategic exercises and, 113
   *See also* missiles; nuclear weapons;
     war potential
Milosevic, Slobodan, 176
minesweepers, 138, 140, 144, 149
mining of harbors, 137–138
missiles, 105, 113, 174, 175
   mobile, 102, 106, 184
   strike scenario, 130–132

missiles (continued)
    tracking of, 52
    See also specific types
multilateral institutions, 19, 28
multinational companies, 20

Nanjing Military Region, 117
Napoleon, 17
nationalism, 21, 30, 44, 46, 80, 150
Nationalist China. See Taiwan
Nationalist Party (Kuomintang), 5, 57,
        60, 61–65, 73–75
    political future of, 90, 91, 93, 94
    reforms in, 65, 68, 69
National Security Strategy (U.S.,
        2002), 18, 27
NATO, 8–9, 27, 40, 176
natural gas, 151
natural resources. See raw materials
naval forces, 26, 110, 115, 116, 150
    mistakes at sea and, 120–121
    technology trends and, 146
    vulnerability to attack of, 144–145
    See also submarines
Navy, U.S., 144, 146, 147, 159
Newsweek (magazine), 17
New York Times (newspaper), 18
Nixon, Richard, 1, 40, 80
noncommissioned officers corps, 105
North Korea, 9, 28, 40, 95, 152
notebook computers, 20, 21, 172
nuclear weapons, 1, 9, 28, 29
    accidental use of, 122–123, 156–157
    balance of interests and, 109, 147
    Chinese arsenal of, 14, 102
    Chinese industrial espionage
        and, 49
    first strike fears and, 145, 153
    flexibility of plans for, 157
    high-altitude detonation of, 127,
        135, 183
    nonproliferation of, 2, 111, 123
    potential war scenarios and, 10–11,
        36–37, 61, 111, 127, 135,
        153–158, 162, 181–186
Nye, Joseph, 19, 55

October War (1973), 155
Ogarkov, Nikolai, 145
oil, 11, 30, 32, 38–40, 48–49, 51, 173,
        176
Okinawa, 116, 140, 145, 149–150,
        157, 184
"one country, two systems" model, 8,
        70, 71, 89
OPLAN 5077-04, 147

Pakistan, 28, 168
"peaceful rise" policy, 41–42
Peloponnesian War, 30
Pentagon. See Defense Department
People's Liberation Army, 5, 18, 24,
        80, 81, 118
    strength of, 25, 26, 90, 94, 109
    weaknesses/reforms of, 103–106,
        117
People's Republic of China. See
        China
Perry, William J., 5–6, 18, 114, 177
Persian Gulf, 32, 110, 120, 155,
        171–172
Persian Gulf War, 24, 116, 131, 138,
        145
Philippines, 45, 150–151
politics, 5, 7, 73, 86–87
    Taiwan, 89–92, 118, 170
    2012 scenario, 93–97
    war potential and, 79–82, 118–119
poverty, 13, 21, 23, 41, 53
Powell, Colin, 35
power-transition theory, 13, 30–31,
        32, 36
precision-strike weapons, 145
preemptive strike, 134, 143–145, 147
presidential elections. See politics
P-3 aircraft, 140, 153
Putin, Vladimir, 28

Qian Qichen, 4
Quadrennial Defense Review (U.S.,
        2006), 18–19, 54
Quanta Company, 9
Quemoy, shelling of, 61, 65, 113

radar, 146
raw materials, 29, 39, 45, 46, 48, 51,
    104. *See also* oil
Reagan, Ronald, 12, 65–66
recession, 20, 66
regional institutions, 53–54, 170
repression
    Chinese, 19–20, 24, 40–44, 49, 68
    Taiwan Nationalist, 61–62, 63–64
    *See also* human rights
Republican Party (U.S.), 72, 80,
    95–96, 163
Republic of China. *See* Taiwan
revolution, export of, 40, 42
RMA hypothesis, 145–146
robotic submersibles, 140
Roh Moo-Hyun, 150
Roman Empire, 31
Roosevelt, Franklin, 39, 54
Rumsfeld, Donald, 101
Russia, 44, 101, 176
    as arms supplier, 71, 81–82, 102,
        105–106, 107, 113, 146
    Chinese relations with, 28, 32, 152,
        172
    Chinese vs. U.S. relations with,
        42

satellite capabilities, 142, 146
Saudi Arabia, 14, 38, 173
savings rates, 48
Schelling, Thomas, 155
science, 23, 31, 56
seabed resources, 45, 46, 104
sensors, 145, 146
September 11 (2001) attack, 28, 35
Seventh Fleet, U.S., 60
Shambaugh, David, 106
Shanghai Cooperation Organization,
    28, 152
Simon, Sheldon, 45
Singapore, 45, 152, 176
Singapore meeting (1993), 67
Six Assurances, 81
"smart mines," 138
social insurance, 48

soft power, Chinese vs. U.S., 30, 51
Solomon, Richard, 42
Somalia, 1, 110, 147
sonar, 133, 137, 144, 180
Song Dynasty, 31
SOSUS, 144
South China Sea, 45
Southeast Asia, 29, 31, 41, 42, 45,
    151–152, 170
South Korea, 20, 150, 170
    Chinese vs. U.S. relations with, 28,
        41, 42
    U.S. alliance with, 14, 45, 114
Soviet Union, 24, 25, 27, 120,
    121–123, 177, 181
    fall of, 19, 28, 71
    *See also* Cold War; Russia
Sovremmeny class ships, 113
special-forces attacks, 134, 135–136
Spratly Islands, 45
spy satellites, 114
SS-N-27 antiship missile, 105
standard of living, 21, 53
*Stark*, USS, 120, 144
stealth technology, 52
Stewart, Potter, 84
S-300/SA-20 air defense, 105
strategic ambiguity, 78
submarines, 109, 116, 126, 133–142,
    144, 146, 147, 150, 151, 157, 158,
    180, 182, 184
    diesel, 105
    multiple-ship accidents and, 120
    quieting equipment, 52
    Russian-supplied, 82
    Taiwan, 107
Sudan, 40, 95
Suettinger, Robert, 42
Summer Olympics (2008), 91
Sunburn missiles, 180
Sun Zi, 112, 113
supercomputer, 52
surface-to-surface missiles, 107
surprise attacks, 143–145
Su-27/Su-30 aircraft, 105, 113
Swaine, Michael, 144–145

Taichung Harbor, 136
Taiwan
  China fever in, 67
  China's diplomatic quarantine of,
    3, 71
  China's eased relations with, 57, 65,
    93
  China's economic interaction with,
    9, 20, 29, 41, 66–67, 69, 79
  China's escalating tensions with,
    86–87
  China's feared secession by, 14, 72,
    78, 83, 84, 88, 96, 109, 162
  China's goal of unification with,
    6–7, 8, 68, 69, 70, 74–75, 82, 88,
    89, 95, 133, 162, 165
  China's minicrises with, 3, 5–8, 14,
    18, 61, 67, 131
  China's "warm economics, cold
    politics" with, 29
  Chinese migrants to, 58–59
  Chinese-U.S. tensions over, 1–2,
    7–8, 13–14, 15, 44, 161–162
  Chinese war potential over. See war
    potential
  constitutional revision proposal in,
    74, 80, 86, 87, 91, 92, 169–170,
    174–175
  core of Chinese dispute with, 85
  defense spending by, 101–102
  as democracy, 3, 6, 7, 14, 61, 67–68,
    72, 84, 110, 118, 123
  depth of Chinese vs. U.S. interest
    in, 2
  economic wealth of, 14, 62, 65–66
  exiles from, 63, 64
  history of, 57–66, 74–75
  identities configuration and, 57, 58,
    59, 60, 63–64, 70
  independence advocates in, 25, 30,
    63–66, 69, 73, 74, 78, 82, 86, 91,
    94, 95, 97, 100, 109, 123, 135,
    136
  leadership survivability of, 135–136,
    145
  legal identity of, 92–93
  military power of, 71, 78, 100,
    101–102, 103t, 106–107, 118
  public opinion in, 86, 90, 93, 119
  sovereignty issue of, 8, 70, 92–93,
    100, 164–165
  U.S. credibility and, 128
  U.S. policies and, 3–6, 10–12, 14,
    42, 43, 46, 61, 68, 69, 72–82,
    86–87, 95–96, 100, 107–111, 123,
    162–167, 171
  visitors to China from, 65, 66
  war anxiety and, 118
Taiwan Relations Act of 1979 (U.S.),
  81, 108, 171
Taiwan Strait, 3, 12, 56, 102, 118
Tajikistan, 152
Tang Dynasty, 31
technocrats, 21, 43
technology, 13, 21, 28
  Chinese espionage and, 49, 52
  dual-use, 52–53
  surprise attacks and, 145–146
  Taiwan and, 65, 66, 102, 106
  U.S. resources and, 23, 52, 56
  See also specific types
terrorism, 28, 29, 35, 37
Thailand, 45, 152
Thant, U, 177
Thucydides, 30, 36
Tiananmen Square crisis (1989),
  19–20, 24, 43, 68
Tibet, 14
Time (magazine), 17
torpedoes, 144, 146
tourism, 65, 66
trade
  China's commodity needs and, 39
  China's exports and, 13, 21–22,
    47–48, 172–173
  China's fostering of, 42, 50, 151
  China's illicit practices of, 48, 49
  China-Taiwan, 41, 171
  Chinese-U.S. disputes over, 43
  dispute settlement mechanism,
    51
  sanctions and, 173–174

U.S. deficit, 22, 23, 47, 50
  *See also* blockade of Taiwan
    scenario
Treasury bonds (U.S.), 23, 47, 173
Treasury Department (U.S.), 51
Truman, Harry S., 96
turbofan engine, 105
Turkey, 122, 129, 177
two-China status, 3, 4, 60–61, 68, 71,
    75, 78

United Kingdom. *See* Britain
United Nations
  Law of the Sea, 45
  Security Council members, 39, 56,
    170, 175
  Taiwan and, 71, 170, 175, 176, 177
United States
  as casualty-averse, 1, 110, 144, 147
  Chinese crises with, 1–9, 10, 14, 18,
    44
  Chinese debt holding and, 13, 23,
    47, 173
  Chinese economic relations and.
    *See* economy; manufacturing;
    trade
  Chinese relations outlook and,
    55–56
  Communist China's recognition by,
    1, 40, 68
  declining influence of, 27–29, 30
  foreign investments in, 51–52
  global credibility of, 123
  global responsibilities of, 56
  hegemony in Pacific of, 18, 19
  international leadership role of, 56
  military power of, 19, 24, 52, 56,
    101, 103t, 125
  nuclear threats by, 153–155
  oil competition and, 38–39
  regional allies of, 14, 30, 43, 44,
    46–47
  resentments toward, 42
  resources of, 23
  security strategy of, 18–19
  *See also* Taiwan; war potential

UNOCAL, 49, 51
U-2 plane downing, 123
Uzbekistan, 28, 152

Venezuela, 39
Vietnam, 24, 42
Vietnam War, 154, 168
*Vincennes*, USS, 120

Wal-Mart, 20, 172
Wang Jisi, 42
war potential, 3, 10–13, 27, 32–33,
    36–56, 77–97, 99–124, 159,
    161–186
  accidental encounters and,
    120–123, 156–157
  brinkmanship and, 90, 128, 164,
    181, 184
  casualty aversion and, 1, 110, 144,
    147
  cautious assessment of, 91–97
  challenge of rising power and, 13,
    30–31, 32, 36, 38, 39, 56
  Chinese ambiguity and, 83–84,
    85–86, 90
  Chinese assumptions and, 81–84
  coercion option and, 88
  complex dynamics of, 125–142
  costs of, 186
  deterrence strategy and, 78, 82–88,
    100, 123, 153, 154
  diffusion of, 77–78, 118–119,
    164–168
  dual deterrence policy and, 78, 90,
    96, 108–109, 163–164
  escalation and, 99–100, 119, 120,
    127–128, 131, 144–145, 148, 149,
    153–155, 158, 159, 180–181, 183,
    185
  historical examples and, 101, 120,
    121–123, 131, 153
  hypothetical causes and, 33
  ideology's limited importance and,
    40, 44
  inadvertent conflict risk and,
    113–114

war potential (continued)
  informal security partnerships and,
    149–152
  main guidelines for, 182
  massive mobilization and, 117–118
  mediation and, 176–177
  military-military dialogues and,
    177–178, 186
  minicrises and, 3, 5–8, 14, 18, 61,
    67, 72, 73, 77–78, 113, 131, 174
  misperceptions/miscalculations and,
    72–73, 87, 89–91, 112, 119, 128,
    129, 164, 166
  mutual interests vs., 99–101,
    128–129
  mutual mistrust and, 85, 86–87, 90,
    183
  nation-state stability and, 37
  outcomes and, 153–159
  peace trend and, 91
  politics and, 79–82, 118–119
  preemptive strike and, 134,
    143–144, 143–145, 147
  real dangers of, 11–12, 184–185
  reasons for outbreak, 100
  RMA hypothesis and, 145–146
  scenarios for conduct of, 10–11, 45,
    90–91, 93–97, 126–142, 158–159,
    175
  Taiwan's status and, 10, 33, 55,
    57–75, 69, 85, 99

  three-way testing and, 112–113
  triggers for, 15, 32, 38, 40, 49, 56
  as unlikely, 57–58, 66–67, 78–79
  U.S. position and, 11–12, 77–78,
    90, 96, 108–111, 118–119,
    135, 140, 141, 146–148, 163–168
  zone of conflict and, 125–126
  See also military power; nuclear
    weapons
World Bank, 19
World Trade Organization, 19, 37, 51,
    54
World War I, 13, 36, 79, 100, 129
  economic legacy of, 47
  massive mobilization and, 117
World War II, 18–19, 37, 39, 131,
    137, 179
  amphibious assaults and, 126, 129
  Chinese Communists and, 75
  Taiwan's status following, 59,
    60–61

Xinjiang Autonomous Region, 14
Xiong Guangkai, 156

Yeltsin, Boris, 28

Zhang Ziyi, 17
Zhu Chenghu, 156
Zoellick, Robert, 54
Zweig, David, 39